Behind Enemy Lines

Sir Tommy Macpherson was born in Edinburgh in 1920. He now divides his time between London and Newtonmore.

Richard Bath is an award-winning journalist who edits *Scottish Field* magazine and writes for *Scotland on Sunday* on history, politics, food and sport. He lives in Edinburgh with his wife and three children.

BEHIND ENEMY LINES

THE AUTOBIOGRAPHY OF BRITAIN'S
MOST DECORATED LIVING WAR HERO

SIR TOMMY MACPHERSON
WITH RICHARD BATH

MAINSTREAM
PUBLISHING

EDINBURGH AND LONDON

To my children, Angus, Ishbel and Duncan, and my grandchildren, Tom, Lochlan, Fiona and Alasdair.

This edition, 2012

Copyright © Sir Tommy Macpherson with Richard Bath, 2010
All rights reserved
The moral rights of the authors have been asserted

First published in Great Britain in 2010 by
MAINSTREAM PUBLISHING COMPANY
(EDINBURGH) LTD
7 Albany Street
Edinburgh EH1 3UG

ISBN 9781845967086

All photos courtesy of the author

A catalogue record for this book is available
from the British Library

Typeset in Adobe Caslon and ParmaPetit

Printed and bound by
Clays Ltd, St Ives plc

9 10 8

Contents

	Introduction	7
1	In the Beginning	9
2	Bundled Off	21
3	Calm before the Storm	31
4	The Phoney War	39
5	The Clouds of War Break	45
6	The Road to Damascus	57
7	Desperately Seeking Rommel	67
8	The Camp for Bad Boys	73
9	Prison on the Eastern Front	83
10	On the Run	87
11	Say Hello to the Gestapo	97
12	Breaking for the Border with Gangster Joe	101
13	Homeward Bound	115
14	Joining the Jedburghs	119
15	'Chef, There's a French Officer, and He's Brought His Wife'	129
16	The Das Reich Are Coming	137
17	Bluffing for Victory	149
18	To Italy	161
19	A Dirty War	169
20	The Turncoats' Comeuppance	175
21	Saving Trieste	179
22	The Dreaming Spires	189
23	An Oval World	199
24	Achilles Heel	209
25	By Royal Appointment	217

26	Domestic Bliss	223
27	Balavil	237
28	The SAS and Dark Arts	243
29	Timber!	247
30	The Boss	255
31	The European Dimension	269

Acknowledgements

Without Richard Bath's enthusiasm, professionalism and discipline, this book would not have appeared. I would also like to thank Jenny Coles, for her help in London, keeping in order my papers and files; Val Hoare, in the Highlands, for typing the tapes and putting random thoughts into chronological order, and, when she left the neighbourhood, Susan Macpherson, who carried on the good work; Susan Moore, who, like the others, helped over a great number of years, not least by keeping the photo albums and writing in their captions. I'd also like to thank Marion Ross for always making a warm and and welcoming home in which to write. Lastly, thank you to my children, Angus, Ishbel and Duncan; to my daughter-in-law, Valerie, and son-in-law, Philip Dayer; and to my wife, Jean, whose encouragement kept my nose to the grindstone.

Introduction

There's a phrase that was used in the years immediately after the Second World War and which was applied to those of us who were in the thick of the fighting but emerged relatively unscathed. People would say that we 'had a good war'. If we had enough medals or mentions in dispatches to our name, we might even have had 'a very good war'.

For those of us who came face to face with the enemy, there was no such thing as a good war, just a war we survived. Our only alternative was to die in some foreign land, and it was a fate I witnessed more often than I care to remember.

I've always taken life as it came to me and tried to make the best of the circumstances I have found myself in. That was never more true than during the war that broke out when I was just eighteen and which consumed almost six long years of my life.

In many ways I had much to be grateful for. By the age of twenty-five, I had become fluent in three languages and had learnt the art of war. I had forged deep and enduring friendships that were to last my whole life, and I had the gongs to prove that I'd done my duty: three Military Crosses, a *Croix de guerre*, a papal knighthood and the honour of being a *Chevalier* of the *Légion d'honneur*. I had fought in Syria and North Africa, escaped from two of the most feared prisoner-of-war camps in Europe and orchestrated guerrilla operations in Italy and France that kept divisions of Germans and Italians busy looking for me rather than killing my countrymen.

So, yes, in most people's eyes I had a 'good war', but it was also a war that kept me awake at night for many years. The memories of the comrades and enemies who were shot, blown up and knifed blighted my sleep. These things do not simply fade away when a whistle blows and

7

peace is resumed. I have no doubt that a whole raft of my generation felt exactly the same.

They say that survivors 'live to tell the tale', but we didn't want to tell the tale. All most of us wanted was to forget, and in the years after the war we didn't really talk about our wartime experiences unless we were asked. Even then most of us would be as self-effacing as possible; even my own children have never really known the details of my war.

Yet now, having just celebrated my 90th birthday, time has given me more perspective on events, and there seems little point in bashfulness. Indeed, 70 years after the event, those of us who are left have a duty to remind the next generation of what war really entails.

I would also like to think that I've had a life that bears retelling. My early years growing up in Edinburgh and the Highlands are a snapshot of a way of life that has now gone, while my university years and my business career give an insight into the growing pains of a nation emerging from the ruins of war.

Most of all, though, I've been blessed to have met some of the most interesting men not just of my generation but of those on either side. The roll call of people whom I've been fortunate enough to meet, occasionally befriend and often work alongside is something that gives me real pleasure.

There are sports stars aplenty, not least my brother Phil, arguably the best rugby player Scotland has produced and skipper of the 1925 Grand Slam side. There are too many to list here, but Emile Zátopek, Harold Abrahams and Eric Liddell all feature. I witnessed the first year rugby was played at Murrayfield and played my part in the 1948 Olympics.

I've also met many statesmen and politicians, ranging from Churchill and Monty through to the Queen, the Pope, Marshal Tito and President Giscard d'Estaing. From the wider world of culture there was Sir Malcolm Sargent, Neil Armstrong, Grace of Monaco and countless others. And in business I've had the good fortune to rub shoulders with many legendary figures from the nation's boardrooms and to have my contribution recognised in 1992 with a knighthood.

Most of all, though, I've lived a life made full by my friends and family, foremost among them my wife, Jean, and my three children, Angus, Ishbel and Duncan. Of course, I have regrets, things that I would have done differently, but as I look back upon my life at least I can boast that it was never dull. What better legacy can there be than that?

I

In the Beginning

I was born in Edinburgh by mistake. Actually, there were two mistakes about my birth. The first was that all my numerous siblings – and I was the last of seven – had been born either in India, where my father worked, or at our family home in Newtonmore in the Highlands of Scotland, but I wasn't. My mother was setting out for the train from Edinburgh to go to Newtonmore when events overcame her. She was taken back home to our house in Edinburgh, where I arrived soon afterwards. The birth itself was not undramatic. My mother was almost 46, a great age for a mother in those days, and both she and I were very sickly after the birth. It was decided that I should be christened in our house in Edinburgh seven days after my birth, as I probably wouldn't survive and my mother might not. However, she lived on to the age of 101, and I am still here a good length of time later.

My maternal grandfather, a retired Church of Scotland minister, carried out the christening. With his white hair, white beard and ecclesiastical manner, he was a remarkable old man. He had enjoyed a very wide education, which was reflected in his extremely interesting conversation, even when I was a boy. He had been at the University of Edinburgh and theological college and had then gone to university in Heidelberg in Germany before finally studying in Paris. He was in the French capital during the siege of 1870–1 when the Prussians were at the gates of the city, having swept the French before them and dismantled their empire. My grandfather harboured a lasting and deep dislike of the French from that time, saying that they behaved execrably towards each other during the miseries of the siege, stealing food and money from their neighbours and helping nobody except themselves. His opinions permeated my youth, but fortunately I came to have another opinion, as you will find out later.

The second mistake about my birth was that it happened at all. It was not until my teens that I fully appreciated that I was what is now euphemistically referred to as 'an afterthought'. My father, working in India as a judge, was a very organised man who had had six children before the Great War and planned to have their education out of the way long before his retirement was due. The seventh was quite clearly an error of judgement during one of his periods of leave, which tended to occur – by boat, of course – every two and a half to three years. He had been away virtually the whole of the First World War so could well have been overcome by enthusiasm on his return. That enthusiasm certainly waned when he found he had a seventh child to educate over the next twenty years, and it was not until I was virtually self-supporting at university that he began to have, I think, some regard for me.

My father returned on leave shortly after I was born, and when I was 18 months old my mother and I went out to join him in India. In those days the tour of duty was two and a half years in India followed by six months' leave, which included travelling to and fro by P&O steamer via the Suez Canal and then train across India from Bombay to Patna, where my father was then stationed. It was the time when senior officials enjoyed 'port out, starboard home' to avoid the strong sunlight, which was a much sought-after privilege. This tour of duty, with my mother spending half the time in India and half at home, set a pattern of family life that was probably even more peculiar for my elder brothers and sisters than it turned out to be for me.

My father had gone into the Indian Civil Service after leaving university and gaining one of the ten best results in his year's Civil Service examination list. Back then, in the 1890s, those would-be civil servants with the highest marks went not to the domestic Civil Service but to the Indian or Sudanese Civil Service. So it was that my father spent most of his career on the banks of the Ganges between Delhi and Calcutta, although by the time I was born he was a judge in the province of Bihar. He had gone there from a traditional Highland family, and he had made his way from the village school via George Watson's in Edinburgh, the University of Edinburgh, Trinity College, Oxford, and Middle Temple. The legal training was very much in his blood, so he quickly gravitated to the legal side of the Indian Civil Service, becoming a judge of the High Court and chancellor of Patna University.

When my mother joined my father as his bride in the 1890s, he was a junior district magistrate living a modest life in remotest rural India, and I can only begin to imagine what a traditional Scottish daughter of the manse thought of being parachuted into such an extraordinary life. I have a photograph of her a few years later when she had three very young children, mounted with them on a howdah on the back of an elephant, ready to accompany my father on a circuit of justice through his district. He rode ahead of her on a white horse, carrying a rifle for protection from wild animals and wearing a white topee on his head. Behind them was another elephant, carrying the huge marquee in which they both lived and from where he dispensed justice, and, behind that, a whole queue of bearers with enormous bundles on their heads, carrying whatever was needed, from cooking pots upwards.

My father acquired his first motor car relatively early in his career, with his Ford Model T one of the first cars on the Indian subcontinent. Yet, with so few passable roads to travel on, he still generally travelled by elephant. He got to know the country well, not least because he was an avid linguist who acquired all sorts of Indian language and dialect certificates.

My father rose to the top of the Indian judiciary, but we were not always so grand. My paternal grandfather's family was from the district of Badenoch, where we still live and which is traditional Macpherson country, the home of our clan since we were driven westwards down the Spey Valley in the late 11th century and settled amid the lush Speyside pastures around what is now the village of Newtonmore. My grandfather was born in the little township of Strone, just outside Newtonmore, and inherited a croft there. His wife, Anne Stewart, had an uncle who worked for the Caledonian Bank in Inverness, and my grandfather was much more interested in learning about this than crofting, so in due course the croft passed to his sister. He concentrated almost wholly on trading and building up a business selling coal, hay and straw, while also acting as the local transport contractor – which in those days meant horse and cart or carriage.

My grandfather was apparently a natural and very successful businessman, and he soon became prominent in local affairs. One of the friendships he struck up – perhaps, in those days, above his station – was with Mrs Brewster Macpherson of Balavil, the widow of the major landlord in the area who had retired to the dower house of that family in the village of Newtonmore. She strongly encouraged him to send his very promising sons from school at Newtonmore Primary and Kingussie Secondary to George Watson's, which gave them the flying start to go on to university.

So successfully did my father and his brothers seize the chance that had been given them that there is a story that remains famous in Badenoch. It's about a wealthy Englishman who took his holiday in Newtonmore in 1916 and was being driven in a carriage from his hotel to the station by my grandfather. On the way the visitor talked at length about his family and the success of his sons and then, rather condescendingly, asked, 'Have you any sons, and what are they doing?' to which my grandfather replied, 'Well, yes, sir, I have three sons: the youngest is a serving officer with the Queen's Own Cameron Highlanders in France, the second is a minister of the government and a member of the War Cabinet and the third is a judge of the High Court in India.'

My father was small and thick-set, so it came as a surprise to me that he had been a seriously good athlete and a noted shinty player in his youth. He was not a patient man and found domesticity, when he came home on leave, more than a little trying. He had particular doubts about my behaviour and upbringing, which was largely conducted in his absence, and we did not see eye to eye until my university days. It was sad that I got to know him so late.

My mother, born Helen Cameron in Arbroath in the reign of Queen Victoria, lived for a century and enjoyed a life that spanned everything from the Tay Bridge Disaster to man walking on the moon. She was an able woman who met my father at the University of Edinburgh, where she was the gold medallist in the university's first class of women, but her early years in India were not easy ones. My father was often away and always busy, so she had to fend for herself, while her staff could spot a greenhorn at a thousand paces and ruled her with a rod of iron.

She eventually asserted herself, however, and went on to become a very distinguished figure in her own right in India. When I went through my mother's papers after her death, the picture that quickly emerged was of a woman who felt deeply about the lot of Indian women. She was one of the reformers who helped women on the subcontinent develop a real role outside the home by campaigning against the tradition of purdah, which decreed that many Indian women stayed inside their family home so that they would remain unseen by men. Despite local opposition, she even more controversially became the first secretary of the Women's Council of Bihar and Narissa, a new branch of the National Women's Council of India. Her work in this area led to the award of the Kaisar-i-Hind gold medal by King Edward VIII and several other honours.

I remember little or nothing about the first three years of my life, which were spent in India, although I've been told the stories of how my stout ayah, or nanny, killed the huge cobra that appeared out of a big earthenware jar in the bathroom while I was being bathed, and of the huge 'sacred' python that lived in our cellar and would emerge once a week looking for food.

Instead, my earliest memories are of our home in Edinburgh, which was a large red-brick detached house called Edgebrook in East Fettes Avenue, right next to Inverleith Park. Our road led up to the imposing Gothic tower of Fettes College, and in many ways my childhood came at a time when the old-style Victorian upbringing was giving way to a more modern way of life. Early photos of my sisters as children show them resplendent in long white lacy dresses and black stockings, while my elder brothers were dressed in sailor suits or velvet jackets in their early years, clothes that neither I nor my contemporaries would ever have worn.

At Edgebrook we rose early, and even before breakfast there were prayers in the living room, with my mother reading a short Bible passage and playing a hymn on the piano. My mother was a true believer who, when home, insisted on personally putting each of us to bed with a prayer. That Christian vision – a prayer for oneself and for others – has remained with me absolutely, and I believe I have uttered this legacy of my mother's firm Christian faith to myself in bed every night of my life, even when sleeping rough, in hospital or in a prisoner-of-war camp. Mealtimes were absolutely rigid, and woe betide anyone who was a second late. We would say grace before meals and have bread and butter first at teatime – never butter and jam together. Jam or honey could follow on the second piece, but, if so, no butter was allowed.

Soon after my fifth birthday I was sent to a dame school called St Monica's with my sister Rhona, who was fourteen. We would walk to school up the cobbles of Comely Bank Hill, but on the way home I would perch on her bicycle and we'd coast dangerously down the steep hill, bumping over the uneven cobbles and hoping not to collide with the horse-drawn cabs that were everywhere in 1920s Edinburgh. My only other memory of that school is of a parents' musical day, when we all had to go dressed in kilts and my mother forced me to wear my sister's outgrown green-serge bloomers. Oh, the shame of it!

After a year at St Monica's I graduated to the Edinburgh Academy prep school, which in those days was with the main school in Henderson Row in Stockbridge, a short tram ride from home, although I cycled on a third-hand fairy-cycle with solid tyres, which my mother bought for seven pence. At this time I also graduated to the enormous privilege of pocket money to the amount of one penny a week. I would often save up to buy something from the new Woolworths that had opened at the east end of Princes Street – 'Nothing over sixpence' – but just as often I would dive into the shop near the Academy that had huge bottles of sweets on its shelves to taunt the schoolboys. I also developed a lifelong obsession with steam trains after a doctor friend of my parents, Dr Parth, gave me a Hornby model railway set for my sixth birthday, and much of my money went on catalogues and magazines to fuel that enthusiasm.

At the Academy the main games were the traditional ones of fox and geese, and hailes, a very old Edinburgh game played with a type of short wooden bat with a long handle and pancake-like end on which you balanced or by which you hit a ball, endeavouring to run round or hit round your opponents. We didn't really understand the rules, but we had great fun grazing our knees on the gravel playground.

Virtually all of the teachers were grey-haired old women, except for Miss MacGillivray, who counted as young on account of her flame-red hair. All the classrooms had oak desks and benches, which had been there since the school was founded well over a century before and onto which we were unceremoniously crammed. I doubt the method of teaching had changed much since the school was built, but it certainly produced results. There was a great deal of mental work, oral work, spelling bees, mental arithmetic, fast question and response, reward and punishment, and I am quite sure it has been helpful to me right through my career. I certainly thrived, finding myself top of the top class.

My eldest brother, Jim, an extremely kind man who was probably the nicest of my brothers, had qualified as a doctor at the University of Edinburgh and left home, but the others were present to varying degrees.

My second eldest brother, Phil, a rugby hero known throughout Scotland as GPS, was an accountant and an enormous personality in Edinburgh in the 1920s and early 1930s. I remember a letter from overseas being addressed simply to 'GPS Macpherson, Scotland' that was unhesitatingly delivered to our door. He was widely reckoned the greatest centre ever to have played for Scotland and one of the greatest anywhere in the world. He had an extraordinary capacity to flash past an opponent with a burst of speed, along with a devastating swerve, sidestep or dummy, and he had a tremendous eye for the game. He captained not only Scotland but also the Edinburgh Academical Club, so our drawing room became a gathering place the evening before each match, with the leading players congregating to discuss tactics.

My elder brothers may well have felt overshadowed by Phil, but for me it was marvellous having such a famous brother, not least because it meant that I had the privilege of going out to Raeburn Place and kicking a ball around with world-famous international players. I sat on the knee of one of the early visitors, Eric Liddell, the Scotland rugby international and Olympic sprint gold medallist who later became a missionary in China and was to die in a Japanese prisoner-of-war camp. I must be one of the few people alive – if not the only person – who actually met both the men whose feats were immortalised in that great film *Chariots of Fire*, since I later got to know Harold Abrahams very well.

It was very much a rugby atmosphere, and there are several other strong personalities who really stand out in my memory. The great Glasgow Accies, Scotland and Lions stand-off Herbert Waddell was an unforgettable character who not only played with great skill but was also a true amateur who insisted on taking a glass of port in the dressing-room before every game as he said it eliminated staleness. A third member of those famous teams, the Heriot's, Scotland and Lions full-back Dan Drysdale, was later a business colleague of mine, so it is not really surprising that rugby football has been the dominant sporting hobby of my life.

Had there been any doubt about my predilection for rugby, then my journey through Edinburgh's educational establishment removed it entirely. Edinburgh Academy was the birthplace of the game in Scotland and the school's Raeburn Place ground the venue for the first-ever game of international rugby, in which Scotland beat England in 1871. My first headmaster at Cargilfield School, which I attended after Edinburgh Academy, had been an international stand-off, and so too had his successor, H.J. 'Dinks' Kittermaster, who was my sister Sheila's husband, while in turn his successor, K.L.T. Jackson, was yet another Scotland stand-off. Finally, my headmaster at Fettes was former England stand-off A.H. Ashcroft. Clearly, I was destined to be a rugby player and a stand-off at that.

At Edgebrook, in the back garden, I used to take my small oval ball out, and in every spare moment of dry weather I would be kicking the ball against a blank piece of wall, drop-kicking it, punting it, catching it, dummy passing and swerving round bushes. I even devised an indoor game for darkness or bad weather when I was on my own in the household, which I also played every Thursday, when I was sent off after school to spend the evening with my grandparents at their enormous flat on Dundonald Street. My grandfather was, as I have said, a retired minister, a splendidly prophetic figure, tall and white bearded; my small, dumpy grandmother was memorable only for her kindness and her habit of putting pepper instead of sugar on her strawberries.

Often on Thursdays Aunt Margaret, the youngest of my mother's four sisters, would take me to Queen Street Gardens and act as a touch judge while I played rugby until it was time to go home for tea. Aunt Margaret was a very good-looking lady who was by then a spinster in early middle years and represented a tragic generation of women. She had been engaged to a soldier during the First World War, and he had been killed. When her sisters married and moved away, she ended up looking after her aged parents, feeling not any bitterness but an emptiness. This was later forcibly brought home to me when I looked back on one of the rare times I was allowed to actually stay the night at Dundonald Street, when I was about seven. Aunt Margaret was bathing me before I went to bed and, almost absent-mindedly, touched my male organ and said, in a whisper to herself, 'Isn't it extraordinary that that little toorie will give such pleasure one day.' It was a moment that laid bare the frustration of a generation of women whose men lay dead on the battlefield.

Between 1930 and my father's retirement in 1936 my mother spent an increasingly large amount of time with him in India, which was very much required for his social and professional life. We were looked after by various ladies and always spent the summer holidays at Speyville, my grandfather's house in Newtonmore, which is why I've always considered it to be my home village. My mother always seemed to come back for the summer holidays, which I remember as a time of endless enjoyment and almost continuously good weather. I lived outside in those days, creeping out of the house at seven o'clock and running down the hill to the railway station, where the delightful, roly-poly, elderly Miss Budge, one of the kindest souls I have ever come across, presided over a small newsagent's hut. After checking to see that nobody was looking, she would usher me under the counter and let me read all the comics that I was not allowed to buy or to have at home as they were considered educationally inferior.

There was a train at eight o'clock each morning from Newtonmore that would take shoppers to Inverness for the day, with the return train arriving back at about seven o'clock in the evening. It was named 'The Johnstone', after some long-dead railway tycoon, and fascinated me because it turned Newtonmore village station into a veritable terminus. As I got older, I was allowed to ride on the footplate of the engine and help hook up to the carriages, and in my teens I even got the odd chance to drive it, an experience that gave me a deep affection for steam trains and some knowledge of how they worked, which came in useful during the war.

I spent the rest of the day doing chores, which for me meant picking the raspberries, gooseberries, blackcurrants and redcurrants that grew prolifically in the vegetable garden. If I could get away, I would go down to the river, hack my way around the golf course or picnic in the glen. My mother was a strict disciplinarian who thought nothing of pulling down my trousers and giving me several strokes with a wooden-handled hairbrush, but she could also be very tender and would sometimes take me to a small hill called Craggan at the back of the village, where we would sit on a big rock at the top while she read to me from Kipling's *The Jungle Book*.

Back in Edinburgh we had a series of housekeepers. At one stage my sister Sheila, who was studying for a degree in physiotherapy, was put in charge of the household for over a year, which meant that the poor girl had to look after me, plus Archie and Rhona when they came home from school, while Niall was at Edinburgh University and Phil was resident and very demanding in his time and his guests. Occasionally I was even allowed to bring a school friend home for tea, which usually meant my closest friend Bill Normand. His family returned the favour, taking me off on several holidays with them to Boat of Garten or the rather grand hotel of Greywalls at the doors of Muirfield golf course, although I had no idea how lucky I was.

Various members of the family would also come to Speyville, with the most memorable visit being from my Aunt Jill one summer. She was married to my father's brother Ian, later to become Lord Strathcarron and at that stage a cabinet minister. Aunt Jill was English, dramatic, extrovert and, to me, wholly delightful. By some error of judgement I was allowed to sit next to her at tea and was amazed when she lit up a cigarette. I turned to my mother and in a very audible stage whisper said, 'I thought you said that ladies don't smoke,' to which my mother, in an equally audible stage whisper, said, 'They don't, dear.' Aunt Jill thought this was hilarious and shoved a ten-shilling note down my shirt, which was the biggest note that I had ever seen.

One morning towards the end of that year's spring term, my mother woke me, and I must have looked or behaved extremely strangely because, instead of hustling me through the usual hurried morning routine, she tucked me into her own bed and sent for the doctor. Unfortunately, before the doctor arrived, she decided I needed to be strengthened with my first ever breakfast in bed – kippers – which I promptly threw up all over her best quilt after a couple of mouthfuls. After taking some throat swabs, the doctor diagnosed streptococcal diphtheria and more or less told my mother to prepare for my funeral. This turned out to be premature, but, aged nine, I did spend the rest of spring and early summer of 1930 convalescing at Newtonmore.

Three sisters called the Campbells were in residence at a house called Croftdhuac and even though they were in their sixties they still provided some company for me while I awaited the arrival of my parents. At Speyville there were two maids, and in spite of having to share the double bed in the downstairs bedroom this was a much sought-after job because it was the quickest way for young local girls to better themselves, with the next stop a job in a hotel. During my convalescence one of the maids was a girl from Glasgow called Flora MacDonald who was so small that she had to stand on a box to reach the sink for washing-up. Not allowed to do any chores because I was recuperating, I would potter about the kitchen, often sitting down next to her and talking to her. She would stand on the box, and it was only a matter of time before I realised that I could look up her black skirt, at which stage I discovered that she had the idiosyncrasy of never wearing any knickers. I was never allowed to touch, though.

By the summer holidays I was well enough to take part in the fun and games that Newtonmore in the summer had to offer. In those days it was very much a holiday town, with the villagers moving out of the comfortable houses where they spent the winter months and into the wooden bothies at the back, letting their houses at hefty prices throughout July, August and September to families from Glasgow, Dundee and Edinburgh who would take them for a whole month at a time. This meant that there were a lot of young people around, which led to swimming in the dark peaty waters of the River Calder during the day and evening parties at Speyville, where the youngsters would crowd round the dining-room table and play vociferous and exciting games of racing demon. Other evenings my mother would suggest a sing-song, and my brother Niall, who became a fellow of the Royal College of Music and was a brilliant pianist, would play while we stood around the piano and sang the old folk songs of the Highlands in Gaelic and English. The quality may not have been superlative, but the enthusiasm and the volume were impressive.

On Sundays we all went to church, the boys leaving on the first stroke of the five-minute bell and trying to arrive, desperately out of breath, on the last stroke. The minister, Dr Dugald MacFarlane, who later became moderator of the General Assembly of the Church of Scotland, travelled over from Kingussie and was like a primeval Old Testament prophet. Tall, white-haired and with a heavy white moustache, he spoke with deliberation and slowness in a splendid accent from the Western Isles, condemning us or threatening us in every sermon with damnation if we didn't mend our ways. Splendid traditional stuff, and I miss it nowadays.

2

Bundled Off

Convalescing up in Newtonmore in the spring of 1930, and then having a riot of a time during the summer, I was blissfully unaware that my life was about to change dramatically. My parents were spending most of their time in India, but with my father's retirement just six years away he and my mother had decided to leave Edinburgh and base themselves permanently in Newtonmore. This involved selling Edgebrook, our family home, as all my brothers and sisters had either left or were away at boarding school. There was, however, a fly in the ointment: me.

Despite the fact that my father really resented the expense, and thought that boarding prep schools were inherently snobbish institutions best avoided, they decided that the most sensible option was to send me to board at Cargilfield, in Barnton, on the outskirts of Edinburgh. That way my brother and sister who were at university in Edinburgh, or my grandparents and dear Aunt Margaret, would always be handy.

The first I knew of my imminent departure to Cargilfield was the arrival during the summer holidays of a list of essential clothing, followed by the inevitable arguments about what should be worn under my kilt. The fact that I was less than enamoured of this turn of events was neither here nor there: my parents assumed that I would be resilient enough to cope, and they were right.

The headmaster, who was new at the time I arrived, was former Scotland stand-off Rufus Bruce Lockhart, a remarkable man from a remarkable family. His brother R.H. Bruce Lockhart was already a famous diplomat and intelligence man, having written a splendid book about life in Moscow at the end of the First World War. The headmaster's four sons would also prove to be special men: the eldest, John, was in charge of pumping propaganda into enemy-held territories in the Second World War; Rab and Logie both played rugby for Scotland, and alongside me for London Scottish, and also became headmasters; Paddy, the youngest and lame from birth, was a very fine squash player and went on to be a celebrated surgeon in Canada. Logie remains a good friend to this day.

Bruce Lockhart had a French mother and was extremely gifted in the teaching of that language. He enthused us all with it, and he instituted, at lunch twice a week, a French table, where only that language could be spoken. Those of us who came under his spell there learnt a quality of French that passes in France and retained it all our lives. In fact that was probably the lasting legacy of my time there.

My new headmaster was also an excellent musician and created a fine musical tradition at Cargilfield. Every two years he and Mr Randolph, the music master, produced a Gilbert and Sullivan opera. I took part in two of these, *Iolanthe* and *Patience*, learning the score off by heart and being so inspired that I wrote the words for an operetta of my own. This proved to be highly embarrassing when Archie and I spent an Easter holiday with my Uncle John at his home at Keppoch, near Spean Bridge, in the Highlands. The two of them discovered my notebook of writing and rewrote it in ribald fashion, greatly to my shame and discomfiture.

Uncle John was a kind man – and Aunt May was even kinder – but he liked to present a rough exterior. He had been severely wounded in both arms during the First World War, and his claw-like hands were locked in a particular position. He still farmed, and both he and May were expert with dogs – he with sheepdogs and she with Labradors in field trials, at which she became an internationally reputed judge. They were never very good with money and always seemed in some sort of problem. They were peripatetic from farm to farm, and Keppoch was one of their longer stays. Their money problems had started at an early age when, after the war, they borrowed from my father and my Uncle Ian for a farming enterprise in the Hebrides, which failed. When they were unable to pay back the loan or guarantee, relationships soured in the family, particularly with Uncle Ian, for many years. Uncle John had an extremely fast-growing beard, and he would be quite bristly by lunchtime, whereupon he would seize me and rub his cheek on mine, a gentle form of teasing to which I reacted with fury and dislike. But they were happy holidays for all that.

I didn't really enjoy my early years at Cargilfield. I conformed well enough and worked hard, but somehow it wasn't a happy place until I became quite a senior boy, and then it took off, particularly in the last year. I found the academic experience of Cargilfield a very different one from that at the Academy. The classes were smaller, and the exercises in mental gymnastics that had characterised the Academy were replaced by a good deal of learning by rote, but my time at the Academy meant I was well equipped to deal with that. Either way, the standard of teaching must have been remarkably good, because, of the top form, which was taught by the elderly Mr Woodsmith, all but two boys got scholarships to public schools.

But of much more interest to me was sport. At the Academy we played football and touch rugby, but proper rugby was played at Cargilfield. My constant solo practice stood me in good stead, and Bruce Lockhart soon put us through real training: swerving, sidestepping and dummying at full speed; learning to give and take a pass; and lots of goal-kicking practice. But it wasn't until my penultimate year at the school that my rugby came of age, when, after hanging on to a place in the first fifteen by the skin of my teeth for most of the season, I put in a rugged performance in the Melrose mud against St Mary's and was congratulated by the games master, Mr Foster, which bolstered my confidence so much that I never looked back.

The big novelty at Cargilfield was cricket. The master in charge of cricket was Mr Rowley, a former Somerset wicketkeeper whose mangled hands were a constant source of fascination and admiration. Several of us even tried to prepare ourselves for life as professional cricketers by copying the way his fingers had been affected, and I still have one little finger that is distorted at the top joint, which I did quite deliberately at the time to prove my commitment to the game.

My enthusiasm for this new game knew few bounds, and summers at Speyville now saw me setting up a packing case against the back of the house and spending hour upon hour bowling a tennis ball, both fast and with spin, against the wall. If I could find anyone to bowl at me, I would bat with the clachan I used to play hailes at the Academy. I had a good eye, and my constant practice paid dividends as I became one of the few boys of my generation to score a century while at prep school. I was even making a decent score in the fathers' match once – the fathers used to bat left-handed with a shaved-down bat but still tended to defeat us – until my sister Rhona appeared around the sight screen with such a ludicrous little hat perched on the corner of her head that I momentarily lost concentration and was bowled.

My brother Archie was inextricably involved in my life at Cargilfield, mainly because he was studying at the University of Edinburgh. He had intended to follow the examples of Phil and Niall, who both got open scholarships to Oxford to read Classics, but failed his scholarship examination. So instead he went to the University of Edinburgh and studied medicine, later becoming one of Britain's most distinguished surgeons and lecturing in the United States. I looked up to Archie not because of his academic achievements but because, despite being the smallest of the Macpherson boys, he captained the university at rugby and cricket and also played hockey for them. He played rugby for Edinburgh District, narrowly missing a Scottish cap, hockey as an international and opened the batting for Scotland on seven occasions, including scoring 40 against the MCC at Lord's.

Archie might have done even better at sport had it not been for a series of bizarre accidents. The first happened when he was going skiing with my sister Rhona at the height of his rugby and cricket career and they were due to meet at Victoria train station. Archie was already on the train with his gear, but Rhona was delayed and was running up the platform as the train started to move, so Archie, realising she was going to miss the train, was stupid enough to jump out, falling over backwards on the platform and fracturing his skull. The next accident came on the rugby field when he was captaining the University of Edinburgh against Oxford University at Craiglockhart and was tackled into a wooden corner post that broke and impaled itself in his midriff, penetrating his kidney. Finally, in the first winter of the war, he was skiing alone down the Monadliaths at the back of Newtonmore and dislocated his knee.

Yet Archie was a byword for sporting excellence, and as I progressed at Cargilfield, and showed signs of being good at sport, I picked up the nickname of 'Archie', much to the puzzlement of my Aunt Margaret, who thought they were calling me 'RT', as those are my initials – my Sunday name being Ronald Thomas Stewart Macpherson.

Highland dancing was also a speciality of Cargilfield and something I really enjoyed. I had won some medals at the school dancing competition shortly before Archie and I went to stay with our brother Jim in Orkney in the Easter holiday of 1934, and Archie demanded that I teach him the dances. Archie was naturally light on his feet, and his enthusiasm was fired by my demonstration to the point that he became an enthusiastic dancer and later a judge of Highland dancing.

Orkney was a happy place. Jim was well dug in as the parish doctor for the little town of Evie and, being extremely jovial, was very popular. The house was lamp-lit when we first went there, but by our last visit there was a small windmill that produced enough electricity to run the lights and a primitive radio. My main memory of Orkney is of the constant wind and the fact that the only trees were around the ancient cathedrals in Stromness and Kirkwall, which meant that tree birds like blackbirds and thrushes nested in hedges or dry-stone dykes because they couldn't find their natural habitat. The island itself was fascinating, whether it was the Pictish brochs of Skara Brae, the ancient town of Kirkwall, with its strong Viking overtones, or the huge cliffs of Marwick at the other end of the island, which fall nearly a thousand feet into the sea and stare unblinkingly at the spot where Kitchener drowned in the sinking of HMS *Hampshire*.

The Easter holidays in Orkney were the highlight of my year, although getting there and back often was not. We went from Leith docks in small ships named after Orkney saints like St Magnus and St Ronald, leaving at around four o'clock in the afternoon and arriving in Aberdeen at dawn before heading on through invariably stormy seas to Kirkwall. I suffered badly from both carsickness and seasickness and had usually turned green before we were out of the Firth of Forth, the point at which I would retire to my bunk with one of those hideous clip-on things that you were allowed to be sick into. Occasionally the seas were calm, and when that happened the journey was a joy. I remember one particular southward journey when the leg from Aberdeen to Leith was accompanied by brilliant sunshine and dead-calm water. We cruised effortlessly down the east coast of Scotland with marvellous views of Dunnottar Castle, the Firth of Tay and round the butt of Fife. You couldn't do better in the Mediterranean.

If I was seasick in the bigger boats, then the smaller Orcadian ones didn't seem to affect me, which was a good thing because there were frequent journeys with Jim to Rousay and the other islands that didn't have a doctor. We would buffet through stormy seas in the open, heavy timber-framed post boat with Orcadian seamen of great skill who respected the sea but knew that they could master it. I would also accompany Jim on his frequent social invitations in the evening. The format of these was invariably the same: a gigantic tea at six o'clock, followed by conversation and songs in front of the fire until another gigantic meal appeared at ten o'clock, leaving us to stagger home just before midnight.

Opposite Jim's house was the tiny uninhabited island of Eynhallow, between the mainland of Orkney and the island of Rousay, and on each side of Eynhallow there was a tremendous tidal rip where the North Sea and the Atlantic met in narrow waters. Archie was a keen and hugely knowledgeable birdwatcher, so we would often go by boat to Eynhallow to photograph birds like the eider duck, puffin and petrel, and even after he went back to university I would still go over on my own.

All our lives I had a very close affinity with Archie, and we did a great deal together. We also avidly photographed birds at Newtonmore, where we concentrated on birds of prey, photographing kestrels, peregrines and golden eagles on their nests and in the air. As the nests were invariably on steep cliffs, Archie would hold the end of a rope while I climbed down the cliff to do the actual photographing. That wasn't necessary for photographing the golden eagles that nested by Loch Dubh on Cluny Castle land, where we had permission to go. Although difficult, their nest was accessible via a narrow, flat ledge that brought you to within three or four feet of the nest itself. We soon discovered that, while eagles can see everything, they can't count, so we constructed a hide into which two of us would crawl on our tummies, with one then leaving so that the eagles would think we had left.

That allowed us to get some amazing photos: of the eggs, of the chicks hatching and of the adult eagles feeding the chicks rabbit, hare or grouse. At first they fed the chicks the carefully chewed tender innards. Then they opened out the carcasses and allowed the chicks to get in for themselves, and, finally, they let the chicks tear the birds apart. The nest was formed of two halves: the one in which the mother bird sat and in which the chicks hatched; and the one called 'the shambles', where they did their butchery and which was coated with feathers, skin, bones and blood. There were two eggs, which is normal with the eagle, and only one hatched, as is again quite normal. We chronicled the way in which the chick, which had snow-white down when born, gradually changed colour and then acquired its feathers and, finally, the flying lessons, where it was encouraged by its parents to glide off the top and then, when it refused to jump, was forcibly pushed over the edge.

I knew how that little chick felt to be pushed around, because in those days, when Archie and I would go out for a walk in our beloved hills around Newtonmore, Archie was older and far stronger than me, and on the steep climbs I constantly struggled to keep up with him. It must have helped build me up, though, because when I operated in mountainous regions during the war I realised that most people struggled to keep up with me.

If school was about rugby and cricket, my summers in Newtonmore widened my sporting horizons considerably. There was obviously a great deal of walking, but the village was also famous for the Highland game of shinty, a particularly fierce version of hockey. Despite the relatively recent emergence of Ronald Ross's magnificent Kingussie sides, Newtonmore Shinty Club, of which I am vice president, remains a giant of the game, and as a boy many of my sporting heroes were the local men who wore their blue-and-white-striped shirts, especially those who played the day in 1931 when my Uncle John took me to Inverness to see Newtonmore beat Inverary 4–1 in the final of the Camanachd Cup. Each morning break the schoolchildren in the village would practise shinty on the slightly hollowed flat area by the golf course's 18th hole, and in the summer evenings up to 25 youngsters would descend on the same spot, which belonged to the Miss Middlemisses, to play bicycle polo using their camans, or shinty sticks.

We all played golf, too, and I still have my old wooden-shafted clubs from those days. Being ten years younger than any of my siblings, I quickly became disillusioned at trying to keep up with Phil, Niall and Rhona in particular, who all played to low single-figure handicaps. Rhona, who was also an accomplished tennis player, later picked up all sorts of medals in India, although she was helped by what they called a forecaddy out in front, whose naked toes would pick up her ball from a nasty patch and put it in a good lie without anybody knowing. If I struggled to fall in love with the game, my father killed off any prospect of my becoming a golfer. He really was the most discouraging person to play with, because as I grew stronger and hit the ball further so he hit the ball less far but always dead straight down the middle, and when he got near the green it was one chip, one putt. I have never been a patient person, and the frustration this sparked in me was so overwhelming that my enthusiasm for the game has never recovered.

On the days when the sun didn't shine, I was also extremely busy. While at Cargilfield my pocket money had increased to ten shillings a term for incidental expenses, which included twopence a week for sweets and bus fares home. There were, however, always a few shillings left, which went on extending the huge Hornby model train set that I established in the loft of the old stables at Speyville. I managed to add to the layout whenever I received gifts from family or birthday presents, and once I made a killing charging old ladies sixpence each to carry their bags from one train to another after a railway accident at Newtonmore blocked the line.

Summers in Newtonmore were an endless succession of old faces and new experiences, but one incident particularly sticks in my mind. It was the summer of 1934, when I was 13 and had just left Cargilfield. It was a very hot day, and Rhona and I had set out to climb Allt a' Chaorainn. We had barely got into Glen Banchor and were crossing a burn when Rhona fell in, going in right up to her neck in a deep, brown, peaty pool with shade on one side, where she had fallen in, and bright sunshine on the other. It was such a nice day that we decided to swim and lie in the sun for the hour it would take her clothes to dry, so we both stripped off. At that time I had been familiar with Greek classical statues in all their shiny stonework, and although I had on one occasion seen naked ladies in the theatre in Edinburgh, the Lord Chamberlain only allowed them to appear naked provided they were totally hairless and did not move. I had therefore always assumed that women were totally hairless head to foot, so it was a great shock to behold my sister's comfortable triangle of attractive dark hair. It was a long time before I got over the shock.

The last two years of Cargilfield were a crescendo of enjoyment. My brothers were such high-achievers that much the same was expected of me, so when I got a scholarship it brought me kudos at school but little comment at home. Much the same was true of rugby and cricket. Phil was still a legendary figure in Scottish rugby, while Archie was in his prime, so managing two years in the firsts for rugby and cricket barely registered with my family. I did, however, take a lot of satisfaction from

the final sports day, when I'd obviously grown bigger and stronger, with
the result that I won all the events except the high jump and was awarded
the cup for the top performer of the games.

It was a tinge of glory that provided a deeply satisfactory note on
which to end my time at the school. Not that I was feeling nostalgic
about the place. I never remember looking back and regretting leaving,
because this was a step that was inevitable, and the time had come to
move on to the next chapter of my life.

3

Calm before the Storm

In September 1934 I went to the Edinburgh boarding school Fettes College, and it was only years later that I discovered from my father's correspondence how close I came to being sent south of the border. Although I had the top scholarship to the school, that provided only about a third of the annual fees, and my father – still annoyed at having to cough up for me – was pushing Fettes to cover more. He sent countless letters on the subject, mentioning that Eton and Winchester were offering better terms, until the headmaster of Fettes finally told him to take it or leave it. Knowing that there were others waiting in the wings, he took it.

Fettes was a totally new world to me. In those days the wake-up bell from the college tower rang at seven o'clock, and you were to be dressed and in school by half past seven. There was a break from two to four in the afternoon for games and then lessons from four to half past six, followed by supper and two hours of prep. Wednesday and Saturday afternoons were for the major internal or external school matches: rugby in the winter, hockey in the spring, cricket and athletics in the summer. On Sunday you got up an hour later, wore a top hat and tails and carried a black, carefully rolled umbrella under your arm as you made your way through the streets of Edinburgh to St Stephen's Church, an impressive building in the centre of town where the equally impressive minister, Mr Thompson, dispensed fire and brimstone from the pulpit. We were not allowed to leave the school before a quarter past ten for the eleven o'clock service, and had to be back for lunch at one o'clock, so there was no possibility of detouring into town or for any other nefarious diversions.

But if everything at Fettes was shiny new, this was also a world in which my brothers cast long shadows. I went into Glencorse boarding house, where Archie had been a dominant figure not very long before, and it was made clear to me that I was expected to perform. I was also appointed as a fag – basically a servant – to an elegant and sophisticated senior prefect called Laurie Boston, who had the distinction of being in the rugby first XV. He was a bit of a dandy, and my job was not only to clean his shoes and make his toast but to make sure that his suits were well pressed and laid out for him for the following morning.

Laurie Boston was the captain of rugby and endeared himself to me by selecting me for the house junior team, known as the House Belows. This meant that as a 14 year old I would find myself pitted against boys of 17 or 18, and although I acquitted myself well in a comfortable win over a house called Kimmerghame, I had the misfortune for the game to be refereed by the headmaster, who saw me take a heavy tackle from a much older boy. After the game he sent for Boston and told him that I was not physically strong enough to withstand this level of rugby and that it might destroy my future confidence in the game. This was a huge disappointment because playing for the House Belows had given me an enviable status among the other new boys. I was instead put in the Colts, which was for boys of seven and a half stone or under, and found myself playing against similar teams from other public schools but also against the prep schools that we had recently left.

If I enjoyed Colts rugby enormously, I wasn't being challenged academically. That began to change when Freddie Macdonald, a housemaster who had been a contemporary and close friend of my brother Phil, made a point of pushing me pretty hard in class. But one day in Latin my life was to change when, halfway through a particularly thorny passage of prose, I suddenly keeled over. Freddie Macdonald moved with astonishing speed from his desk and caught me before I hit the floor, but I woke up in the sanatorium. I didn't know it then, but I would be spending a lot of time in there.

I had displayed no prior symptoms, so it was only when the areas of pain developed that I was diagnosed as having osteomyelitis and taken to a private nursing home in Drumsheugh Gardens. My knee, hip and wrist were operated on by David Band, a distinguished surgeon in whom my surgeon brother Archie had great confidence. The operations, which involved open-wound draining, were quite lengthy but were apparently successful, and I was once again dispatched to spend the summer term convalescing in Newtonmore. That August Mr Band, who also holidayed in Newtonmore, decided to take me to Edinburgh for more tests, and we set out in his sports car only to have to quickly abandon it when the back wheel burst into flames as we crossed the Drumochter summit. The fire was quickly extinguished, at which point it became apparent that he had been driving at 70 miles an hour with the brake on.

Changing a red-hot wheel proved tricky, but we eventually found our way to Edinburgh, where I was declared sound of body and available to go back to school that September. Rugby was out, of course, but at least I was allowed to play golf. A local GP, Dr Silver, played out of town and was happy to have a playing partner, and he probably thought that he was doing me a favour when he invited me back to his house for tea and cakes after one of our rounds. However, it meant that I was returned to school later than normal, with the result that I got six of the best from my housemaster, Mr Edwards, and was banned from golf for a month as a punishment.

In December 1934, shortly before I plunged into these bouts of osteomyelitis, my family had decided that it would be good for me to travel and to practise my French, so they dispatched me to Switzerland, where I was to stay with my mother's younger sister, who had married a Swiss pastor from Lausanne. A distant cousin of my mother's, Marjorie Boyd, who owned a printing works in Belfast, was also visiting friends in Switzerland and had no experience of foreign travel, so I was to travel with her from London. Phil put me onto the sleeper at Waverley Station only to find I had been put in with a lady. As she knew Phil, she didn't mind, although I think she may have changed her mind as I noisily suffered the effects of travel sickness on the top bunk all night.

Pale and shaken, I made my way across London to the Grosvenor Hotel, Victoria, where I met the formidable Mrs Boyd at twelve o'clock sharp. We left from Victoria that afternoon, crossing the Channel on a steamer and then travelling through France into Switzerland, and sleeping in a couchette compartment where the seats turned into very smart blue, velvety beds at night. With the exception of the first three years of my life, which were spent living in India, this was not only my first experience of going outside Britain, it was the first time I had been outside Scotland. We duly arrived in Lausanne, our taxi delivered Mrs Boyd to her hotel and I went on to my aunt's. Most of the visit is a blur, although my 21-year-old cousin Evelyn took me up into the mountains, where she and a group of her friends had rented a chalet. I was lent ski gear and set about teaching myself to ski, an experiment that almost came to grief when I hit a ditch at full speed.

Back in Scotland the first two Easter holidays from Fettes were again spent on Orkney, where they coincided with the Silver Jubilee of King George V and the coronation of King George VI. The latter occasion led to huge celebrations in Kirkwall, with a ladies' hockey match between Orkney and Shetland. It sticks in my mind because I wrote a match report that I sent to the local paper, *The Orcadian*, which to my astonishment was published in full.

Eventually we had to confront the osteomyelitis again, and I was taken to the school sanatorium for a second bout of operations. This involved heavy sedation and considerable pain followed by a journey to the Western General Hospital, where my brother Archie was a resident surgeon. I was put into the care of a Mr Robert Stirling, a genius of a surgeon who was so versatile that he also operated on my mother's knee when she suffered from severe arthritis. He was a hearty man and set about combating the osteomyelitis that riddled my anatomy. He was successful, and I haven't been bothered since, but it was a long job, which meant that I had to be moved to a small private greenhouse in the hospital garden where I spent the spring and early summer in splendid isolation. I gradually recovered from the various operations and had twice-weekly treatments from the surgeon, whose main task was to keep the various holes in me open so that the drains removed all the nastiness from my system.

I passed the time reading an enormous number of novels by authors such as Sapper, Buchan, A.E.W. Mason, Rider Haggard and Dornford Yates, often as many as five books a week. Archie looked in when he could, and various other Edinburgh relatives bounced in from time to time, but I was strangely content, happy to let events run their course, as I have done all my life. I had time off for good behaviour between operations and was up in the north for Christmas and again later on with my right leg in plaster, right up to the hip. Equipped with a pair of shoulder crutches, I could outrun many of the boys of the village and even learnt to pole-vault over a low fence.

When I got back to school, it was to the dignity of the lower sixth form. The most surprising thing is that it didn't feel to me as if I had been away at all, and although I couldn't play games, by Easter 1937 I was pretty active again. Having had lots of time to read the papers, I was well informed about a world where everything was changing for the worse. In the sixth-form common room there were always copies of *The Scotsman* with detailed reports of momentous events, such as the invasion of the Rhineland by Hitler. Even then we found it difficult to believe that neither the British nor the French government thought fit to oppose this, and we shared our disillusionment with our masters. A lot of the future could have been changed if that move had been opposed, particularly as Germany was so short of equipment that those soldiers marching into the Rhineland triumphantly had only ten rounds of ammunition apiece.

Every day seemed to bring us closer to a war that we all suspected was not long coming. As we read of Mussolini's sweep into Abyssinia, and studied Hitler's incursions into Czechoslovakia and Austria, there was a general atmosphere of despair among masters and boys alike. Some people may have felt that Hitler and Mussolini were changing the face of central Europe for the better, with Mussolini making the trains run on time and Hitler revitalising a Germany shattered by the First World War, but even then we knew it was all a sham, and so did our schoolmasters.

I spent the last two and a half years of school in the upper sixth, a period when life was really dominated by the classroom on the first floor of the Gothic building. We would sit on a horseshoe of sloping oak desks that had been there since the school was founded in 1870, from where we would look out through huge windows over the panorama of Edinburgh, dominated by the castle, the spires of the churches and Calton Hill, with its Nelson monument and pillared folly.

From half past seven, when school began, we would go over the two hundred lines of Greek or Latin classical text we had learnt the night before, ready for the moment when the headmaster would rise to his feet, go to the gap in the horseshoe and select a boy at random to translate from memory twenty lines of the passage. I eventually came to the conclusion that all this sweat of careful translation was a waste of time and effort and instead bought myself extremely good translations, which meant that I had only to look up the words that really puzzled me each morning before quickly committing the passages to memory. Such was the concentration on Classics that even on Sunday, when we had a divinity lesson at five o'clock to add to our previous visit to church in Edinburgh and our subsequent visit at seven to the college chapel, we would study the New Testament in Greek.

It must in any case have worked fairly well, because the vast majority of Fettes boys won scholarships to Oxford or Cambridge.

I had travelled to Trinity College Oxford in December 1938 to sit the scholarship examination but was far more excited about staying with my sister Rhona and her husband at their flat in Dolphin Square in Pimlico. I had only really been to London once before, which was for Niall's wedding to Peggy Runge, the daughter of a London county councillor whose constituency was Bermondsey, where they were married. My two brothers and I had turned up in our morning coats and top hats and had a pub lunch of steak and kidney pie and a half-pint of beer before going to the wedding, which turned out to be great fun. The Bermondsey people, many of them cockneys working at the docks and for all the world like the chorus in *My Fair Lady*, turned out on the streets to cheer the bride and bridegroom on their way.

As I waited to hear from Trinity, I was determined to see as much of London as possible. Rhona took me to the Houses of Parliament to see the Commons in action, and one evening we were entertained to dinner by one of her friends and I was given my first glass of wine while my sister looked on disapprovingly – I later discovered that she had promised my parents that I would remain completely teetotal. The next morning we were able to treat my glass of plonk as a premature celebration, because the telegram came through from Trinity College to say that I had won the top scholarship in Classics there, a fact that we immediately conveyed in another telegram to my relieved parents.

Having been denied the chance to play any sport by my illness – although I was put in charge of the Colts rugby team, an independent command that I really enjoyed – I tried to cram in as much as possible before leaving Fettes. I was not allowed to play rugby, but hockey and cricket were both permitted. I became vice captain of the hockey team, but my cricket life was not so successful, mainly because I stupidly volunteered the information that I could bowl leg breaks, when in fact my forte was batting. Fortunately, after the end of the summer term in 1938, Archie, who by then had already played seven matches for Scotland, invited me on the Warriors cricket tour of Inverness, Nairn and Elgin. I was allowed to do some batting, as they had a strong bowling side that included my brother and a remarkable Edinburgh Accie called Gibbie Hole, who was almost 60 and had been a first-class bowler in his day. He still could twist the ball into a state that baffled many a batsman, and it was a privilege to watch him. It was fun being in a touring team whose ages ran from my own 17 to over 60, and I felt very grown up.

In my last term at Fettes I decided that I would really target the school sports day and set about training from as early as the Easter holidays in Newtonmore. I equalled the school record for the half-mile in the heats with a time of 2 min 8 sec, and although I won the final I was disappointed with a time of 2 min 16 sec. The next day was windless, and I took eight seconds off the old school record for the mile, which had stood at 4 min 48 sec, before winning the quarter-mile. I was beaten into second place in the steeplechase by Goldie Scott but won the cup for best athlete at the end of term the following day. If my sporting career had been a profound disappointment at Fettes, at least I finished on a high.

Yet, even though it seemed important at the time, something as trivial as sport couldn't mask the fact that we were in very dangerous times. Like everyone in the school from the age of 16 – the point at which I had returned to school after my operation – I joined the Officers' Training Corps, where we wore the MacLeod tartan, an army khaki jacket with brass buttons and the Fettes OTC badge on the lapel. Although I was so ambivalent about the whole exercise that I joined the pipe band in an effort to avoid the most militaristic aspects of the OTC, I quickly progressed to the rank of sergeant and was put in charge of the younger boys who came into the OTC for the first time. This basically meant teaching them elementary skills like drill, weapons training with a First World War Lee–Enfield rifle and map reading, a brief taste of leadership that was to come in handy when I found myself in His Majesty's forces proper.

That time was coming faster than any of us could have dreamt. In the April holiday of 1939, when Niall and I were at Speyville with our parents, a Captain Tweedy, who was adjutant of the 4th Queen's Own Cameron Highlanders Territorial Army, came visiting. The government had belatedly decided they needed to double the size of the TA to give some credible reserve, so Niall and I were signed up as officers for the regiment with the rank of second lieutenant – we both qualified because we had been sergeants in the OTC and had a magical thing called Certificate A, which said that we were competent in various forms of military arts. Our commissions came through at the beginning of June

1939, and I found myself simultaneously a sergeant in the OTC, a second lieutenant in the Queen's Own Cameron Highlanders and a corporal in the pipe band. The pipe band, as an aside, was very good fun and the best way to avoid so-called field days, weekend manoeuvres and the annual summer camp, which I regarded as a tragic waste of good holiday time. I did, however, come to really enjoy piping for its own sake.

At school we were allowed what was called Sunday leave three times a term on stipulated days, when we went 'up town'. In my last term I was allowed two special visits up town on a games afternoon to visit Andersons, the regimental tailors for the Queen's Own Cameron Highlanders, on George Street. The government had given me, like all officers, an allowance of £104 to acquire our uniforms, and for that Andersons would supply your regimental kilt, day stockings, evening stockings, various forms of footwear, shirts, khaki ties, a khaki brass-buttoned service jacket for day wear, a Sam Browne, evening blues (a tight-fitting jacket with a high collar) and evening tartan trews. How Andersons produced all that within the budget remains a mystery, but the fact that they did so meant that when I went from school to the training course at Cameron Barracks at the end of term I was able to go fully equipped.

My companion on this training course was a chap called Simms who worked for British Aluminium in Fort William and was four or five years older than me. At the end of the course Major Riach, who was the officer in charge, kindly said that I'd done well and had been a pleasure to have in the officers' mess, before adding, 'Pity the other chap wasn't quite a gentleman.' Those were the extraordinary judgements and rules of those days in closed circles like the officers' mess of the Army, which thankfully were changed quickly by the effects of war.

That was a rare bad note in what had been an enjoyable experience. The barracks was full of the first and second intake of the so-called militia, most of whom came from Glasgow and were a joy to be with in their enthusiasm and innocence. They were welcoming of anyone of their age who was prepared to take the lead, and while in most activities I joined them as a trainee under the watchful eye of Corporal MacLean, in drill and any other ceremonial things I was their officer. We were all starry-eyed back then, but as the war clouds gathered we were soon to lose our innocence.

4

The Phoney War

By the time the officers' training course at Cameron Barracks drew to a close, it was late August 1939 and the preparations for war were obvious everywhere you went. The politicians kept saying that it wouldn't happen, but every dog in the street knew that it was coming and that there was very little we could do about it.

That was the atmosphere in which I briefly went home to Newtonmore. As a boy and young man I had walked the hills round Newtonmore virtually every day and knew the surrounding countryside intimately. Our right to roam may have been formalised recently, but back then as long as we didn't interfere with the shooting, fishing or stalking we always had unrestricted access to all the hills and moors, and I took full advantage, walking long distances and improving my fitness, speed and stamina. During this brief interval between leaving Cameron Barracks and listening in silence to Chamberlain's solemn declaration of war, I remember climbing up A' Chailleach, the majestic Munro that towers more than 3,000 feet into the skyline behind Newtonmore, and breathing in the magnificent view. On a clear day you can see virtually from coast to coast across the broken land of the Highlands, so I committed the view to memory, wondering whether I would ever see it again. My generation had been brought up at the knees of fathers and uncles who had fought in the First World War, and we had absorbed an absolute belief that the lifetime of a second lieutenant at the front did not exceed three weeks.

The dreaded call to arms wasn't long in arriving. One day at the end of August the local post boy pedalled down from the village with a telegram for me. It simply said, 'Macpherson, Cameron Highlanders.' That was all. The whole preparation for war, the whole personal drama, was encapsulated in a single sentence.

I had been given charge of the Kincraig platoon of the Badenoch Company of the 5th Queen's Own Cameron Highlanders. Badenoch is the area that covers the hills on either side of the Spey Valley, encompassing the three villages of Kincraig, Kingussie and Newtonmore. My brother Niall, being older than me, had priority and chose the Newtonmore platoon, while Hugh Cameron was already established with the Kingussie platoon – so Kincraig was for me. The first three days after the famous telegram arrived were spent in Kingussie, where the company was headquartered and where our commanding officer, an old friend of the family, had his personal base. It was there in his drawing room that I and several of the other officers heard Chamberlain's famous broadcast at eleven o'clock on 3 September. The sound of the wailing of the siren in London could be heard clearly in the background at the end of the broadcast and emphasised with chilling effectiveness that this was going to be a long and frightening period.

The following morning the orders came to assemble the battalion and to proceed northwards to Tain, on the Ross-shire coast, just across the firth from the famous Royal Dornoch golf links. My father had lent us his car, and one of the young men of the village who had yet to be called up drove me to join my platoon at six o'clock in the morning. My feelings as I walked into the drill hall in the centre of Kincraig village in the early light of dawn on that September morning were of intense nervousness. I can imagine that up and down the country there were extremely young officers who felt exactly the same as they arrived to meet the platoon they were to command, never having clapped eyes on any of them before. At the time I thought that the platoon sergeant, Munro, was an old stager, but I guess he was about 36. I can only begin to imagine what he thought when this whippersnapper from Fettes arrived out of nowhere to take over his command. The platoon itself turned out to be a pretty even mixture of men in their 30s and those closer to my own age; happily, we hit it off from a very early stage and shared a mutual loyalty that sustained us in the months to come.

From Kincraig we boarded the train and travelled the 40-odd miles north to Inverness, where we held our first full parade on the platform. I was very amused to see several Fettes boys who were younger than me and who lived in the Inverness area peering back at me from the large crowd, staring with absolute astonishment at their immediate past house prefect standing in full uniform at the head of his platoon.

To help us gain experience as quickly as possible, officers were moved about quite a bit, and at one stage I found myself moved to Headquarter Company, who were short of young officers. The company's commanding officer was Gordon Monro, an Inverness solicitor whose regular ill health meant that he delegated a good deal. That's how I found myself in charge of the books of Headquarter Company, quickly becoming adept at the extremely old-fashioned system of Army bookkeeping, a form of double-entry accounts known as imprest. Even more fortunately I also found myself transport officer, which came in handy because the driving test had become compulsory in 1935 and I had yet to pass it. Not that this presented much of a problem when I became an official testing officer: I passed myself with flying colours, awarding myself a licence that I have held ever since.

It wasn't the only time that I acted on my own behalf. At another stage I was drafted to be assistant adjutant of the battalion, providing me with not just a further insight into the arcane workings of military law but also a welcome opportunity to increase my personal comfort. I had always done my hillwalking in heavy studded shoes, and I hated Army boots. Being assistant adjutant, I was able to sign myself a certificate excusing me boots for the duration of hostilities. I didn't always exercise this exemption, because on battalion parades I continued to wear boots and putties, but when I left the battalion and joined the Commandos, then later the Special Forces, I never wore boots again, waving my certificate at anyone who had the temerity to suggest that I should.

I was also the battalion's intelligence officer, although I realised how much I had to learn when I was instructed to devise the perimeter defences of the Inverness airport of Dalcross – thank goodness my amateur plans never had to be put into operation. Being intelligence officer did, however, allow me to get my hands on lots of equipment. It's difficult to appreciate in this time of plenty, but back then all equipment was so scarce – ammunition was used so sparingly that each man could fire just three rounds on the range – that this was a plum job. I used it to commandeer on the battalion's behalf an Austin Seven with two seats and a small flat body at the back, which was one of just six or seven vehicles at our disposal. More importantly my position meant that I had access to the pool motorbikes, because it was my job to familiarise myself with all the roads that the battalion could be called upon to use. This was fantastic fun, although I'd never ridden a motorbike before and our Triumphs and

Enfields were so solid that you could hardly pick them up when they fell over. I did, however, have a great deal of freedom while I learnt how to use them – freedom that I grabbed and used as often as possible.

As intelligence officer, most of my supporting troops came from the pipe band, while my intelligence sergeant, a man who was certainly not noted for his intelligence, was the pipe major. Some civilians reported to him that they had seen strange lights out in the Cromarty Firth and, later, in the Dornoch Firth. Just outside Tain there is a steep pyramid-like hill that has a good view over the Dornoch Firth, and I was instructed to take, for three nights running, two men as bodyguards or runners and to mount this hill. Given the danger, I was allowed to draw from the battalion armoury one of the few pistols we possessed. It turned out to be a First World War Webley revolver, heavy as lead and with an extremely long barrel, and I was allowed only the six rounds that the chamber of the revolver actually held. With my revolver handy, I and my two companions were dispatched up this steep hill in the pitch dark on a freezing winter evening, the three of us spending three nights gazing out over the water. No one ever bothered to explain quite what action I was supposed to take if we saw any strange lights out to sea, but at that stage I wasn't experienced enough to ask the obvious question.

Very soon after the outbreak of war one of the officers, Captain Ian Davie, got married to a young lady whose family had a large house in the vicinity, and all the officers were invited to the wedding party. It was my first introduction to champagne, and I thought it tasted like a very nice, very cold, fizzy lemonade, especially as it was a scorching-hot summer day. It seemed like the perfect thing to slake our thirst, and by the time I got back to the officers' mess I was in no shape at all and, sitting down in an armchair, started to snore prodigiously. It was only when I was shaken out of it by a senior officer and suddenly remembered that it was my job to change the guard in the evening that I snapped to. The sergeant major of the company, who was a great ally, took one look at me and asked if I would like him to take charge. In my fortified state, I firmly said no, I would do it myself. I'm not sure what sort of a fist I made of it, but by that time the guard knew exactly what to do and all went off reasonably well. The same sergeant major was on leave in Newtonmore just before Christmas, and my father and mother met him in the street. My father said to him, 'Well, Sergeant Major, how are my boys getting on?'

'Oh,' he said. 'Mr Niall is very well respected, but the boys would go anywhere for Mr Tommy.'

Momentarily stunned, my father said, 'Wait a minute. Surely you've got that the wrong way round?'

But no, he insisted, he hadn't. My father said nothing about this, but my mother repeated it to me some months later.

My father would have been appalled had he heard of an incident that happened six weeks after I joined the battalion when I was sent for by the commanding officer, who, with a very grave face, said, 'Macpherson, I have heard from your bank that you are overdrawn.' To be overdrawn in those days was so serious a matter that, in peacetime, you would have been either cashiered or sent to the Tower to await beheading for treason. I was totally astonished because, apart from a weakness for jaffa cakes and liquorice allsorts, I had no vices and was almost completely teetotal, so lived very frugally. Thankfully, we eventually discovered that my brother Niall, who had been commissioned on the same day as me and had a similar Army number, had been receiving both of our pays while I got nothing. It took a bit of sorting out, but eventually I was exonerated without a stain on my character.

The winter of '39 passed slowly, with the only change in our circumstances the company's northwards move from Tain to Edderton, where we were billeted in the Balblair Distillery, which was at that time out of action but which has sprung heroically back to life recently. When I was at Edderton, the commanding officer sent for me and told me that there were serious deficiencies in the accounts of the officers' mess at Tain. Would I look into them and recommend what action should be taken. I can only assume that I received this deeply unpopular task because, as a virtual teetotaller, my mess bills must have been among the lowest. What I found was not dishonesty but a degree of over-optimism and miscalculation, so that people were simply being charged too little on their bills. At the commanding officer's behest I had the unenviable job of issuing to every officer in the mess a surcharge on his bill. Fortunately, the unpleasantness was quite short-lived.

In the small mess at Edderton we were still solemnly changing into ceremonial blues and trews every evening for dinner, and occasionally, when visitors came from the main mess at Tain, we even went in for light entertainment – which included dancing. I was the piper from my days at Fettes, so I was easily persuaded to pipe Highland waltzes, but we had no women and the hardest thing was piping while keeping a straight face at the sight of middle-aged officers in high spirits waltzing together.

That year is a patchwork of memories, and among the most vivid of these was the time when my brother Archie had a serious accident while skiing up above Newtonmore. Foolishly, he had gone out on his own and had severely twisted his knee, but with characteristic courage he had bound his skis together to make them into a toboggan and then propelled himself five miles down the hill. It must have been agonising, especially as there were sections that were uphill, but he eventually made it down to the remote glen road and continued tobogganing down until quite by chance he met a car coming the other way. He was carted off to hospital in Edinburgh, and on one occasion, when I was sent in my capacity as intelligence officer on a course for training of defence against gas warfare in Edinburgh, I was able to visit him with my sister Rhona. We went first to the old Café Royal in Edinburgh, which was a great haunt for fresh oysters, and paid buttons for a small sack-load of oysters and several bottles of Guinness, a combination that I knew for certain would have been his last meal had he been a condemned man. We took them up to the hospital, where they were happily consumed with a little help from some of the doctors and nurses.

The only other excitement of that period was my purchase from a brother officer of an open, dark-blue Ford Ten banger for the princely sum of £15. It was already on its third engine, but it chugged along very satisfactorily and seemed to consume remarkably little petrol. I've never been a great mechanic, and shortly after I had bought it I was travelling north with a transport sergeant who immediately discovered that it was running on only three cylinders. When he put that right, the upturn in performance was astonishing. But if things were going well on the vehicular front, the prospect of any action in the war seemed further away than ever. That was literally true, because in the early spring the whole battalion moved yet further northwards, this time to within spitting distance of the northern coast of Scotland, between Thurso and Wick. From there we were to defend the whole of the north coast against the possibility of invasion from Norway via Orkney. Most of the time, though, nothing happened, and it would be difficult to be more remote than our lodgings at Halkirk, the seat of the Sinclair family.

5

The Clouds of War Break

In May 1940 the war began in earnest with the German blitzkrieg, and in a very short time indeed the British Expeditionary Force was driven from the field, the French had capitulated and Dunkirk was evacuated. Very shortly afterwards the 51st Highland Division, containing the 4th Cameron Highlanders, in which I had originally been commissioned, was captured at Saint-Valéry, and I always thought I was extraordinarily fortunate that I was not with them, otherwise I would have spent the entire war in a dreary German prison camp.

The stunning German successes marked the end of the so-called Phoney War. In some extraordinary way the defeat in France and the amazing events of Dunkirk seemed to stimulate the British Army at home and to energise the British public. It was no coincidence that Winston Churchill had just become prime minister: he seemed to breathe new life into the nation and to give our preparations for war a shot of impetus that they badly needed. That was to have immediate implications for me, because Churchill had already decided that he was not going to accept a totally passive role in the long years of preparation that had to take place before Europe could be reinvaded. He sent for Admiral of the Fleet Sir Roger Keyes of Zeebrugge, a First World War hero who had conducted an extraordinary raid on Zeebrugge in 1917, and told him to raise a force of commandos – irregularly organised and rapidly mobile – with which to 'set Europe ablaze'.

Churchill had fought in the Boer War and was a great admirer of the Afrikaner Commandos. He felt that a similarly disruptive British force – which, as we are an island, would have to be amphibious – should be created not just to attack the underbelly of German occupation but also to act as a morale-booster for the British public. And in Keyes, a naval officer with a proven record, Churchill had just the man to translate thought into deed. Keyes set about following Churchill's orders with an incredible enthusiasm, and within days the order went out for volunteers. Among the first three commando units to be formed was No. 11 Scottish Commando, which called for volunteers from the Scottish and Highland regiments. The take-up was huge, and I was among the men who volunteered as soon as the call went out.

From the very beginning, entry into the Commandos carried with it huge kudos, so I was incredibly pleased when, in due course, my name was accepted and I was ordered to report to Galashiels, in the Scottish Borders, early in July. I was also told in advance that I could recruit up to a platoon from my own battalion of 5th Camerons, and, while the battalion limited me to 20 men, the soldiers I chose were some of the very best I ever fought alongside. I'm not aware that many regretted the decision to join the Commandos, but for any who might have had second thoughts there was a powerful incentive to succeed, because being returned to your unit, or RTU'd, was a humiliating mark of failure for soldiers who didn't make the grade.

The idea behind the Commandos was that they should be lightly armed with no administrative tail so that even during their training all 600 men were billeted on local families. Each man received 13s. 4d. per week for his billeting and his rations, which was more than enough for the host families to keep and feed them in country districts where non-rationed food was available. This compared favourably with the lot of regular troops such as the Camerons, where the pay of a private soldier was 14s. per week, but a parsimonious Ministry of War retained 4s. of this against possible damages caused by the soldier to his chargeable equipment, which meant that the normal pay for a bachelor soldier was 10s. per week. A married soldier, however, had to allocate 5s. to his wife as what was called an allotment, so the married soldier received the princely sum of 5s. a week.

In those early days in Galashiels there was a lot of organisational work to do, but things were not so intense that we couldn't get away regularly. One of my fellow officers was Kenneth Greenlees, who was considerably older than me but of a similar rank. He worked in the City of London and was a contemporary of my brother Phil, who worked as a stockbroker. One day he asked if I would go to Edinburgh to dine with him and a young lady. It seems strange now, but such were the proprieties at the beginning of the war that it would not have been, in his eyes, correct to go and dine with this young lady on his own without its appearing to be a commitment rather further than he intended to go. He had a very smart car, so we tore through the Borders countryside, thrashing along the A7 on our way up to the Malmaison restaurant in the Caledonian Hotel, which was the smart place of the day in Edinburgh. No sooner had we got there than an elegant lady in her mid 20s appeared, and we proceeded to have a very pleasant dinner – especially as Kenneth was paying! The rule in restaurants in wartime Britain was that you could not charge more than 5s. for the meal, which, of course, did not go down well with the smart restaurants, who either charged through the nose for wine or slapped a heavy cover charge onto the bill for the privilege of your attendance, and sometimes both.

Just as I was settling into life in Galashiels, I was singled out to go on the Commando training course at Lochailort in the north-west of Scotland, near Arisaig. This was, I think, the first or second course that had been staged, and it was fascinating to meet officers from the other Commando units that had, like us, just been formed. I was detailed to share a tent with a Londoner called Basil Henriques, another city man who was 30 years older than me and of a build that did not bode well for any form of athletic activity. In fact, he had served with distinction in the tank corps during the First World War and went on to be knighted for his support of Jewish charities and his work with poor children – not that I knew any of that then. But despite the fact that the two of us could not have been a greater contrast, after initial suspicion we got on extremely well together.

The staff were a very interesting collection. There was a burglar – who I don't think was fully retired – who taught us the mysteries of locksmith work and the opening of safes. There were demolition experts who gave us instruction in blowing up things of every nature. There were also weapons-training people, including a really remarkable First World War veteran called Captain Cyril Mackworth-Praed, who won two Olympic gold medals and one silver medal in Paris in 1924 and was probably the best shot I have ever seen. He was able, with a Lee–Enfield rifle, which held nine shots in its magazine, to fire eighteen shots in a minute, changing the magazine on the way, flicking the bolt with his little finger and getting every single one into the bull at two hundred yards – an astonishing achievement that inspired us to work hard on the accuracy of our shooting.

There were also two complete thugs who taught us unarmed combat, which tended to be a very rough lesson indeed. Major W.E. Fairbairn, who had been the Shanghai chief of police, and his sidekick Eric Sykes were famous throughout the military world for creating 'Defendu', which is generally credited with being the first 'kill or get killed' modern fighting system. Fairbairn later wrote a book called *Get Tough*, which included his famous 'how long to die' charts, showing the effectiveness of various stab wounds in killing an opponent. They also designed the long, dagger-like Commando knife, with a sharpened seven-and-a-half-inch blade that was designed to slip in between the ribs, and which had a knurled brass handle so that it handled well even when bloody. As you can probably imagine, they were a couple of real charmers.

On the mountain training and fieldcraft side was Simon Lovat from the Lovat Scouts. His father had formed the Lovat Scouts in 1900 during the Second Boer War, and they were a remarkable fighting force that became the British Army's first sniper unit. The Scottish gamekeepers who made up most of the force's members were famous for pioneering the use of the ghillie suit, a sort of camouflage suit coated in leaves and sticks that allowed them to operate unseen in heavy foliage. In fact, their motto – 'He who shoots and runs away, lives to shoot another day' – was the guiding principle that helped me survive the war. I was quite soon detailed to assist Lovat because I was accustomed to hills and fieldcraft and was probably among the fittest of the officers there, and we formed a bond that lasted many years. He later became Brigadier Commandos UK and led the famous – or infamous – Dieppe Raid, which may have brought home a certain amount of information but certainly cost many lives. He died in the 1990s as an old man in rather sad circumstances, as his two sons had died one year and two years before, most unexpectedly.

The permanent staff of the training school lived in Lochailort House, where we had our mess, while the rest of us were tented. The weather was relentlessly awful, as you would expect on the west coast of Scotland. At one stage Ian Glennie, one of the other officers from Scottish Commando, went on an exercise up Loch Morar's silver sands before crossing some of the mountain passes and coming back to attack a small bridge on the road up the coast. This proved to be more of an endurance test than a military exercise, and by the end the men were so exhausted that they had to rest. But they found it had been raining so hard that the only place to lie down was in the middle of the road, which is exactly what they did. Oh, for those days where one could sleep anywhere!

At Lochailort we were also encouraged to use the boats that were available in the sea loch. As we were allowed to supplement our diet by having on our own plate at breakfast any mackerel we caught, I went out regularly and enjoyed these generally successful excursions enormously. On one occasion the steward brought my mackerel out on my plate for breakfast, and I had made a start on it before I realised it was in fact a succulent sea trout caught by one of the senior instructors on rod and line late the previous night. I finished my breakfast rapidly and departed.

At the end of the course it was back to join my Commando unit, which, in the meantime, had marched across Scotland from Galashiels to Ayr. From there they had been taken by special train to Fairlie, where they had been loaded onto the *Glensannox* for the journey across to Lamlash before heading on to our new training base on the island of Arran. Ian Glennie took a day or two's leave, but I headed straight to Ardrossan, only for our extremely crowded train to be so late that I missed the last boat, a regular occurrence in those days of unreliable rail travel. As I arrived late at night in the middle of a blackout, the only place that was open was the cop shop, so I spent the night there, the only time I have slept in a British police cell. It wasn't bad, either: a very comfortable bed followed by a handsome bacon and egg breakfast in the morning before being escorted down to the boat by a young policeman.

Arran has become known as 'Scotland in miniature', which is pretty accurate and the reason why we were moved there. It certainly provided a fantastic training ground thanks to the sea and lochs, where we would practise boat handling and swimming in full kit; the mountains like Goat Fell, where we would rock-climb and go for cross-country runs; the roads, where we would practise map reading; the bridges, where we would simulate detonations during explosives lessons; and the roaming uplands and its coastal plain, where we would stage initiative tests and mock operations. We undertook all those tasks carrying about us a morphia tablet and a short length of rope with a bight at one end and a toggle at the other, which could be used for climbing rock faces, constructing rope bridges or fording rivers in spate.

It was on Arran that we were really forged into one united unit, but I also remember Arran for the great attachment we formed to the islanders. The whole island was awash with commandos, with the 9th Scottish Commando at Whiting Bay and 7th Commando at Lochranza. As commandos, we lived among the local population, paying them for board and lodgings. I remember on one occasion having to do the weekly pay-out, which meant lugging 600 ten shilling notes and huge bags stuffed full with so many shillings, florins and coppers that we could barely lift them.

I made an acquaintance on Arran who remains one of my dearest friends. The lairds of Arran were the Duke and Duchess of Montrose or, more properly, the Duchess herself, who had been a Hamilton, and the island was a Hamilton property inherited by her. They had two daughters, of whom the younger was Jean, who was just a few weeks older than me and very prominent in entertaining the young officers. My friendship with Jean, which my wife now shares, has been a constant in my life since that time, and we still see her often, whether in Arran, in Inverness-shire or in London. As chance would have it, Jean Fforde, through her Hamilton ancestry, was also a cousin of Prince Rainier of Monaco, with whose family we established a connection, but more of that later.

We officers also rented a building known as The White House from the Duchess of Montrose, as an officers' mess, and took some shooting so that we had something to do on our one day off a week. If we socialised on Arran, the training was hard but enjoyable, although our shared adversity forged extremely close bonds between all of us. The harsh conditions also brought soldiers of all ages together, even if the age differences between us were not as wide as we might have thought at the time. I remember at the end of one very arduous exercise, when the latecomers were being brought in, sitting in the dawn sunshine with Ian Robinson, a 19-year-old officer, and watching the arrival of a troop commanded by Major David Blair – later a famous Walker Cup golfer – who was at that time 26. Ian turned to me and said, 'I'm amazed that these older people can do it.'

Ian, an English Gordon Highlander, later had a romantic life. After the war he returned to his job as a clerk in the Cunard office in London and fell heavily for the daughter of an American couple who came in to book their passage back to the United States. He saw a lot of her during her stay in London but was formally warned off by her parents as not wholly suitable for this quite eligible lady. Undeterred, he arranged with Cunard to sign him on as a temporary assistant purser on one of their transatlantic vessels and turned up at the lady's home in the States, which the parents found so romantic that they agreed to the wedding bells. The couple lived a long and happy married life, the later years of it in Kilcoy Castle in Ross-shire, not too distant neighbours of ours.

As Christmas approached, there was a feeling, fuelled by constant rumours, that we were about to go into action. That seemed to be confirmed when one day in Lochranza we were put on board a fast ferry ship called *The Royal Scotsman*. We were so keyed up that we barely noticed that the officers had been given the most elegant cabins, instead focusing on the whispers that we were heading for the coast of Norway. We were assured several times that it was purely an exercise, a statement that we simply refused to believe because the preparations had been so thorough. Yet after we were at sea whatever operation or exercise we were on was cancelled, and we were taken back to Arran but warned to be ready for an imminent departure that never came. It later turned out that our destination had been the Italian island of Pantelleria off the coast of Sicily but that we had been pulled out of what was a very risky operation when it was discovered that the Germans had just stationed dive bombers on Sicily.

However, just after the turn of the year we were taken to Gourock on the Firth of Clyde, where we boarded three commando ships called Glen ships. These had been used as fast traders out to the Far East and were owned by the Glen Line. They were capable of up to 23 knots and had been converted completely to battleship grey, with their holds cleared to make accommodation for troops and their decks hung with landing craft on which we had already done a lot of training. There were three Commando units going out – 2, 7 and 11 Scottish – and our unit was split between two ships, with me and one half of the 11th Scottish on the *Glenroy*, the rest of the 11th Scottish on the *Glenearn* and the other commandos on the *Glengyle*. It was clear to us all that a convoy was assembling, and late one dreary January day we set sail from the mouth of the Clyde, moving past the northern tip of Ireland and out into the Atlantic.

With us was the *Queen Mary*, the converted liner that could carry 16,000 men and which, Churchill believed – in tandem with its sister ship, the *Queen Elizabeth* – shortened the war by a year. The *Queen Mary* accompanied the convoy until we were clear of the immediate hazards of submarines and other attacks close to the coast and then departed into the distance at almost 30 knots, far faster than even a destroyer could travel. That impressive speed was her best defence against U-boats. Hitler was so keen to sink the *Queens* that he offered any U-boat captain who could do so an Iron Cross and a reward of $250,000. Shorn of the *Queen Mary*, ours was a general convoy that was led by the cruisers *Kenya* and *Dorsetshire* and surrounded by frigates and destroyers for protection but which proceeded at a fairly sedate speed across the Atlantic, despite the fact that most of the cargo ships were empty, ready to bring valuable supplies back from the States.

On the third day, our Glen ships, accompanied by a cruiser and two destroyers, changed course and started heading due south down through the middle of the Atlantic. For days we heaved our way through the stormy ocean under grey, rain-swept skies. The weather was so vile that all we could do with the men was to make sure that they kept their quarters clean and remained alive, even if many of them were so ill that they felt they would rather die. Then suddenly, gloriously, the sun came out. The skies, hesitantly at first, went from grey to blue, and before we knew it we were off the African coast. We eventually put in to Sierra Leone for supplies, fresh vegetables and water, and although we were forbidden to go ashore or have any truck with the locals, because of the extremely dubious security situation in the country, it wasn't long before Sierra Leone came visiting. As we lay off the deep-water harbour in Freetown, we were immediately surrounded by Africans in canoes of all sorts trying to sell us things. Even though we were confined to ship, it was still wonderful to see the green waving palm trees above the sandy beaches, to feel the warmth of the sun and to see fresh fruit and vegetables coming aboard in the sort of quantity that nobody had seen in Britain since the very earliest days of the war.

Duly provisioned, we left Sierra Leone, heading southwards as we followed the western coast of Africa. The seas were pretty placid now, with the destroyers changing places from time to time while we watched the dolphins and flying fish that followed in our wake, even occasionally spying an albatross gliding silently overhead. In the evening everyone was up on deck, where we had rigged up a tiny swimming pool and where there was space to exercise. We filled the time by carrying out intensive weapons training and gun drill for the troops so that by the time we arrived at our destination they knew their weapons inside out, even being able to dismantle and reassemble them in the pitch dark. In the late evening, when everyone was off parade after the evening meal, the troops used to gather on the forecastle deck under the tropical moon and sing. Even in my unsentimental youth it really brought a lump to my throat listening to them sing 'Loch Lomond' when they came to the passage:

> Ye'll tak' the high road, and I'll tak' the low road,
> And I'll be in Scotland afore ye;
> But me and my true love will never meet again
> On the bonnie, bonnie banks o' Loch Lomond.

It just seemed unbearably prescient, and so it proved. Of the 600 Scottish commandos in that convoy, by the end of the war only 60 had not been killed, wounded or imprisoned.

Slowly we came towards the southern point of Africa and sailed one brilliant morning into the great bay of Cape Town, with the towering mass of Table Mountain on our right as we came in. With its crescent cliffs at the top and flat plateau on its summit, it was so like a large-scale version of A' Chailleach, the hill behind Newtonmore that I had climbed so often, that it made me feel quite at home.

In Cape Town our first expedition ashore was a march through the main streets of the full battalion in the Commando tropical uniform of rather baggy shorts and khaki shirts. Each of our tam-o'-shanters, which were khaki in those days, sported the Scottish Commandos' black hackle – a clutch of black feathers – backed with the badge of the respective regiment. With bayonets fixed, we marched through crowds that were, I think, cheering with genuine enthusiasm.

After the parade everybody seemed to be picked up by friendly South Africans, with the Ulsterman Blair Mayne a particular catch because he had excelled as a rugby player for the popular British Lions team that had toured South Africa in 1938, winning the first Test match in Cape Town but losing the other two in Johannesburg and Port Elizabeth. Although not quite as sought-after as my friend Blair, Ian Glennie and

I were collected by a Mrs Moore, a lady who seemed to us of about middle age and who we later found out was the editor of *Cape Argus*, the country's leading English-language broadsheet newspaper. She looked after us extraordinarily well, ferrying us around the city and putting us up for the two nights that we were there. We left on the third day, but instead of getting straight on board to continue our voyage we stopped off at the Mount Nelson Hotel, which was then the best hotel in Cape Town. Ian, I and two other officers gave ourselves a tremendous dinner but made the serious mistake of finishing off with peach brandy, which caught up with us very badly as we rounded the Cape of Storms the following day. I've never met a cape that lived up to its name more fully, nor have I ever felt sicker than I did that day.

Not that my torment lasted too long, because there were soon reports that the German pocket battleship *Admiral Scheer* had been sighted, which sent us scurrying for the cover of Durban, where we docked. Eventually, accompanied by the cruisers *Dorsetshire* and *Glasgow*, we headed towards Suez, where we arrived on 7 March 1941. During those days at sea Piper Lawson set about composing a tune to replace 'Scotland the Brave', which had been our anthem until then. He came up with a two-part composition that he called 'The 11th (Scottish) Commando March', to which he added the following words:

> From a' the crack regiments cam oor men
> The pick of the Heilands and Lowlands and a'
> And stout-hearted Irish frae mountain and bog
> And gunners and infantry gallant and braw
> And noo we're awa, lads, to meet the foe
> We'll fight in the desert, the hill and the plain,
> And though as yet we've no honours to show,
> They'll ken the 'Black Hackle', afore we cam hame.

By now we were all desperate to fight, yet circumstances kept conspiring against us. Less than a month after we arrived in El-Geneifa, on the Sinai peninsula, where we began to make preparations for the invasion of Rhodes, the whole balance of the war in the Mediterranean shifted: the Germans invaded Greece and Yugoslavia, and Rommel's Afrika Korps began to reoccupy large swathes of the Western Desert that had previously been captured by the Desert Rats. Confusion reigned, and we were sent from Alexandria to Palestine in mid April, only to be diverted via the port of Haifa to Cyprus, which was thought to be vulnerable to invasion – and this was before the successful, if exceedingly bloody, aerial conquest of Crete by German paratroopers. I still have vivid memories of the train journey from Alexandria, when the train chuntered its way quite quickly across the desert and then slowed almost to a halt when it hit the lush fruit groves of Palestine. In fact, it went so slowly that several of us were able to leap from the officers' car at the front of the train, rush down the side of the embankment, fill our shirts with oranges and grapefruit, and get up in time to leap onto the last car, which was the sergeants'.

Thanks to a mulish reluctance on the part of the military hierarchy to accept the imposition of the word 'commando' by Churchill, the collective noun for our commandos was officially 'Force Z', followed swiftly thereafter by 'Layforce', named after Lieutenant Colonel Robert Laycock, who was in overall command. My crew, 11th (Scottish) Commando, were known as C Battalion.

When we landed on Cyprus, our first camp was on the site of the ancient city of Salamis, which was a fantastic source of water, not to mention local wine and brandy. From there we moved to a camp based at the ancient fortress of Famagusta, which had been repelling foreign hordes since its construction in 1490. At first we had a grand time, swimming in the sea and mooching around on the beaches, but when Crete fell to a daring attack by 15,000 German paratroopers in late May 1941 the whole atmosphere changed overnight. All of a sudden we were rushed up to the Karpasia peninsula at the north-east of the island, where we built dummy tanks hidden beneath the olive trees to confuse German reconnaissance planes about the strength of our defences. With just the Commandos and the Norfolk Regiment to defend the island, we felt incredibly vulnerable.

However, our stint of manual labour in the Cypriot sun didn't last too long, because on 3 June we unexpectedly got the order to get to Famagusta and embark on the two destroyers *Hotspur* and *Ilex*, which were both just back from the Battle of Crete, and that night we set sail for Port Said in Egypt. As soon as we docked, our commanding officer, Lieutenant Colonel Richard Pedder – the man who had placed the original call for men looking for 'special service of an undefined hazardous nature', which had launched the Scots Commandos – was off to Jerusalem to be briefed on our mission. There was a rising expectation that we were finally about to see some action, a feeling bolstered by the fact that we all knew the situation in this part of the Middle East was particularly precarious. With Field Marshal Sir Archibald Wavell fighting fires on several fronts, the Germans had fomented a rebellion in Iraq, which was at that time a British protectorate and the source of the oil that kept our war machine running. The pro-German rebels had become the de facto government in Basra, and although the revolt was eventually crushed when Indian troops under Auchinleck were sent from Delhi, augmented by a division from Palestine, the issue of Syria had come to the forefront.

6

The Road to Damascus

Syria, which then also included Lebanon, was at that stage under the command of the Vichy French. As soon as the Anglo–Iraq War drew to a conclusion, the British learnt that General Dentz, the commander-in-chief of Vichy French forces in Syria, had allowed German planes to refuel at airfields inside the country en route to bombing raids in support of the rebels. This would have given the Luftwaffe access to the Suez Canal and was something we couldn't allow. Although Dentz insisted that he would resist any notion of allowing the Germans to take over strategically crucial Syria, we weren't remotely satisfied that was the case, and Churchill ordered Wavell to send in an army under the leadership of General 'Jumbo' Wilson in Jerusalem.

I think we hoped that the Vichy French, who had plenty of armour and 53,000 troops – half of whom were regular French and colonial forces, while the other half were irregular Algerian, Senegalese, Foreign Legion and light horsemen from across North Africa – would put up no resistance, but we had to work on the basis that they would stand and fight. A small force would come in from Iraq, but the main thrust would come from the port of Haifa and a force spearheaded by the 7th Australian Division but also including the East Africa veterans of the 5th and 21st Indian Brigades, plus the Free French and two brigades of British cavalry. This army, with help from the Jewish Palmach fighters who were later to form the basis of the Israeli Army that defeated its neighbours in 1948 and 1967, was to invade from Palestine and move up the Lebanon coast, advancing north until it had taken Beirut.

The main obstacle between Haifa and Beirut was a well-defended river called the Litani which was where we came in. The original plan was for us to land on the beach to the north of the Qasmiyeh Bridge, which we knew was mined, and try to capture it intact so that the Australian-led forces coming up from the south could advance quickly along the road to Beirut. On the night of 7 June the entirety of 11 Commando set off from Port Said aboard the *Glengyle*, with the two destroyers, *Hotspur* and *Isis*, acting as our escort throughout the 250-mile journey. Our progress was remarkably good, because not only was the Mediterranean Sea particularly calm but there was also a full moon, making navigation very easy. We were finally going into battle, and the sense of anticipation on that boat was almost palpable.

An illuminated sea, however, doesn't qualify as the ideal condition for a covert amphibious assault, and within minutes of reaching the bay where we were due to land we ran into trouble. For a start, while the sea was calm, there was a hell of a swell that night where the waves hit the beach, as is often the case when there is a full moon. Just getting into the landing craft was fiendishly difficult as they pitched to and fro alongside the *Glengyle*. All that remained was to await the all-clear from the naval reconnaissance party led by Lieutenant Potter and Sub-Lieutenant Colenut, who had been serving with the Palestinian police and knew the area extremely well. But when they pulled alongside in their naval launch, the news was dire. Potter informed us that the surf was so strong that there was a likelihood of the landing craft's being overturned and lost before we reached the beach. Even worse, we'd been spotted eight miles out from the shore, which had given the Vichy forces plenty of time to get organised, and the area around the beach was crawling with the enemy, who were busy setting up mortars and machine-gun emplacements so that they had a perfect killing arc. Colonel Pedder had his orders and was determined to press ahead, but the final say belonged to the skipper of the *Glengyle*, and he simply shook his head and ordered the landing craft to be retrieved. This was done with incredible difficulty, as was getting the men back on board after we'd spent an hour sitting in the landing craft ready for the off. Then we simply turned around and headed back to Port Said.

The sense of anticlimax as we chugged off southwards, heading away from the fight, was unforgettable. So, too, was the reception the skipper of the *Glengyle* got when we returned to Port Said. Suffice it to say that we had barely arrived at the dock when we turned around and headed back towards the same beach we had left just hours before. While we had aborted our operation, the Aussies had ploughed on and broken through from Palestine, pushing the Vichy forces before them. But, with no commandos to stop them, the Vichy forces had blown the mined bridge over the Litani and established the river as a heavily fortified front line that included at least two gun batteries and countless machine-gun positions.

By the time we got back to the beach, we were 24 hours behind schedule and a running battle was already under way as the Aussie skirmishers probed and tried crossing the Litani under heavy fire. The good news was that, with all the Vichy forces busy repelling the main advance, the beach was largely undefended. This turned out to be extremely lucky because, by the time we arrived back on 8 June, dawn had already broken and we would have been sitting ducks had there been a significant welcome party in place. During the journey Colonel Pedder had reappraised our situation and come to the conclusion that, as the vital Qasmiyeh Bridge had already been blown, our tactics would have to be modified slightly. He decided that we would split into three groups, all to be landed north of the river. His second-in-command, Geoffrey Keyes, son of Keyes of Zeebrugge, would land 800 yards north of the Litani and lead an assault on the Vichy troops defending the north bank to enable the Aussies to construct a pontoon bridge. Pedder himself would take a force another 800 yards further north and move inland to attack the Vichy barracks north of the river and deal with a battery of 75-mm guns. I was to be part of the most northerly of the three parties, consisting of two troops; our job was to attack the Kafr-Badda Bridge, which spanned a significant tributary of the Litani almost two miles north of the Qasmiyeh Bridge, and capture it intact. After that we were to knock out the battery of 155-mm howitzers to the east of the bridge and generally cause enough chaos to draw as many Vichy troops as possible away from the main battle.

The northern party was under the overall command of Captain Ian Macdonald, with me leading 10 Troop. Unfortunately, our group's radio fell in the water during the landing and was completely useless, which meant that Captain George More, the adjutant of the Commandos who had been designated as the liaison officer between the two northern troops, had to spend most of the Battle of the Litani River delivering messages by shuttling around on a motorbike liberated from the Vichy forces.

As soon as we were off the boat, we headed directly for the bridge.

At first we encountered virtually no resistance, except for the odd bullet whining overhead, even though we were crossing a lot of open ground. As soon as we started getting closer to the bridge, however, things began to heat up, and not only did we come under fire from enemy outposts, but we also started to be shelled and machine-gunned by enemy armoured cars. Yet, if our progress was slowed, it was by no means halted, mainly because our opponents had little stomach for the fight: with four machine-gun nests surrounding the bridge and a number of armoured cars at their disposal, the French Vichy officers would certainly have fought us to a standstill if they could, but the largely Algerian and Senegalese conscripts who were congregated at the back of the main force to the south were less inclined to lay down their lives. In fact, so keen were they to surrender that we quickly found ourselves with an embarrassing number of prisoners; at one stage they comfortably outnumbered the commandos guarding them.

So, by ten o'clock that morning, little more than four hours after clambering onto the beach from the landing craft of the *Glengyle*, and with just one dead and two wounded, we had taken the Kafr Badda Bridge, which we found hadn't been mined. I had very nearly joined the casualty list, when, as we were accepting the surrender of a group of Vichy prisoners, a French sergeant broke ranks and tried to stab me. He only managed to graze me – I still have a deep scar on my wrist – before he was dispatched by an alert trooper. As soon as we had secured the bridge and dealt with the prisoners, we consolidated our position on the high ground to the north of the bridge and waited for orders. The expected counter-attack by Vichy forces came at around noon, when eight armoured cars appeared and tried to dislodge us from our positions around the bridge. That was the scene for a fierce firefight, but at the end of it we were still in place. Another six armoured cars also approached from the east, engaging the other troop and allowing many of the Vichy prisoners to escape. Apart from that, there were several other attempts by the Vichy to dislodge us during the day, but they were largely ineffective, including the amusingly inaccurate shelling by three very smart-looking French frigates.

While we held the northern bridge, the battle to the south of us was raging. Geoffrey Keyes quickly found he had been landed on the wrong side of the Litani, but, showing the commendable bravery and resourcefulness that would later win him a posthumous VC after the Rommel Raid, the first won by any commando, he made contact with the Australians and persuaded them to lend him seven small inflatable boats, which he used to ferry his troops across the river despite intermittent rifle and mortar fire. Once across, Major Keyes's men secured the northern bank, which allowed the Australians to build a pontoon bridge at midday.

Further inland and sandwiched between Keyes's troops and my own, Colonel Pedder was having a far harder time of it. Attacking the barracks, he came under heavy and sustained fire from machine-gunners, snipers and mortars and was forced to withdraw. Before he could get back to the shelter of the gully along which they had approached the barracks, Pedder was one of several commandos to be killed. Regimental Sergeant Major Tevendale collected the remaining men and headed for some high ground despite being under continual fire, but they were so badly outnumbered that it was only a matter of time before they were surrounded and captured, to be released the next morning when the surrender of the Vichy troops marked the formal end of the battle.

We were ordered to withdraw south of the Litani at half past six that evening, and, not wanting to be encumbered with prisoners we couldn't adequately guard if we needed to fight, I let them all go as we left. I was careful to disarm them and remove their trousers and boots so that they couldn't fight, not that they were showing any appetite to do so. We didn't face any more Vichy while heading south, but the journey wasn't without incident. By the time we reached the river, it was dark. We didn't have a map, and we didn't know that the Australians had constructed a pontoon bridge, so we forded the Litani further downstream, where it was at its highest. As we tried to cross the river, one of the last men in line – a huge, lanky Inverness man called Hughie MacKay, who carried the heavy and unwieldy anti-tank rifle – lost his footing and his nerve, fell over and disappeared downstream. There was a moment or two of delay, because I hadn't been watching, but I dived in and was able to catch him up. It took all my strength to drag his large, panicky body to the side of the fast-moving stream as he struggled violently in the water, but I had just about managed to manoeuvre him to the riverbank when Sergeant Anderson and Sergeant MacCulloch came rushing down to the rescue and managed to grab hold of him as I pushed him to the edge.

When he heard the report, Geoffrey Keyes initially censured me very heavily for losing weapons in the crossing but then recommended me for a George Medal for pulling MacKay out of the water at a point where there was a better-than-evens chance that the enemy would be present. Unfortunately, as the Commandos disbanded, the recommendation was lost, although Geoffrey's father, Admiral Lord Keyes, did his best to pursue it.

Having crossed the river, we went up the hill to what I felt was a safe distance and then turned right towards the shore and came down the hill. At that point we heard noises in front of us and prepared for more action, only to come across a very large encampment of Australians who were clearly in no hurry to continue their advance in spite of the way having been cleared for them. Like all good Aussies, they were in the middle of having a party, even though it was about two in the morning. So our boys got down to the cookhouse, got a good few bottles of beer and, I think, were glad to be there.

In fact, whenever we came across Commonwealth troops, we were amazed at how easily they took to their surroundings and how inventive they were in their pursuit of beer, happiness and sport. At the Mriya camp in Libya, for instance, the South Africans had very powerful Harley-Davidson motorcycles, and occasionally I had the good fortune to be invited by them to go on one of their regular gazelle hunts. This consisted of trying to pop off these fleetfooted beasts with your Colt 45 automatic pistol while riding a Harley-Davidson across rough terrain or sand at speeds of up to 30 miles an hour. It was an incredibly exhilarating pursuit full of thrills and spills – luckily, I got plenty of the former but none of the latter, being one of the few non-South Africans not to fall off, even if I never shot a gazelle either.

The morning after we met the Australians, word reached us that the Commando units were to regroup at a rendezvous on Mount Carmel, just outside Haifa. That gave us an opportunity to assess our casualties and to unwind after a tough campaign. It soon became clear that Pedder's group had sustained by far the heaviest casualties among the Commandos. By the time the Vichy forces surrendered the next morning, to bring the battle to a formal end, we found that we had lost 123 commandos killed or wounded, while a total of 3,500 Allied lives were lost in that action. The Syrian campaign was later adjudged to have been a resounding success and an operation of major tactical significance, but it didn't feel like it at the time. It was, however, the first time virtually any of us had seen action, and the hard edge forged by that Lebanese river would later have a profound effect on the course of the war. One small element was the fact that, because we had the good luck to have a couple of artillery-trained soldiers in the unit, after we captured the Vichy guns that had been shelling the beach we were able to turn them on the French. After the Litani campaign a course on the use of enemy weapons became a standard subject in Commando training at Achnacarry.

More important than that, though, was the fact that many of the men who fought at the Battle of the Litani River went on to assume positions of great responsibility. Of none was that more true than Lieutenant Blair Mayne, who went on to form the SAS in conjunction with David Stirling and win a superhuman tally of four DSOs, plus the *Légion d'honneur* and the *Croix de guerre*. Like me, his first action was the Litani River, but he would go on to become one of the most famous and feted warriors in the history of the British Army.

Blair was a proud Ulsterman from Newtonards and a rumbustious rugby player of great renown who would have won far more than his six caps had the war not intervened. As it was, he was one of the main players on the 1938 British Lions tour of South Africa, and our shared love of the game was one of the many reasons we got on so well from the time we first met in Galashiels. Blair was a heavyweight boxing champion and an utterly fearless man who so enraged the Germans that at one stage they had 10,000 men out looking for him. When David Stirling was captured by the Germans, Blair ran the SAS, pioneering the tactic of driving in through the front gate of German compounds with all machine guns blazing. Stirling was definitely right to call him 'a fighter of satanic ferocity', as he proved in Syria.

But if he had a reputation as a brawler and a drinker with an explosive temper, there was also another side to Blair, a more thoughtful, contemplative aspect that few people ever got to see. When I think about him, I think about the softly spoken lawyer with his love of reading and poetry rather than the cardboard cut-out from the history books. Few people will remember him like that, but I was privileged to get to know Blair very well in Galashiels, Lochailort, Arran and then Syria, and I was sad to see him leave 11th (Scottish) Commando after the Battle of the Litani River.

I caught up with Blair on Mount Carmel, and he seemed to be in his usual high spirits. That time up on the mountain was a glorious respite from the searing heat of the valley, and in any case it was good to be at altitude once again, with the cool evenings freshening us up. Mount Carmel is home to some of the original cedars of Lebanon and their descendants, and, for someone brought up on the forests of Strathspey, they were magnificent trees. After our first night on Mount Carmel, Ian Glennie, a group of other officers and I went down to Haifa for breakfast.

Most of us had actually been to Haifa before – when we first went to Cyprus, we were sent up there by train from Alexandria to catch the boat to Limassol – but this was an altogether more memorable trip, indeed one of those unforgettable culinary experiences. I suspect that we would have been pleased with our breakfast at any time, but, having been in the grip of indigestible rations for some time, the grub served up at the Apollonia Hotel remains one of the most memorable breakfasts that I have ever had. The other great spot in Haifa, which I didn't actually attend but which my brother officers told me about, was the casino. This was a type of nightclub cum gambling den that was presided over by a lady with the splendid name of Cashdown Kitty, who sounded an absolutely formidable proprietor. I never got the chance to visit Ms Kitty, because after a few days we were told to re-embark for Cyprus, where the priority was to regroup after the casualties and see how we stood on officer appointments.

After Litani the Commandos lost more than half their men and officers to other sections of the Army, with Blair going off to form the SAS with David Stirling. With the drifting away of officers, Geoffrey Keyes became desperate to do something that would fix the Commandos in the public imagination so that they wouldn't be disbanded, at least in the Middle East, although at home they seemed to be going strong. I think he felt a certain loyalty here to his father, who was head and founder of the Commandos, and that he mustn't let Lord Keyes's legacy simply fade away. I was sent off on one little operation – just before an intended attack by our main forces in the desert – to protect an oasis away into the desert that was to act as a water-pumping station to help the southern flank of the advance. We were there for only three or four days before we were relieved by ordinary infantry with rather heavier defensive equipment, but on one of those days or nights we had a stand-to because there was shooting out in the desert, possibly Arabs chasing birds or gazelles, but it turned out to have nothing to do with us.

Shortly after I came back, I was rubber-stamped by Geoffrey in the post of adjutant. This went in the daily orders of the Commandos on 7 October 1941, just three days after my 21st birthday, but it was backdated to 10 July, when I had started to do captain's duties, which was fortunate as it later enabled me to be confirmed in the rank of captain when I returned from abroad in 1943.

So there I was, barely past the age of majority and already a seasoned veteran. I was ready for the next stage of my war but had no idea that the Battle of the Litani River was just the beginning.

7

Desperately Seeking Rommel

Our adventures in the Litani River campaign were my first taste of action, and it was a formidably steep learning curve. One of the things that was brought home to me very forcibly was that all soldiers detest pretensions and self-serving behaviour. Geoffrey Keyes, for instance, had a fairly scathing opinion of Lieutenant Colonel – later General – Laycock, who commanded the Commando group that had gone to the Middle East and which he called Layforce to show this. He was, perhaps, a little too smooth a cavalry man for the taste of the Scottish Commando officers, but he also developed a reputation of endeavouring to take the credit for anything that was successful and distancing himself from anything that was not. As Crete was about to fall, he was instructed to cover the rear with 9 Commando under his command yet instead pleaded with the general to let him abandon his commandos and come back to Egypt, on the pretext that he could be more useful there. With his wish granted at the 11th hour, he was the last man aboard the last ship to leave successfully.

The unflattering portrait this paints was to be borne out by his conduct during the abortive Operation Flipper, more commonly known as the Rommel Raid. This raid on Beda Littoria on the Libyan coast in November 1941, carried out in the hope of capturing Field Marshal Erwin Rommel, would have been a disastrous enterprise whatever happened, but it certainly wasn't helped by the fact that Laycock insisted on complicating command issues by joining the expedition, then remained on the beach before removing himself rapidly as soon as it was clear that things had gone badly wrong.

After we got back from Haifa, Geoffrey was up and down to Cairo to General Headquarters a great deal but was very secretive about what he was doing, although he did let slip that an operation that he thought would go down in history was in the wind. On one of these absences, in the latter part of October 1941, I was suddenly ordered to report to the submarine depot ship HMS *Medway* in Alexandria. I presumed it was simply preparation for another amphibious exercise, so I set out in my ordinary daily uniform with my pistol but was otherwise unequipped. Yet, as soon as I arrived on board the *Medway* in Alexandria harbour, I was told that under no circumstances could I leave the ship. That afternoon I was briefed by the commander of the ship, Captain Dewhurst – known throughout the Navy as 'Dogberry' – who informed me that I was to be sent on a submarine patrol up the North African coast to reconnoitre a landing spot whose location I was not allowed to know. I was also to reconnoitre the territory behind that and investigate the escarpment, which involved a steep climb to the top of the Djebel Mountains, from where the desert plateau ran inland. My ultimate aim was to see if this was passable at night for a medium-sized force arriving in landing craft.

We set out in HMS *Talisman*, commanded by Commander Michael Wilmott, and I quickly learnt the facts about life in the standard diesel T-class submarines. The boats – never 'ships' for submariners – were so crowded that the first lieutenant told me the only exercise he got was running up and down the conning-tower or bending down to tie his shoelaces. There were so few bunks that they were constantly occupied, with the watch coming down to the bunks just vacated by their replacements. By night the subs came to the surface to recharge their batteries and to run on the diesel motors, but by day they were submerged and extremely vulnerable because the sandy and shallow Mediterranean meant that they could easily be spotted underwater by a passing aircraft and depth-charged.

From the submarine the plan was for me to set out to the shore in a folbot, a folding timber-framed canvas canoe designed for two people, each using one paddle. I had never encountered these craft but was in the capable hands of two officers and a corporal from the Special Boat Section (SBS), who had been trained in them. I did, however, request a compass to take with me – but no map, in case I was captured.

On the second night, the submarine surfaced in a placid, inky-black sea to recharge her batteries, and we were told that this was the moment for learning how to manoeuvre a folbot. The two SBS officers, one of whom was called Trevor Ravenscroft and had been a junior officer with me in the Scottish Commando, did not need this practice. Instead, the splendid Corporal Evans and I were dumped overboard in our folbot and told to follow a particular compass bearing through the dark night for two miles, at which stage we should find the submarine waiting for us at the other end. We went one way, the submarine went the other and in moments we couldn't see it. However, it wasn't difficult to paddle in time, and we made good progress, held precisely to our bearing and hit the submarine spot-on – a fact that, as becomes apparent later, was quite significant.

My folbot initiation successfully concluded, we climbed back on board and carried on towards our destination. We had one scare in the narrowest part of the Mediterranean when we heard propeller noises, and we sank to the bottom of the sea to wait motionless, listening while depth charges could be heard banging in not too distant areas. There is a certain claustrophobia in submarines, but, for a soldier accustomed to far greater discomfort, the submarines and destroyers that we sailed in during our amphibious Commando life were the acme of comfort because the sailor carries his bed, his laundry and his warmth with him. Their food wasn't bad either.

Eventually we came to 'the night', and we all climbed down into our two folbots. I was paired with Corporal Evans, while Trevor Ravenscroft shared his folbot with Captain Ratcliffe, who had come into the army from being town clerk of a small town in Lancashire and, by some great misfortune, had been promoted to captain just a few days before my date, which meant that he was in command of the expedition. We paddled towards the beach, crashing through the surf but making a safe landing before camouflaging our folbots in a cave. The four of us headed inland from the beach, straight up the escarpment and onto the plateau before zigzagging our way back so that we could be sure there weren't unexpected obstacles should the landing force, in due course, not land at precisely the same spot as us. There were, however, no signs of any activity, and we were back on the beach and hiding in our cave just before dawn.

The following night we were to make the rendezvous, and, as the appointed hour approached, we got into our folbots, set our compasses in both boats and made our way out. As on our trial run a few nights earlier, we were absolutely precise with our compasses, and, as both boats agreed,

I am convinced that we were precise again. Yet we made our distance, went beyond, came back, zigzagged all night – all with no sign whatsoever of the submarine. We were so determined not to miss it that we stayed until dawn had broken and then realised that it would be madness to go back to the beach during daylight, which meant a hot and thirsty day at sea. Every so often a reconnaissance aircraft would fly overhead, and we'd try to pretend that we were Arab fishermen, and certainly no alarm was raised during that day.

As night finally fell, we circled round and round the rendezvous area, forlornly flashing the signal we had been given and looking desperately for an answer. Suddenly we heard the noise of a diesel engine, only to realise just in time that it wasn't a submarine. We turned off our lights just seconds before one of the wooden transport ships common in the Mediterranean swept past us, laden with German troops going up the coast.

We had been told that the submarine would only rendezvous for two nights, so when dawn broke again we had no option but to get back to shore before it was too light. As soon as we reached the beach, we sliced open our folbots so that they couldn't be used, folded them up and hid them in a cave, taking rather more care to camouflage them this time, as we were abandoning them. Then, taking council of war together, we decided we would split into two parties and try to get back to our lines. We left immediately after dusk, Corporal Evans and I following the coast and Ratcliffe and Ravenscroft heading inland. Unfortunately, the Ratcliffe–Ravenscroft pairing was picked up very quickly while crossing a road, which led to the discovery of the folbots and the knowledge that there were at least two more people at large in the area.

We made rather better progress, although on the second night we eluded a patrol only to find that they had one of those big Dobermann dogs. Unable to see us but knowing from the dog's reaction that we were nearby, its handler slipped its leash, and it came chasing after us. I heard it just in the nick of time, and as it came out of the dark it really looked like the Hound of the Baskervilles, with its black body almost invisible, its eyes shining and its mouth open enough for you to see the reflection of the fading light on its teeth. I didn't want to fire a shot, so the only thing I could think of was to hold out my ever-handy Commando knife at arm's length in front of me, turning towards the dog. It went straight for my throat, and, by sheer chance, my knife penetrated its throat and it collapsed at my feet – all of which fortunately happened in silence.

After that scare we made quite good progress as we moved further inland, even occasionally travelling by day because we had the upper ground. By the next night, however, we were extremely hungry and found ourselves on the edge of a German encampment. We watched the sentries do their rounds and realised it would be quite easy to evade them, so I left Corporal Evans to keep watch and went in search of food. I couldn't find the cookhouse, but there were lots of large tents filled with sleeping Germans in bunk beds. I slipped into one of these tents and soon found two large lengths of French bread on top of a locker. I grabbed them and made for the door. I don't know whether I made a noise or if somebody noticed the movement, but there was suddenly a shout, in German, of 'Who goes there?' Startled, I let go of the tent flap rather too heavily, and it cracked back with a noise like a pistol shot. Immediately all hell broke loose, with people shouting and the sentries on the perimeter firing wildly, although thankfully not at me. I quickly found Evans, and we legged it up the hill, hiding in a remote spot where we could tuck into our bread and the last of our water. Fortunately, later the same night, we came to a little Arab village where we found a well and refilled our water bottles.

We were progressing quite well, despite the fact that Evans had a septic foot and I had a cracked toenail, but we knew that our next big obstacle would be the military town of Derna, just over 50 miles west along the Libyan coast from Tobruk. There were encampments all over the inland side, but I was reluctant to go up to the escarpment because the only thing I knew for sure about it was that the main supply roads ran along it and there would be a lot of troops up there. So we dropped down onto a secondary road nearer the shoreline, diving under a small bridge when a vehicle came along as we were crossing the road. To our amazement we found a major telephone exchange under that bridge, and, thinking it would be fun to sabotage the enemy's telephone system, we virtually destroyed it – in retrospect a stupid act because it had to draw attention to our location. We then hightailed it into the desert up what we thought was a small track, confident that in the clear desert air we would hear any vehicles. Unfortunately, what approached was not a car but a dead silent patrol of 20 Italians on bicycles who simply emerged out of the night and surrounded us before we could react to their sudden presence.

8

The Camp for Bad Boys

So that was that. I managed to remove the magazine and pop it into my pocket before handing over my pistol, and then we were taken off to Derna to be incarcerated in a barn, where we found Ratcliffe and Ravenscroft already there, more or less awaiting our arrival. As I had never expected to find myself on a mission, and had turned up underdressed, I was still in my gym kit and was freezing in the desert cold, so the Italians produced some slightly warmer clothing for us to stave off the winter nights, as well as military boots to replace our battered shoes. I just had to have some exercise, and I remember marching up and down that barn, imagining myself in the glen at Newtonmore and counting every tree as I went by, so clearly could I see it.

We were then split up before a very prolonged interrogation, which was conducted in pidgin English and French because we didn't speak a word of Italian – although I was later amazed to find in my file at the prisoner-of-war camp a transcript that referred to me speaking fluent Italian at that interrogation. In my room there were six *carabinieri*, the armed police of the Italian state, and four interrogating officers, who seemed to spend most of their time arguing with each other. At one stage the argument got so heated that one of the interrogating officers brought in my Colt automatic and ordered me to show him how it worked. As I still had a magazine in my pocket, I quickly loaded it up and held up the embarrassed Italians. My plan was to break out and grab the big staff car that I'd seen sitting outside the police station, but after walking for so long across the desert, and then sitting on a stool for a few hours, as soon as I tried to move, both my legs spasmed with cramp and I had to sit down, at which stage I fell to the floor and was jumped on by the whole lot of them.

As I was clearly a bad boy, I was put in solitary confinement at Apollonia and left to my own devices. After three days of trying to find a way out of my cell, I eventually managed to break the lock and was almost clear when I was caught trying to start a motorcycle in the garage yard. This time I wasn't to get another chance to make a run for it. As high-priority prisoners, we were loaded onto the Italian destroyer *Ugolino Vivaldi* after just a few days and sent at full speed across the Mediterranean to Sicily. This was actually a pleasant experience, because the Italian naval officers were extremely amiable, gave us good quarters and – if you like pasta, which I do – gave us extremely good food on the crossing. We spent our first night on Italian soil in the police cells at Reggio di Calabria, but once again the *carabinieri* were almost welcoming. From there we went on an extremely slow and heavily guarded train to the south side of the Po Valley near Piacenza, to our final destination, the castle of Montalbo.

Montalbo was neither a photogenic castle nor a particularly comfortable one, being absolutely stuffed with prisoners from North Africa as well as sailors and air crew captured in the Mediterranean. One of the most notable was Major T.A.G. Pritchard, who had been captured after successfully destroying the Tragino aqueduct near Taranto in a daring raid. I also found myself alongside various submarine crews, including some from T-class submarines who were rather scathing of their colleagues when they learnt why we had ended up in the camp. I later found out that, when Geoffrey Keyes went on the Rommel Raid, which was what we had been reconnoitring, the same submarine failed to make its rendezvous, so I rest my case.

In the winter of 1941–2 Montalbo was not a pleasant place to be. The influx of prisoners had exhausted the resources of our Italian jailers and of our food suppliers, the Red Cross. Food was very scarce indeed, and, with no food parcels coming through at all, there were times when we were reduced to just potato soup, served twice a day, and nothing else. Amazingly, our ration of two cigarettes a day remained uninterrupted, and, with virtually everyone except me smoking back then, it was possible to swap cigarettes for food. I gave my cigarettes to an elderly, red-bearded merchant seaman called Piggott in return for the peelings of his potato soup. We both benefited, but because of the poor diet I got jaundice that winter. I shared my dormitory with a young naval lieutenant called Dixon who had been a medical student and was absolutely fascinated by my condition, demanding that I should present him with samples of what he called my 'stool' in a cardboard box for him to examine in detail.

There were occasional attempts to escape from Montalbo, but none of them was likely to get far. I once managed to get past the inner perimeter by climbing over a roof, but from there it was clear that I could get no further, and I was pleased to get back to my cell without any of the Italians discovering the presence of a night-walker. The closest anyone came was through the simple plan of sticking a pole out of the window with a rope at the end of it from which the potential escapee would swing until he could propel himself right over the wire and pray that he would land in one piece from a considerable height at the other side of it. An inmate who had been a tailor ran up some imitation Italian uniforms, and a couple of officers even got out through the gate using this method. One of them, Dean Drummond, got right up to the Swiss border before he was brought back to solitary confinement, but in very heroic mood.

I decided that if I was going to escape successfully it would be vital to be able to speak Italian, so I set about learning the language and had made pretty good progress by the following midsummer of 1942. That was the point at which those of us who were commandos or any other brand of so-called 'bad boys' were stuffed into a guarded bus and transported across Italy to the province of Liguria, which runs down to Genoa by the sea. The journey was getting rather lengthy and boring when, as we swung round a corner, I saw a magnificent medieval castle poised on a rock high above us, and, in what was intended as humour, said to the guard, 'Aha, I suppose we are going there.' The guard beamed delightedly, pleased at my comprehension, and said, '*Si, Señor*. Yes, we are going there.' We were barely 70 miles from the French border at the castle of Gavi, a medieval hilltop castle that had had a little bit of plumbing put in but very little else for the past 600 years. It was reputed to have been used to house convicts for many years, and the guards took great pleasure in telling us that nobody had ever escaped from it.

We were lucky that it was a fine day when we arrived at Gavi, otherwise the entrance to the castle would have been even more depressing. After the bus stopped, we were unloaded in the village and then walked up a long, steep, winding road until we eventually reached the massive doors of the castle. Behind those impenetrable doors was a long tunnel, with an equally massive metal-grille door covering every inch of the opening at the other end. Just to emphasise that escape through this tunnel was absolutely impossible, there was a series of guardrooms between the two gates. This second door opened into what we discovered was the lower courtyard. This was larger than the upper courtyard, where I was to be housed, but only about 12 yards by 20 yards was reasonably flat, with the rest sloping in various directions on bedrock.

The lower courtyard housed the other ranks, who performed the supply duties, the cleaning duties and the cooking duties of the officer camp. They were in the rock side of the courtyard, so their quarters, which housed ten men per room, had no windows whatsoever, making them baking hot in summer, freezing cold in winter and highly insanitary all year round, especially when the door was closed. On the other side of the courtyard was the kitchen and vegetable-preparing area; above that was the mess room for all the officers, and above that were the rooms for those officers who were accommodated in the lower courtyard.

Gavi was known to the Italians as Camp 5 (P), the 'P' standing for *pericolosi* or 'dangerous'. If we were all treated as dangerous, the prisoners such as me who were considered to be the gravest danger were escorted up the steep ramp that rose about 150 feet, winding its way around the edge of the rock before reaching the upper courtyard. This ramp also went through a tunnel before it opened into the sunlight, but even the open part allowed you to walk not more than two abreast, while it had a brick flooring laid on top of base rock, so that there was no chance of any tunnelling. This triangular upper courtyard, which measured about forty yards on each side, twenty yards at one end and about eight at the other, was to become our main exercise area, our only chance to keep fit. On the inside, the rock side, the more junior officers were housed eight to a room in conditions that were very damp indeed, and they did not have a happy time. I was extremely lucky – partly from being one of the first arrivals, partly from being a captain when there were so many lieutenants – and was allocated a space in the 'new' block. It was only about 60 years old, and it was on the open cliff side of the courtyard, looking out over the picturesque little village of Gavi.

Being at Gavi had its compensations. As the prisoners there were almost exclusively commandos or attempted escapees, there was a very good community. The upper level, which was guarded most heavily, housed officers only; the lower level, where we ate our meals and played sport in the courtyard, was for other ranks. We soon developed fitness programmes and played volleyball and our own version of basketball, which quickly became highly competitive. In each case my team was captained by a fellow Scot called Iain Muir, who had been a noted distance runner at Glasgow University just before the war, and we were successful in both sports: the basketball, which was played in the lower courtyard, and the volleyball, which was played in the higher one. I also used to keep fit on the steep path that ran between the upper and lower levels. There was a locked gate and a sentry on it at all times, other than when we were allowed through for meals or sport, but there was enough of that steep path to give good exercise if you walked down and ran up it lots of times.

As the autumn drew on that year, the village was an intensely colourful sight because the peasants laid out their ears of maize on the cob to bronze on the many flat roofs, where they went a marvellous red colour in the sunshine. We could also see grapes being harvested outside the village and taken to the cooperative wine press; every now and then, in still weather, the glorious scent of the pressed grapes floated up to us. I never tried the local wine while I was there, but I later discovered that the white wine from Gavi is almost certainly the best in Italy.

Compared with the other prisoners at Gavi, our living conditions were almost salubrious. We had quite big windows on the village side of our dormitory and individual iron bedsteads with enough room between them to get up and dress in reasonable comfort. The windows were, of course, heavily barred, but they needn't have bothered because there was a sheer drop of about 150 feet to the next level.

Despite Gavi's formidable reputation, there was still a constant stream of attempts to escape. Only one had a seriously satisfactory outcome when, in the spring of 1943, officers in the lower courtyard managed to locate an old drain by assiduous tapping, broke into it and found their way down into a water-storage tank, which was full. By working out the course of the drain on the surface, they were able to break through a chimney breast and bypass the full storage tank, with the drain then leading them right out to near the ramparts, where they were able to break through a final thin layer of rock and reach the outside. The sound of all that digging had to be masked, so the other ranks in the lower courtyard would make as much noise as possible during the digging times so that no guard would hear what was going on.

Once they had broken out, they still had to get down over the third level, which meant crossing a courtyard, scaling a wall and dropping about 30 feet over that wall and onto what looked like a steep, grassy slope. A rope was made out of plaited sheets and baggage cords to bridge that drop, and we waited for a night that was so wet and windy that, we hoped, the guards would not be too enthusiastic in their work. A team of 12 had been selected, necessarily from the officers in the lower courtyard, to break out. The first six got clean away, but the other six were waiting in the shadows in the courtyard after the rope broke under the strain, and Lieutenant Cram fell the last twelve feet, severely damaging his ankle. The rope was in the process of being repaired when, with a tragic inevitability, a corporal of the guard came out for a smoke and saw the six prospective escapees skulking in the shadows and raised the alarm. Very quickly, of course, the hunt was on for the others. Cram was picked up quite close to the castle, because he could move only slowly due to his injury. Four of the others were also collected fairly soon, although one got quite a distance and was arrested on a train. The last, Pringle, in whom we had great faith because his Italian was excellent and he knew the country, got to within half a mile of the Swiss border and was hiding, waiting for darkness, in some bushes when a patrol found him, and he was brought back to a heroic welcome – but we were sad indeed that he had not got away.

We who had come from other camps were presumed to be 'clean' – in the sense of free of weapons, maps or coins – when we arrived, but any new arrivals after our time were strip-searched with great thoroughness when they arrived. The camp had a fearsome reputation throughout Italy as a punishment camp, but the atmosphere was not too bad because our morale was high, despite the fact that the winter of 1942–3 was a cold and hungry time. It was, I believe, less cold than at Montalbo, but there was no heating and a great deal of damp, except, fortunately, in our sleeping rooms on the open side of the top courtyard. I am sure the experience of no heating at Fettes stood me in good stead, because at Gavi I was not that uncomfortable, while the complaints from English, New Zealand and South African officers were fortissimo, and I think they suffered considerably.

In the spring of 1943 the Red Cross appeared to find us and parcels began to arrive. They were stored in one of the damper dungeons, so anything that was not tinned deteriorated very quickly indeed. Newer arrivals to the camp were amazed that the older stagers, we of the first batch who had known the privations of the previous winter, hoarded a great deal of the food against what we thought might be a rainy day, but which turned out to be of assistance to us when we needed supplies for later escapes.

The first roll call was at eight o'clock each morning in each courtyard, when an Italian officer would come with a guard of half a dozen armed soldiers. We were supposed to be properly turned out and smart for it, but our objective was to make these roll calls as shambolic and as difficult to check as they could possibly be. We emerged – piecemeal, slowly, reluctantly and in all sorts of dress – from our sleeping quarters, and it was rare that there was a roll call without the Italians losing their tempers and certainly losing count. At night, in spite of the total security of the castle, we were all locked in our sleeping quarters and did not emerge until the sounding of the bugle for roll call in the morning. There were frequent and unpredictable checks by the *carabinieri*, who were very thorough. They looked for any sign of work on escape routes; they looked under mattresses, in beds, among clothing for any instruments of escape, and these visits, of course, were very tiresome.

Whenever they were upset, the Italian officers would make an arrest and cart off some victim to the punishment cells, where they would be alone, allowed out for only half an hour a day and had no light in their cell, no reading matter and no water. During the whole time we were there, until the Italian armistice, there was only one day when the punishment cells were not occupied, and that was Christmas Day in 1942, when Colonel Moscatelli, the commandant of the prison, declared an armistice. The Swiss Red Cross representative came, to my knowledge, twice – or at least he emerged twice in the upper courtyard – and on the second occasion he said firmly that he had reported that the camp was unsuitable for officer prisoner accommodation, but, of course, nothing whatsoever happened.

I was determined to keep fit against every eventuality, so I used the ramp for exercise regularly, both morning and afternoon, and I took a full part in team games when they began to develop. My other preoccupation was to learn Italian, which, at first, almost flattered our captors, who gave me various books from which to study. I would spend a good chunk of the day talking to the guards at the bottom of the ramp, and they seemed quite pleased to pass the time of day with me. Although I have no doubt they had a variety of regional accents, they nevertheless gave me a great deal of oral practice with the language.

From this developed my principal public task in the camp, which was, every evening, at the end of dinner, to give the officers what the author George Millar called a 'blimpish' version of the news as it appeared in the Italian press – or as could be deduced from hints and omissions in what were heavily censored newspapers. We received two papers each day at the camp, the *Corriere della Sera* and *La Stampa*, which were both delivered to my table as soon as they arrived. I studied them from cover to cover and, from them, endeavoured to keep the camp informed. The papers were heavily biased and full of propaganda for internal consumption, portraying what they called the 'Anglo-Saxons' as demonic and almost cannibal capitalists determined to subvert the saintly virtues of fascism. Gradually, the full debacle of the Russian situation began to appear, because there were several Italian divisions sent to that front, and they suffered greatly. And, of course, inevitably, the news came of Allied victories in North Africa. We waited with tension and expectation for the move into Europe, and finally word of the Sicily landings reached us.

I tried to end each of my daily bulletins with something amusing, which wasn't particularly difficult because some extraordinary incidents would appear in the papers, such as regular reports of peasants accidentally shooting each other while hiding in ditches during the migration of birds. The recounting of all sorts of complicated and intimate marital difficulties also raised a laugh here and there, but the mounting excitement after the invasion of Sicily and the question of what we would do if the Allied armies moved sharply up Italy absorbed us greatly.

Finally, at the beginning of September 1943, came the definitive news that Benito Mussolini had been deposed and an armistice signed with the Allies, including a total ceasefire between Italian and Allied troops. We had little doubt that the Germans would have earmarked our camp as one that should be taken over as quickly as possible and its inhabitants whisked off to Germany, and we tried to persuade Colonel Moscatelli and his officers to simply open the gates and let us go. The Italians, however, still had an underlying feeling that important British officer prisoners were somehow a bargaining chip. This was a total illusion, as they were to find out to their cost.

Throughout our time at Gavi it had been the practice of Colonel Moscatelli to march a party of soldiers down to the village square each morning, where they would drill and parade, presumably to impress the Germans. On the fine morning of 9 September 1943 the castle and village were surrounded by a company of Germans, but the Italians didn't seem to appreciate their intent. When one of the Italian soldiers pointed his rifle at a German, the trooper opened fire with his machine gun, killing two Italians and wounding many more. The German officer also gave the signal for dummy mortar rounds to be fired – it was only moments before Moscatelli's second-in-command appeared holding a white sheet, at which stage we passed from Italian to German hands. The Germans kept a hundred Italians to do fatigues and let the others go, although within two days they were rounded up and all the Italians sent to an internment camp at Novi.

So that was that: the Germans had simply appeared and, with their usual efficiency and preparation, taken the place over. There were, however, obvious opportunities to arise from this takeover. The Germans did not know the routine of the camp and had only a sketchy knowledge of prisoner numbers because, in the confusion of the takeover, we had broken into the office and removed most of the files. Nor did they know that it was customary to lock the gate between the upper and lower courtyards, and we managed to persuade them that we had been allowed regularly to go up still further from the upper courtyard to the ramparts on the roof, from which, although escape was unlikely, we could assess very much more easily what lay below us and what lay between the top and the bottom courtyards.

We immediately started to have large numbers of absentees from the roll calls, so that there would not be any firm knowledge by the Germans of how many prisoners were in the camp. Our plan was to hide away a sizeable number of officers in hidey-holes throughout the castle, so that, when the prisoners and Germans moved off, they would remain behind. This is where the Red Cross reserves proved vital, because those of us who were to be hidden away behind the panels that covered hollowed-out walls and half-completed tunnels had enough supplies to last for several days. Unfortunately, the plan broke down when several officers who didn't have the authorisation to stay behind decided to chance their arms and hide away.

When the Germans made their final parade before marching the prisoners out to transport, prisoners were so thin on the ground that they immediately requested to talk to the senior officer, a New Zealander called Brigadier Clifton who was about the only officer well known to them. Unfortunately, he had himself decided to hide away at the last moment, and when he couldn't be found all hell broke loose: the Germans lined a number of officers up against a wall and said they would be shot if the others could not be found. The brigadier was soon discovered and decreed that the situation was too dangerous, so he sent criers round the camp summoning the officers to come forward. One or two did stay behind, and as the numbers were so uncertain this did no harm, but the majority obeyed the order, coming out and climbing aboard the transport with sinking hearts.

Still, we all knew that there could be no more difficult place to escape from than Gavi, so we had little option but to look upon our departure as an opportunity. More importantly, much of Italy had already been liberated, and we knew that the endgame had begun.

9

Prison on the Eastern Front

The end of Italy's alliance with Germany was the beginning of a new chapter in my war. That much was obvious when we were marched from our mountain redoubt in Gavi, loaded into buses and lorries and taken through the Piedmontese countryside to the railway station at Alessandria, 15 miles to the north. Drawn up in the station was a train of covered metal goods wagons, which had the notice 'Eight horses or forty men' stencilled on their sides and had obviously been used for troop movements in the recent past. We were piled into the wagons before it was discovered that the train would be delayed for some time, so we were allowed out onto the platform on this beautiful sunny afternoon.

I was constantly looking for chances to escape, and as far as I was concerned there had to be a reasonable possibility that one would present itself during the journey, so I dressed as much like a civilian as I could, wearing a blue shirt, corduroy trousers and walking shoes. When the call eventually came for everyone to get back into the wagons, I stationed myself near a gap by the fence that ran along the back of the platform, which was edged with stone and covered with dark ash, rather like an old-fashioned tennis court.

There were German soldiers about every ten yards along the platform, but they were virtually all busy trying to herd the officers back towards their trucks. The officers, as usual, were not cooperating very fully, and with the guards apparently distracted I made a dash for the gap. My friends later told me that had I slipped quietly out rather than making a dash for it I might not have been seen, but the unbelievably loud scrunch of my boots as I ran across the cinders immediately drew the guards' attention, and the firing began almost as soon as I made my move.

The ground on the other side of the fence appeared to slope upwards, but it also looked pretty broken and I thought it would offer me some shelter until I reached a row of houses in the distance. That assessment was, unhappily, completely wrong, and I quickly found myself scuttling from one bit of insufficient cover to another. Another of my colleagues afterwards said it looked a little like a walked-up partridge shoot, with the guards' rifles going up to the shoulder and down again as I sprinted back and forth, fading in and out of view as I zigzagged my way up the hill.

By now I realised that every guard on the station's elevated platform could see me, and it was only a matter of time before I would feel the stinging thump of a German bullet hitting home. Bullets were kicking up bits of turf all around me when I ran past an old peasant who was out on the hill. No sooner had I passed him than he was shot in the foot, at which point his enraged dog came haring after me, only to be killed by another bullet, literally at my heels. I'd been going for what seemed like hours, and still there was no cover, while the horizon seemed as far away as ever. Just as I reached the skyline, at which stage an endless succession of bullets was pinging past my ears, a German vehicle came over the top straight towards me. Hearing the firing, they jumped out, and I almost literally ran into their arms.

Panting heavily from the exertion, I was marched back to the station by a sergeant and three men who had been sent up to fetch me while I was held by this other patrol. The sergeant was extremely irritated, and although his English wasn't up to much he expressed his feelings very clearly by emptying his rifle in single shots between my feet as I walked, which was not an entirely confidence-producing experience for me. Things almost got worse when I was back at the station, as the angry *Feldwebel* ordered me to be put up against the wall and shot as a warning to any other would-be escapees, only for an officer to countermand the order, to my intense relief. His angry reaction was, however, in stark contrast with that of several of the other Germans; back on the platform, a smiling officer greeted me warmly in English and actually wished me better luck in the future. My only damage at that stage was a bullet graze on my wrist, although I picked up a world-class collection of bruises when the sergeant and men who had been forced to tramp to the top of the hill to collect me literally kicked me into a wagon.

As soon as we left the station on our long journey, the prisoners in virtually every wagon staged attempted breakouts. Some of the wagons had ventilators that led onto the roof, and several of these were successfully detached; others had a trapdoor at the end of the wagon that could be opened up; and every wagon set about trying to dislodge the chains holding the doors shut. Only one succeeded in forcing the door open, and unfortunately they did that just before the train arrived in a station, so the guards immediately refastened it and made sure it couldn't be reopened.

Those who got onto the roof – each wagon had a senior officer who decided what could be done and who could do it – quickly found that most of the wagons had a little sentry box attached to them, where the seated guards could see along the roofs. The guards hadn't been expecting any trouble, but once the first prisoners were spotted they were alive to our escape attempts and the shooting along the line of the roof was virtually continuous. Night-time offered the best opportunity to go out via the roof, but others got out through the end of the wagons and onto the buffers. A steady stream of men were jumping from the roofs and the buffers, with 18 officers getting out that way. Sadly, half a dozen were killed, either by the shooting or by an unsuccessful jump from the moving train. The guards became significantly unimpressed and at one stage lobbed a hand grenade against the side of a truck the prisoners were trying to open. When a Greek officer rolled off the train into a ditch, he was shot for his trouble. A good number got away, however, and some of those with broken limbs were very warmly looked after by Italian countrymen who found them and took them to their farmhouses. In all, it was one of the more successful mass escapes.

The journey threw up a few moments of levity, including a bizarre episode near the border between Italy and Austria, where our train drew to a halt behind a stationary train full of Italian prisoners. The Italians, it turned out, had just been let out to relieve themselves in a field alongside the tracks, which had a small stream running through it. The extraordinary spectacle of 500 Italian soldiers crammed into a small field, all with their trousers down as they did what they had to do, was one that stayed with me long after the war. After the Italians had gone, we were allowed out in the same field in groups of five or six, both for natural purposes and to get a drink from this stream, because we had no water on the train.

Needless to say, we all headed as far upstream as we could, and while I have no idea how salubrious the water was, it went down extraordinarily well, as we were all truly parched.

Finally, the train crossed the Austrian border, turned westwards up a valley and reached the town of Spittal, where we were disembarked and marched under very heavy guard to what was clearly a transit camp. On our arrival we were formed into queues to be extensively searched for any articles that might aid a future escape, which was done typically methodically by the German troops. Their planning turned to farce, however, because there were already British other-ranks prisoners present, and their quartermaster sergeant was allowed to take part in the organising of each queue on the pretext that he had to take down all the names, ranks and numbers. Instead, he just said to each officer, 'If you've got anything with you that you don't want to be found in the search, give it to me and I'll give it back to you on the other side,' which is exactly what happened.

10

On the Run

As soon as we were through the gates, we were trying to work out how to get back out again. Transit camps, with their temporary huts, constant comings and goings and lax controls, were far easier to escape from than permanent camps, particularly in Germany. In short, this was our big chance. I was particularly keen because, having mastered Italian at Gavi, I had begun to learn a little German from books and felt that if I could get out of the camp then I stood a good chance of remaining at large. I could even see how I was going to get out. On one side of our temporary huts was a camp of Russian other-ranks prisoners of war, with a camp of French on the other. The prisoners in both camps were allowed out each day to work as agricultural labourers for the Germans. The wire fence between the French camp and ours was easily breached, and it occurred to me that it would be easy simply to go out with the French and not come back.

The quartermaster sergeant had already found out where the fence could be breached and had made the necessary arrangements with the French, who were willing to play along in return for access to our Red Cross goods. Unfortunately, Colin Armstrong and Alan Yeomans, two New Zealand officers who were ten years older than me but whom I knew from Gavi, had already come up with the same idea. We compromised by joining forces and waited for the right moment. Everything was in place – we knew exactly how the French groups left the compound, we had three British other-ranks prisoners to take our identities and cover us at roll call and we had maps ready of the outside – but, as often happens, there was some hitch in the work rota and the usual French free passage in and out was suspended. The French very kindly hid us away in one of their huts during those two days, but early in the morning on the third day we took our places at the back of a small column of French workers who were leaving the camp, with three Frenchmen who should have gone staying behind. We simply marched out of the camp and, when the French turned off in various directions to go to their own place of work, carried on going. If escaping had been unbelievably easy, getting back to Blighty was going to be altogether trickier.

As soon as we left the Frenchmen, the rain began to lash down as we trudged along the road towards the one bridge over the River Drava, which was the only practical route that would take us south towards the Italian border. We were slouching along, walking out of step and generally trying to look as if we were a trio of French prisoners on our way to do some agricultural work, when we suddenly saw a pair of familiar figures: two South African officers from Gavi, who were also disguised as French workers and who had decided to make a break for it without seeking official clearance. We were horrified, but in the event it may have worked to our advantage, because as soon as we split up from them they were captured, and any discrepancy in numbers back in the camp would have been blamed on them.

We were equally horrified when we eventually reached the river to find two German sentries guarding the bridge across the Drava. There was, however, no other way across what was a formidable river, so we pressed on and were pleased to discover that the guards were two elderly soldiers. They were not terribly keen to let us pass, but I confounded them with a torrent of French that tumbled from me, its fluency born of my sheer desperation and nerves. Once on the other side we were, we really felt, on our way.

By now we were outside the area permitted to the French workers, so our first priority was to get off the road. We took the first track up the hill, which in turn took us up into the first of the three ranges we had to cross to make the Italian border. Even this path was very risky, so we quickly branched off and made for the rougher wooded ground. It may have provided us with invaluable cover, but it was really hard going, and it wasn't until about four that afternoon that we cleared the first ridge. From there, our map showed that we had to follow the line of a road southwards up a very narrow valley to a track that would lead to the second range, but we couldn't risk going anywhere near the road, which was dotted with houses, villages and timber-working camps, so we clambered along the hills. It was incredibly hard going, with the frequent streams running down to the valley posing a particular problem. Negotiating these often meant lengthy detours and steep climbs, until finally it got so dark that we had little choice but to camp out for the night. We simply lay down as we were, the three of us huddling together to keep the bitterly cold September night at bay, taking turns to be in the warmest spot in the centre. Somehow we got some sleep, but it was no surprise that we rose shortly after dawn and made a very early start in the freezing morning.

Eventually we were over the second range and had a view down into the valley to a town called Hermagor, which lay directly in our path. In the light of dawn it did not seem very easy to bypass it, so we paused and had breakfast, which, like every other meal, was based on what we had been able to carry from the Red Cross parcels. We had taken advice from the camp's only doctor as to what would keep us going and yet be the minimum to carry, with the result that every meal consisted of one teaspoonful of butter, two teaspoonfuls of sugar, two of powdered milk, one of cocoa and three of oatmeal – all mixed up in a little water and eaten out of our only container, which was a disused margarine tin. Twice a day we ate in solemn succession, in slow motion and in dead silence, savouring every mouthful. Our only other sustenance was a quarter of a pound of chocolate spread over the rest of the day.

Unsurprisingly, we were paranoid about avoiding habitation and open areas, which made movement so difficult that we wondered if we'd ever get to the top of the ridge. We were at the stage of weariness where civility, even between ourselves – let alone a sense of humour – had long departed. And yet, when we reached that range and had ten minutes' rest, all was forgotten and forgiven. At the summit we planned the beginning of our next route by the last of the evening light and then lay down to get what sleep we could. An hour before dawn we were off again, working on the basis that the police had been warned we were at large and would be watching every bridge and crossroads, which I think was a sensible precaution. We did creep up to and cross one wooden bridge over a small torrent in the semi-darkness, striking across country until we reached a narrow defile in the foothills five miles away. We felt sure there would be controls, so we kept off the track and continued past an old mill before carrying on up the mountainside. Although we had seen nobody that morning, the maps we had been given by the camp's escape committee said that this cart track led to a customs barrier at the border and that the crossing was regularly patrolled by Austrian customs police with their dogs. We weren't at all keen on the dogs.

Suddenly we got a bonus, finding what looked to be a little-used track that led up a side stream in a direction that might take us to the border without passing the customs house. We followed it, and by dawn we had climbed up to the ridge. We had been on our feet for 36 of the last 48 hours, but our incredible weariness was offset by our belief that we had only to get across the border to be free, and that this track, which was obviously built by some pre-war alpine club, would take us there undetected. Yet a mile further up the track we found a notice in German saying that anyone passing this point was in mortal danger, followed 200 yards later by a deep, impassable gorge with sides that had a sheer drop of 300 feet. There had been a wire-rope causeway, but it was broken and quite unusable, so we had no choice but to go back and clamber up the loose shale sides of the ravine before rejoining the path. Three and a half hours later we re-emerged, two hundred and fifty yards from where we had started up the tiny path that morning. Truly shattered, Colin lit up his one cigarette of the day and was lying back enjoying it when a black dog suddenly rushed out of the trees, barking furiously, and then rushed away again. The echoes hadn't even died down before we were packed up and at a full run, feeling like hunted men.

We never discovered where that dog came from or whom he belonged to, but we weren't taking any chances and didn't stop until we had cleared the hill. Finally, in the early afternoon, we came out onto a grassy clearing on a high saddle of summer pasture where there was an empty wooden-plank building and a few rough sheds, beyond which was a clear view across the valley. We could see the cart track that we had left in the early hours, and ahead of us the customs hut that marked the border was clearly visible. We were close, but it was apparent that any attempt to cross the valley would be in clear view of the hut, which was obviously manned. Our only option was to follow the ridge and hope that it joined the main ridge that constituted the border, something that I thought unlikely. We rested for a couple of hours, moving on when we were hit by a combination of snow and biting wind.

Our decision not to cross the valley was immediately vindicated when we glanced down onto the main cart track and saw a blue-uniformed border guard with a rifle in one hand and the leash for a large Alsatian dog in the other. He was less than a quarter of a mile away but hadn't seen us, and, with the wind blowing towards us, his dog hadn't scented us. We quickly crept under cover, the guard stopping right opposite us before sitting on a rock and casually sweeping the face of our hill with his field glasses. We lay still, and the glasses swept right past us, the guard then lighting a cigarette while the dog crouched at his feet as we crept over a small skyline on all fours and out of sight.

The hill was bare except for stunted mountain pines. Just five or six feet high, their lower branches were interlaced on the ground, which made progress difficult and painful. The valley was getting deeper, and the slope steeper, and sometimes we had to struggle up almost to the crest itself to avoid sheer rock. Some distance ahead of us a single huge crag rose up on the crest of the ridge, many hundreds of feet above us, and clearly we had somehow to pass this, otherwise we were stuck. We struggled on and skirted it on the west side, and just when it seemed as if we were going to be halted by a great ravine, we passed the end of the rock, and there, as narrow as a razor's edge, was the ridge's summit, with a rough goat track covering, like a bridge, the last 200 yards, going down sharply to a gully and up to the main ridge.

As the sun set behind the mountains on the west, the main ridge would have been a magnificent sight regardless. But, to the three of us on that day, the sight of a line of white-painted stones, each about 100 yards apart and running all along the ridge, was one of the most welcome views of our lives. Those stones clearly marked the border, and it was inconceivable that anyone would be guarding such a wild and lonely spot. The final few yards were still pretty hairy, because any slip would have seen us fall hundreds of feet to our deaths, but then we finally crossed that line of white stones and slipped over the skyline and into cover, secure in the knowledge that we were back in Italy again. What a marvellous feeling it was.

Every journey consists of a series of milestones, and all three of us had been completely focused on crossing the Italian border. It had taken us three days and two nights to achieve that aim, and here we were, back again on Italian soil. We believed it would be plain sailing from here to find our way southwards to the Allied lines or south-eastwards into Yugoslavia to join up with the partisans and repatriate from there. Things, however, did not go so smoothly.

Our plan had been to avoid the Italian town of Pontebba, skirting around to the west. As we moved through the hills around the town, however, we saw movement that we believed was likely to be hostile. The first thing we saw was two uniformed men carrying packs and pistols approaching a hut. In the half-light we couldn't make out what their uniforms were, but we feared the worst. However, no sooner had they entered the hut than they came out again and headed up the hill straight towards us. We moved, almost silently, deep into the undergrowth, and they passed right by us before disappearing into the forest. We never found out who they were.

Our sense that these woods were a dangerous place for three fugitives to be wandering around was confirmed just two hours further on when we were approaching a track and heard movement. We instantly faded back into the undergrowth before, moments later, two men and a dog came ambling past. They stopped almost exactly opposite where we were hiding, at which stage one went on and the other remained with the dog, the two of them staring into the forest. We were convinced that we had been spotted and that the man with the dog had been left to watch while the other went for help, yet after he had dallied for the best part of an hour he suddenly upped and walked away.

After that we made excellent progress, especially when we got beyond Pontebba and found, to our astonishment, a curving, totally deserted tarmac road heading down towards the valley. It went absolutely nowhere and was clearly long abandoned, so it must have been built as a military road. Not that it mattered, because it was marvellous to be able to move so quickly and easily.

We also had a mind to the fact that we were entering a far more densely populated part of the country. This was important because it increased the chances of running into civilians, and we were very aware that fugitives were often caught simply because they looked like fugitives. So, when our military road crossed a pleasant stream in some beech woods, we went off the path, found a sunny clearing, had a thoroughly good wash in the stream, shaved and washed our socks. I even cleaned my shoes, which led to a worrying discovery. The shoes had been through a good deal of wear during my two years as a prisoner, and there was now a hole in one sole, and the other sole, as I cleaned it, showed serious signs of coming away. They weren't going to last long, but, somehow, they had to carry me another few miles.

We had decided at this point that we needed to go down towards the valley, because, beyond Pontebba, where the valley narrowed severely, the hills on our side looked pretty well impassable, whereas those on the other side had some tracks that went visibly up towards the ridge lines. Crossing the valley was a deeply worrying prospect, because it was the main route to Austria, so heavily populated with German guards and crawling with soldiers. Nevertheless, unless we wanted a huge detour, we had very little choice, so we decided to wait until dark.

We arrived at the valley in good wooded country at a point where the main valley road and river both went under a viaduct. Just before dusk, we slipped down, with Colin leading the way some 200 or 300 yards in front of us. The idea was that he would sound the alarm if he ran into trouble, so that Alan and I, who were following behind, could make ourselves scarce. Our first obstacle was a small village, and, after Colin passed through it, Alan and I followed him, finding him waiting for us, lying up under a culvert before the viaduct itself. On the viaduct there were two German guards, and it was clear that no further movement was possible before dark, but as soon as the sun went down we slipped through under the arch, curved past the remaining houses of the village and got back onto the main road.

It was vital that we got through the bottleneck of the valley in one night, so we followed the main road for eight miles until we reached the key town of Chiusaforte, which closes the valley at its narrowest part. We made good progress, although we had to dive off the road on the infrequent occasions when vehicles, which were mostly military, passed. That was sometimes more difficult than it sounds, as the mountain side of the road was often sheer rock, and on the other side there was a retaining wall that fell straight into a big river. On three occasions we found ourselves hanging over the retaining wall, holding on by our fingertips until the vehicles had passed.

By this time Alan had taken the lead, with Colin and me following behind. Chiusaforte was our final major obstacle, but we felt certain that when Alan reached the town our system of warning would allow us to take our evasive action. That's not the way it worked out, though, with Alan passing a small row of houses without realising that he was in Chiusaforte, and then suddenly finding himself in the middle of the town. He took a snap decision to go on and got through the village without incident, waiting for us in a very cold and muddy ditch.

His wait was in vain. Colin and I were well behind him but confident – or perhaps that should be overconfident – that we would be warned before we hit any danger. So we strode happily on, passing the same outlying houses that Alan had failed to realise were part of the town before coming upon the centre of Chiusaforte with the same abruptness that Alan had earlier experienced. We, however, weren't as lucky as him, and as we passed a door it opened. It was clearly an inn or winehouse, and out poured a complete German and *carabinieri* patrol, literally on each side of us. We must have been very conspicuous as fugitives because at once there were loud cries of, 'Halt!' and 'Hands up!' and in the blink of an eye we were prisoners again. We later found out that, with the purest of bad luck, we had been passing the entrance to that inn right on the stroke of nine o'clock, which was the witching hour when the curfew began and the Italian and German patrols came on duty.

When we didn't appear, Alan moved on quickly, eventually finding his way out of the valley. He took shelter with some friendly Italians before moving down into Yugoslavia and joining the partisans, where he found four other ex-Camp 5 people. They fought for about a month with the partisans and then were given the opportunity to move, in two parties of three men, to the Adriatic coast. One party, which included two men I knew, New Zealander Dan Reddiford and Englishman Stump Gibbon, successfully found their way to the coast and were repatriated by ship. Alan and his companions, unfortunately, were recaptured and spent the rest of their war in Germany.

As for us, when we were marched off by the patrol, I decided, sotto voce, to make a clean breast of it to the marshal of the *carabinieri* – a marshal is a sort of sergeant major – and he dramatically uttered typical Italian exclamations and groans and said, 'If only you had told us, we would have been able to hide you away.' He then asked the German sergeant if he could lock us up in the *carabinieri* prison, with the obvious implication that we would be allowed to escape. The sergeant, unfortunately, was having none of it, and we were immediately taken to the guard headquarters of

Chiusaforte, where we were put in the care of the Austrian *Alpenjäger*. There we maintained stoutly that we were prisoners of French–Croatian extraction and were on our way to Laibach – which is now known as Ljubljana – to work in the locomotive sheds. As we didn't communicate in any language that was known to them, the Germans didn't quite know what to make of us, and it was not until nearly 36 hours later that they finally decided we should be thoroughly searched. I had nothing incriminating on me, but Colin, unfortunately, had been unable to resist bringing with him his last air letter from his lovely wife, who is still one of our friends. The cat was out of the bag.

As ever, humour is found in the most unlikely places. Colin and I were forced to sleep in the Austrians' barrack-room and were almost speechless with laughter when it became clear that these very young soldiers kept their long blond and extremely Aryan hair looking luxuriant and shiny by storing it in a hairnet overnight. As well as entertaining us with their effete ways, the Austrians treated us perfectly well, except for the obvious total deprivation of liberty. On the second complete day, the sergeant in charge of the headquarters took us to the town of Tolmezzo to be interviewed. It soon became very clear that we had no information to give him, except that we were prisoners of war and where we had come from. With the prospect of a huge amount of paperwork to explain our presence and arrange for us to be sent back to a prison camp, he was not terribly amused.

Yet another day passed before we were taken down to the railway station, where we immediately found ourselves the focus of half a dozen very attractive young girls of the town of Chiusaforte. They had come to talk to us, entertain us and tell us yet again that, if only they had known that we were at large, their families would have hidden us until the end of the war. I have to be honest and say that that was not the impression we had set out with: we felt that in a time of change and turmoil a large number of Italians would be only too anxious to curry favour with the Germans by turning in prisoners. Perhaps I am being unnecessarily cynical; perhaps if we'd been more straightforward and simply approached the nearest Italian, we might have been clasped to his bosom, hidden away in a comfortable farmstead and then seamlessly repatriated through Yugoslavia like so many other British were. But, then again, maybe we'd just have been handed straight over to the Germans.

Either way, we were back in the smelly stuff, pushed into yet another cattle wagon to God knows where, this time with two new companions about whom I remember absolutely nothing at all. All I knew for certain was that I was alive, the Germans were losing the war and I was on my way back to prison.

II

Say Hello to the Gestapo

After so long on the run, being back in captivity was a deeply chastening, not to mention occasionally uncomfortable, experience. Sitting in a covered metal wagon being shunted across occupied Europe like a side of meat will never qualify as fun, but I did my best to keep my spirits up. I was absolutely determined that as soon as humanly possible I would escape again and that this time I would get home. When I got back, I would need to be in a position to furnish our intelligence with as much information as possible, so I went out of my way to try to piece together our journey.

From Chiusaforte, in northern Italy, our train set out on an extraordinarily circuitous route which took it through Austria, into the heart of Germany and, eventually – via a huge S-bend that took us as far west as Mönchengladbach and right around Germany again – across the Polish border and then into East Prussia. Later, when I was back in London being interrogated for my debriefing by British Intelligence, they were interested in the route of that train more than anything, because it helped them identify which railway lines in that devastated country were still working. I had not been able to sleep much on the train, so that all through the long journey, whenever there was a station, I had been up peering through the grille to try to pick up its name. Even now I can remember the signs: Villach, Salzburg, Landshut, Reichenbach, Elsterwerda, Frankfurt an der Oder and then ending up at Hohenstein.

In East Prussia, we found ourselves at a camp run by the *Geheime Staatspolizei*, the secret police better known by their nickname of the Gestapo. This was essentially a transit and interrogation camp, and it wasn't the sort of place in which anyone of sound mind would wish to find himself. We were initially put into a very narrow concrete underground cellar with a steel door, a room that was about the size of a public lavatory. We could sit side by side with our feet extended, but even though I'm not particularly tall there wasn't quite enough room to lie down. It was pitch black, and there was no furniture of any sort, just a bare concrete floor. There was a brief interrogation, after which we were told we would be sent for again, but most of the time we were just left alone. The Gestapo had a fearsome reputation, and we continued to fear the worst, thinking that we could be taken out and executed at any time. Yet when we were eventually sent for again it was to be hurriedly loaded aboard a heavily guarded truck and taken off to another camp, called Stalag 20A, near Torun – which the Germans called Thorn – on the Polish side of the old German–Polish border.

We were still deeply apprehensive about our fate, because, as far as we were concerned, the camp at Torun might simply have been another Gestapo facility. The way in which we were bundled off the closed truck and shoved into a bare hut, where the door was immediately locked and barred, didn't improve our state of mind, and I was mentally steeled for the worst-case scenario of a fairly brutal interrogation by the Gestapo or, at best, being locked away and isolated from any other British prisoners of war and more or less forgotten about.

Nothing could have been further from the truth, as I found out when the door opened and in walked a smart figure in battledress, hat and all, with the insignia of a warrant officer. A smart salute was followed by the unforgettable words, 'Sir, Sergeant Major Howard, Worcester Regiment. I guess you could do with a cup of tea.' We looked at him in almost total disbelief, and then, in seconds, the mood changed from despair to euphoria. Bob Howard quickly described to us the camp that we were in, which consisted of a series of forts for working other-ranks prisoners and a few non-combatant officers.

He gently enquired whether we could do with something to eat, and, when we were very affirmative on this, he said, 'Well, what about bully beef, sardines in tomato sauce, bread, butter, tea, sir?' Sure enough, in about 20 minutes the sort of feast that we hadn't seen since we were back in Britain duly appeared. After we had eaten, he came back, delivered another smart salute and said, 'Sorry, sir, you will have to stay here tonight, but in the morning we'll do something for you.'

Sure enough, at half past six in the morning he appeared and said, 'We are not allowed combatant officers in the fort, but we have arranged that you can join the non-combatant officers' mess in the Stalag Headquarters, Fort 14, for a few days while you're in transit, sir.' At this stage, in came the German administrative officer, whom we knew only as Hans and who was clearly on good terms with Sergeant Major Howard. He was accompanied by his interpreter, a Bavarian lieutenant who made clear his non-Nazi views and who made the most perfunctory attempt to search us. We didn't have any maps or equipment left, but if we had had he would not have bothered to find them.

If I was staggered by what I had seen so far, an even more surreal experience awaited me when I was taken up to the fort headquarters and to the officers' mess to meet the six non-combatant officers. The scene that greeted me was utterly unforgettable, with two English padres, an English doctor, an Australian doctor and two Kiwi dentists sitting down to lunch at a table that was set with a white tablecloth, forks, knives, spoons and clean dishes. Even more incredible was the fact that they were tucking into a splendid meal of potato soup, sausages, eggs, spinach and ice cream, all of which had been prepared by a very small Scotsman called George. I hadn't seen an egg for over two years, and it had been a lifetime since I had last clapped eyes on clean cutlery, crockery or tablecloths.

Domestic electricity was rationed in Poland, but George had three electric hotplates in his kitchen. Unbelievably, out of the cupboard came a bottle of beer for each of us and schnapps for after the meal. What had happened was that Poland had become a country of barter. The reichsmark had fallen into disrepute, and the prisoners of war, through German competence in delivering Red Cross parcels, had become the capitalists of the neighbourhood, able to barter things, like chocolate, coffee and cigarettes, that were absolutely unobtainable in the Polish civilian world and, indeed, to most Germans. We found that the prisoners at Stalag 20A, most of whom had been there since Dunkirk, had a strong hold over the German guards who had accepted bribes, always carefully given in the presence of witnesses, and were thereafter hooked. After dinner the orderly brought in several sheets of foolscap on which, handwritten, was the latest news from the BBC, and Dr Kennedy read this out to us. What a camp! And what a contrast with the ever-present searches in Italy, the *carabinieri* present all night outside our doors and occasionally bursting in. In Torun there were no Germans present in the camp at night.

The next surprise was a sort of variety-show revue laid on by the prisoners, who had made their own costumes. Seeing the civilian suits and dresses worn by the performers immediately reminded me of the possibilities of escaping from this camp. Morale there was very high, in spite of the horrors of the march they had had from Dunkirk in 1940 and the lengthy spell of imprisonment. When we were walking up to the camp from our hut, we witnessed the splendid spectacle of 200 men marching out to work. We had been told by the sergeant major that they would put on a good show for us, and they were perfectly turned out in their battledress. As they passed us, they gave a perfect 'eyes left', which was directed by Sergeant Major Mackintosh, a Cameron Highlander from my next village, Kingussie, who was the senior warrant officer in the camp. We were almost tearfully proud of this body of men swinging by and showing enormous spirit. The contrast with the generally depressed attitude of their own guards raised morale hugely.

One of the New Zealand dentists, the memorably named Captain Cook, was in charge of escape attempts from this Stalag, and he worked closely with the regimental sergeant major. He advised us that the only real practical route would be to get to a Baltic port and cross in one of the Swedish vessels that arrived regularly, carrying timber and iron ore to Germany and going back with coal. In theory, he said, it should be possible to cross the whole width of Germany from east to west, then into Denmark and from there across to Sweden; but, although the train and transport routes were good, such travel for non-Germans would be extremely hazardous. Despite those dangers, I was sure to be moved soon and was desperate for another crack at getting home.

12

Breaking for the Border with Gangster Joe

My 23rd birthday, on Monday, 4 October 1943, brought both good news and bad news. The good news was that a Welsh corporal who was an interpreter for the camp and was allowed a good deal of latitude to go out to the town with supply parties had formed a close relationship with a Polish girl who lived in Gdynia – which the Germans called Gotenhafen – and was able to provide reliable information about when the Swedish ships would be coming and going. The bad news was that the previous night an Allied air raid had blocked both of the Baltic ports, Danzig and Gdynia, for the foreseeable future. That week was one of considerable frustration, but we concentrated on eating, sleeping and getting fitter by the day. We were raring to go, and when on that Friday we heard that the ports had been cleared and further Swedish vessels were expected shortly, our spirits soared. Those spirits were, however, immediately doused by Captain Cook, who informed me that he had long since promised two British sergeants that they would be the first to go. I feared that I would be moved imminently, and knew for a fact that the escape of the two sergeants would see security tightened up, but, in all honour, they had to take priority.

That evening I was in poor form as I listened to Captain Kennedy reading the BBC news from the daily sheet that mysteriously appeared. I barely noticed the regimental sergeant major come in, or stand politely while the bulletin was being read. But, after the reading, as Colin and I were getting into bed, he wandered over to us. 'Excuse me, sir,' he said. 'I came in to ask if the two gentlemen would like to go tomorrow.' Colin and I were transfixed, sitting bolt upright in our beds and staring slack-jawed at him.

He swiftly explained that the two sergeants had come to him saying they had received well-founded stories that Joe Yotkovski – the king of the local black market who would be meeting the escape party the following night – was intending to drive hell for leather to Danzig with machine pistols out of each opening in the van, ready to mow down any German patrol or roadblock they met, a risk the sergeants were not prepared to take. Secondly, Yotkovski's objective was apparently not to help the prisoners escape but instead to accept all the Red Cross bribes and then take the prisoners, for a further bounty, to the Polish resistance fighters in the Forest of Torun who were armed but very short of training, weapons instruction and leadership.

The intrepid sergeants had formally withdrawn from the escape attempt, meaning that the opportunity was open to us. We were under no illusions and realised that the rumours might well be true, but the question of mowing down some German roadblocks seemed to us just one of the hazards of war, while the risk of being delivered to the underground and working with the Polish Resistance was at least more meaningful than being cooped up in a camp for the rest of the war. Colin and I looked at each other and then turned to Sergeant Major Howard, saying in unison, 'Let's go.'

We postponed the preparations until the following morning because we were going to need as much sleep as possible ahead of what was sure to be an arduous journey. Strangely, sleep came very quickly, not that it lasted long, because we were up at dawn, and by six o'clock wee George was serving us a hearty breakfast. At half past six we were in other-ranks battledress and boots and were lining up in the second rear rank of the column that was to go out for work that day. As we left, marching in step and swinging our arms as they always proudly did, Colin and I were afflicted with a good deal of coughing and sneezing as we passed the gate, raising our handkerchiefs to our faces in case any of the guard should, by some awful chance, recognise us.

We knew that if we could get away undetected then we would have a flying start. We had been assured by the officers that they would cover our departure until the Monday, which they did by putting two of the 'ghosts' from the camp into our beds. The 'ghosts' were men who were spare, having never been registered as prisoners, and who were therefore available for this sort of task. They would be lying in our bunks with only their foreheads and hair showing when the German interpreter came in each morning to count the officers, which he did in a predictably haphazard way. Similarly, two 'ghosts' would be used for the roll call when the working party marched back, so that the numbers would add up satisfactorily.

Once past the elaborate main wire, with its towers, searchlights and machine guns, we soon came to the second gate, with its much less formidable single wire fence. There, to our left, just as we'd been told, we saw the two huts from which we were to make good our departure. The rest of the column played their part, milling around as if they'd lost their compass so that we could slip away in the confusion. As with every other aspect of the plan, it worked perfectly, and we were able to leave unseen, slipping into the first of the huts. This was the sleeping and mess quarters of the two young soldiers of the Northumberland Regiment who looked after the camp rabbit farm, which provided an essential part of the diet of both prisoners and guards. They had a great deal of freedom to fetch suitable forage from outside and to wander between the wires where the rabbit farm enclosures were kept, and were well known to the guards. They were quietly drinking a cup of tea when we arrived, and they invited us to join them and rapidly made us welcome.

This was the point at which things suddenly looked like going awry. With that evening set as the rendezvous for us to be picked up by Yotkovski, our chat soon turned to what would happen later that day. To our horror, it rapidly became clear that Glancy and Hutson, the two young men with whom we were supping tea, had decided to come along too. This was not only unauthorised, but it enormously increased the hazards of the enterprise because a party of four would be much more conspicuous than a party of two, even if both of them had been in the camp for so long that they spoke a degree of pidgin German and could possibly help with interpretation at some point.

Our first thought was that our friendly bandit, Joe Yotkovski, was not expecting four escapees but two. Glancy quickly dismissed that line of argument: they were the go-betweens who arranged our getaway, and they had already been in touch with him, persuading him to accept the extra numbers by a further bribe of Red Cross tins and cigarettes. At the time, Colin and I were appalled at this use of Red Cross bounty, especially given the hunger we had experienced in Italy and the way we had become hoarders as a result. On reflection, however, the Red Cross's largesse not only kept the prisoners in Torun in good shape but, because of the dominance of the black market, also gave them the ability to influence events around them, as they had just so ably demonstrated.

We had little choice but to go ahead as planned, except that Glancy and Hutson were now along for the ride. The arrangement was that, shortly after dark, at about half past six, we would cut the external wire and crawl through a shallow dip that had already been prepared and covered with grass. In the meantime, because the hut could so easily be visited by the Germans, Colin and I spent the day in the next-door forage hut, covered with grass, vegetables and other rabbit food. We were suited and booted in smart civilian garb after Sergeant Major Howard had found an excuse to come down to the rabbit hut, bringing in his pack the two tailored suits that had been made for the variety revue we had witnessed some days earlier. Glancy and Hutson were natural spivs and had already acquired civilian clothing from their black-market activities. At the appointed time we cut the wire and crawled through the trench, dragging our packs behind us. These were stuffed with toiletries and food, which we could eat or use as bribes if necessary, plus the cigarettes and coffee that we were to give Yotkovski to soothe the burden of two extra people.

We came to the third and final layer of wire, which wasn't a formidable obstacle in itself but which was supposed to be supplemented by a heavy iron gate guarded by a patrolling sentry. However, the Luxembourger who should have been manning that post had been regularly bribed by Glancy to turn a blind eye when Glancy went down to see his girlfriend in the nearby village and had been told that this was one of those nights. Glancy had always returned, so the sentry must have felt it was easy money – I only hope his punishment was not terminal. My heart sank when I saw that the big iron gate that he should have been guarding had a heavy chain and an enormous padlock on it, but, as I got closer, I could see in the moonlight that the chain was draped over the top spikes and could easily be lifted off. As we carefully removed and replaced it, we looked back at the brilliant searchlights from the towers, which played along the main wire of the camp, and said a short, silent prayer.

With the gate shut, we yomped up the road at double-quick time for about a mile and a half until we came to the wooded crossroads that marked our rendezvous. The plan was that Yotkovski would turn up at seven o'clock in his anonymous van. Except seven o'clock came and passed. So did quarter past. Half past. Quarter to eight. And then, just before eight, there was the rumble of an engine coming to a stop just short of the crossroads – a wise precaution by Yotkovski. We covered that hundred yards in record time and had the back of the van open, ourselves and our packs flung into it and Yotkovski on the move again before we even had the back properly closed. We went through the town of Torun, which had at that time about a quarter of a million inhabitants, with our hearts in our mouths because we felt sure that there must be patrols and roadblocks everywhere. However, from the twisting and turning of our route, I am sure we took all sorts of back alleys. Eventually we were clear of the town and thundering down the main road to our next stop of Bydgoszcz – or Bromberg as the Germans called it – which was about an hour and a half away. When I say 'thundering down', I exaggerate a little; the wartime engine of this vehicle shook us to bits, but we moved at what seemed like a painfully slow speed.

The moon was incredibly bright that night, and as we drove along we were able to peek out through cracks in the canvas sides and see the countryside passing. Finally, we came into Bromberg itself, and despite our worst fears the whole place seemed to be deadly silent, with no movement, German or otherwise. We swung left through some gates, came to a halt and were ordered to get out as quickly as possible; we didn't need to be told twice. There were several men there whom we had heard exchange a password with Yotkovski, and who, I imagine, were his regular black-market distribution gang. They carried off the goods, which they had to hide, and one of them, who turned out to be the nightwatchman of the factory we were now in, took us and Yotkovski up endless stairs to the top floor. We were put in what I guess was the office of the secretary to the managing director of the factory because we had passed an open door with rather better furniture inside it. The blackout blinds were drawn, the door was shut and at last the light was put on. This was the first time we saw Joe Yotkovski face to face, but he was such an open and obvious brigand that I couldn't help but trust him.

We had arrived late on Saturday night, and after a good night's sleep on the plush carpet in the secretary's centrally heated office, Sunday passed pretty agreeably. At lunchtime, Joe and the nightwatchman turned up with a gentleman called Tadeusz, who was to be our companion for the next stage and whom we immediately renamed 'George' at his own request. Joe came for lunch bearing gifts, namely a bottle of cherry brandy and six huge cooked pork chops, each of which must have been more than the monthly meat ration for ordinary Poles. We passed the day eating, drinking the cherry brandy and listening to Joe talking about the conditions in Poland and of his own immense black-market network, which extended to selling goods in Berlin. He said he had seriously considered coming with us, because there had been times when the police network was getting very close to him. On the other hand, he had bribed so many people that he was sure he would get plenty of warning of any serious attempt to arrest him. He decided against it in the end, which was a pity, as the presence of such a confident and reliable guide would have made our journey easier. George proved no mean substitute, however.

That evening we sat in that office and ran through our next moves. It was Sunday night, and the plan was to stay put until very early the next morning, at which stage we would be driven down to Danzig, where a boat was expected. Nothing ever goes completely to schedule, though, and as we sat there gabbing the air-raid siren sounded. Moments later the breathless nightwatchman rushed in and explained to us in garbled German – which, fortunately, we were able to understand – that during air raids the managing director always came and sat in his office until the raid was over, so that he could summon assistance if there was any incident in his precious factory. He closed the door and locked us in. Soon afterwards we heard footsteps, saw the light go on next door and heard someone come in, walk round the room and obviously sit at the desk. We even smelt the smoke of his cigar. We sat in absolute silence, not daring to move and scarcely to breathe. All the time we could hear his little fidgets, a phone call he made, even his breathing at times, and we wondered when he would perhaps require a file from his secretary's office. But eventually the all-clear went, he departed and we all let out simultaneous long sighs of relief. We didn't know it then, but that air raid was to change our plans radically – and may even have saved our lives.

The next morning we left just after dawn in another anonymous van, with George and an old gentleman up front alongside the driver and the four of us in the back. We made good speed down the main road to Danzig and were threading our way through the town when suddenly we felt the driver jam on his brakes, turn sharply down a side street and push on his accelerator equally sharply. After two or three more turns, the van screeched to a halt and the driver opened the bonnet and began tinkering with the engine. George and the old man disappeared, but not before George had hissed over his shoulder at us to sit tight and shut up. As we sat in the back of that van, time passed extraordinarily slowly. We felt that all eyes must be on our driver, who couldn't go on tinkering forever. Finally, the door opened and George, without elaboration, told us to get out. If anyone observed us in this residential suburb of Danzig, they must have wondered what was happening when four men in suits piled out of the back of the van and started walking away. George took over care of Hutson and Glancy and, without a word of explanation, handed us over to the venerable old gentleman, with his black overcoat, dark glasses and umbrella. He quickly shook hands with each of us, handed us a railway ticket each and silently walked away. Completely at a loss, Colin and I followed a few yards behind him, our legs so stiff with cramp that we both walked with a limp at first and felt horribly exposed.

Finally, we came to a small suburban railway station, outside which the old man stopped, leant on a post, fiddled with his umbrella and gazed into space, completely disassociating himself from us. George and the other two were nowhere to be seen, so we had to take the hint that we were not to approach him and to make ourselves as invisible as possible. It's difficult to explain how self-consciously conspicuous we felt, and it was with a huge sense of relief that we suddenly spotted the familiar sign of the gents' toilets. We disappeared into them, wondering what on earth would happen next and whose hands we had fallen into.

When we came out, the first person we saw was George waiting outside for us, and were we glad to see him. He told us that the air raid of the previous night had closed Danzig and had left Gdynia as the only operational port and our only hope. Even more worryingly, a rumour had swept the town that some parachutists had come down in the raid, so there were extra roadblocks in all the cities and along all the roads between major towns. This news necessitated a complete change of plan, which meant that we were now to take the train, watching the old man, who would be travelling in the same carriage but separately from us, and then following him again when he left the train in order to board the same bus as he did to Gdynia. George hoped that this circuitous route would allow us to circumvent the roadblocks but could offer no guarantees.

Eventually the train came puffing in. We followed the old man into an extremely crowded carriage and had to take what seats there were. The old man sat across the aisle from us, again staring into space, while we sat in the only two remaining seats, with Colin on one side next to a mother and small girl, and me, without looking, next to a man facing him. When I became fully aware of my surroundings, I realised that I was sitting next to an SS officer in full black uniform, which set my nerves jangling. Luckily, he paid no attention to me at all, but the little girl did. In the camp I had been given a really superb pair of fur-lined leather gauntlets as a final leaving present by a generous doctor, and I was wearing these on that chilly day. The little girl's eyes immediately latched onto them, and I heard her whisper to her mother the word 'Gestapo' before her mother quickly shut her up. I instantly realised that she had mistaken me, in my splendid gloves, as being with the Gestapo, because only they could afford to flaunt such things. I inwardly prayed that my SS neighbour had not heard a word of this, and, fortunately, he was absorbed in the papers he was reading, which looked of a very official nature. When we got out of the train, the gloves went over the first hedge that we came to.

During the quite short journey, the inspector came round, we thought, for tickets, but it turned out he was a police inspector looking at travel passes. He took only a cursory glance at mine because he had to lean across the formidable figure of the SS man in uniform to reach me, while Colin's document got even more scant attention because, although he was on the other side of the train, he was shielded by a large lady with a baby who had chosen that exact moment to become an extremely smelly baby. Then he moved down the carriage to where the old man was keeping an eye on Glancy and Hutson. Just as he was reaching their row, the train stopped and the old man got out, hurriedly followed by the two boys and ourselves – a nasty moment.

We once again followed the old man down the street to a bus stop, keeping our distance all the time. There was a long queue of people waiting for the bus, but in the mistrustful atmosphere of those days none of them even looked at us, let alone spoke to us. The only time anyone addressed any of us was when the ticket collector said a word or two to

Colin, who didn't understand but smiled and nodded, which appeared to do. The old man preceded us onto the bus and bought three tickets, two of which he handed to us before once again completely disassociating himself from us. We went towards the back of the bus, while he sat in front where we could see him, so that, when he eventually got out at a stop in Gdynia, Colin and I were able to follow him to his home. Somehow, George, Glancy and Hutson had already arrived, and we were immediately taken to a small upstairs room and told to lie up there, be quiet and wait for some food to be brought to us. We thought that the old man's insistence on such extensive precautions inside his own house was a little overly dramatic until he explained that most houses occupied by individual Poles had a German billeted on them and that there was a *Wehrmacht* officer in the room just across the landing from us. After that, we didn't make much noise.

After two days of four grown men living in silence in such a small room, there were still no Swedish ships available. The port of Danzig was still closed after the air raid, and the Swedes had been told to delay their visit. We had no idea of when they might resume. It was becoming increasingly difficult for the elderly gentleman and his wife to conceal our presence, especially with a German living cheek by jowl with them, so on his daily visit George decided that two of us would go to stay with him while the other two stayed put until the signal to move was given. After coins were tossed, Glancy and I went with George, who explained in passing that the delay in getting to Gdynia had probably saved our lives, because the ship that we would have taken, had everything gone smoothly, had received a direct hit and nobody in the hold could possibly have survived.

George, his wife and two daughters were extremely hospitable, even managing to produce a goose one evening, which gave us a succulent and enormous meal. Both the daughters were working, with one employed at the German headquarters. In her conversations with Glancy – who was a good deal less shy with the girls than me – she confessed that she bitterly regretted the absence of Polish boys, although to my intense satisfaction she quickly added that, 'I would never go with the German boys, because they all have horrible diseases.'

At last, news reached us that there was a ship coming in, loading that night and sailing at noon the next day for Sweden. The girlfriend of the

Welsh corporal at the camp who was in touch with George came to the rescue at this point. She lived in Gdynia, and, with George in Bromberg to pick up further supplies, she helped the old man to guide Colin and Hutson to the dock area and showed them through a secret hole in the fence to the docks. As her English was more than adequate, she was also able to give them clear directions on where the rendezvous within the dock would be. This was a very gallant performance by an 18-year-old girl who had nothing to gain and everything to lose by her generosity.

We followed another guide to the centre of the town, and then the old man came back to rendezvous with us. While he walked slowly and apparently aimlessly down one side of the street, Glancy and I pursued him at a distance and on the other side of the street. The darkened streets down by the docks were illuminated only by a fleeting moon, so we couldn't drop too far behind him, but nor did we get close enough to threaten his safety had we been rumbled. We tried to act on George's oft-repeated advice, which was that we should never walk down the street looking glum and never walk in dead silence; so we exercised our German together and allowed ourselves to be amused by the jokes we were not making and not feeling like making.

Eventually we got to the place where we could get into the docks. Glancy and I were told to rendezvous with the other two behind a big pile of telegraph poles lying on the ground not far from the secret entrance. There would be, we were told, a friendly Polish dockworker along shortly who would pick us up and guide us for the last bit. When we got to the rendezvous, there was absolutely nobody there. It turned out that Colin and Hutson had already arrived but were lying as still as dormice because they had heard us come but didn't know who or what we were. As I cast around, I almost fell over them, and, just at that moment, the Pole turned up and gave the password as arranged. We followed him, scrambling over the telegraph poles until we found an opening right in the middle, which the Polish Resistance had left as a hiding place when they constructed the pile. All four of us slid into the hole, and there we were, totally invisible, waiting for the appropriate time.

After what seemed an age, our Polish friend, who never exchanged a word with us but simply waved for us to follow, turned up again, and we followed him along the docks to where we could see a crane loading coal dust onto a ship. Sure enough, as we got closer, we could see that the ship was flying Swedish colours. We were ensconced behind the coal heap while the huge crane, with its searchlight directed at where the scoop would fall, was working between us and the ship. We could see that the gangway was down and that the afterhold was open and being loaded. The scoop of the crane was close enough to us for bits of coal dust to fall out of the air and pepper us, and it can't have been long before we were a pretty sight.

The Pole had brought four sets of the blue dungarees that the dockworkers wore, so that we had some protection. The crane got closer and closer until the rays of it were beginning to flash right across us, which forced us to scrub coal dust on our faces and hands so that the white didn't show up. Then, suddenly, the crane's light went out, and there was dead silence. It was either an air raid or a tea break, and, in any case, it was the moment to try our luck. We had already decided on the order by which we would go on the ship: I would go first, and they would watch me to see how things went and then follow exactly the route I took, with Hutson going second, Glancy third and Colin Armstrong bringing up the rear.

I walked purposefully across the open dock and hopped up onto the gangway, at which point a swarm of people were suddenly milling around me. Some were crewmen, and some were dockers, but they appeared to be conducting a heated altercation in the mouth of the hold and barring my way. George's wife had given us some sandwiches for the journey, and, as I have a theory that nobody who is eating is ever suspected, I took out my sandwiches, leant on the rail and started to nibble at them until, as suddenly as the argument between the dockers and sailors had blown up, it stopped and they dispersed. I raised my hand to wave the others on and went forward to the hold, where there was the usual iron ladder going down to the Stygian black of the piled coal dust. Shortly afterwards, Hutson appeared, followed by Colin, but there was no sign of Glancy, and after a while we feared the worst. More to the point, we fretted that he'd been apprehended and worried that he might confess that there were three other fugitives on the loose. There was nothing for it but to move away from the hatch and dig our way into a hiding place in the remotest part of the coal. Digging in was not difficult, because the dust was soft, but the clouds of coal dust made for an appalling atmosphere, and we knew there was more to come when the crane started working again.

We had already been warned that, before any Swedish ship sailed, there would be a thorough search with dogs – although we suspected that the dogs would have no more fun with the coal dust than we did – and that a pilot boat would come alongside, which would make another thorough search of the cargo areas just after the boat reached the three-mile limit. This was much further than three miles from the port, as there was a long spit of land that protected the harbour, but we made our minds up that we were going to give it a clear three hours before we surfaced.

After about an hour and a half, the trapdoor in the hatch opened, and down came a small party of men calling out in broken English, 'Englishmen, Englishmen, come out. We know you are there.' We knew then that Glancy had indeed been taken and that they were looking for us, but the only thing to do was to sit tight and hope that they couldn't detain the ship forever and would believe that we were either not on board or that we had been suffocated by the dust.

Eventually the ship, which had first got moving on the stroke of noon, set off again, and we began to relax, waiting for our three hours to pass. Almost exactly on the three hours, the hatch opened again and the same calls came forward. This time we said, 'Let's have a go,' and revealed ourselves. We must have been horrid figures, all covered with grime and our noses and mouths full of coal dust. We staggered up the mountains of coal and got to the hatch, finally getting a glimpse of light and a breath of fresh air. There were two Swedish crewmen waiting for us, and one said, 'We've been looking for you; we thought you must be dead.'

As soon as we were in the crew's quarters, we were reunited with Glancy, who had in fact been on board the whole time. He told us how he'd panicked on arrival, couldn't remember whether to turn right or left and had turned the wrong way. He bumped into a Swedish crewman who was, mercifully, friendly – even if he accepted all the reichsmarks that Glancy had on him – and hid him away in a broom cupboard until they were clear of the three-mile limit and the pilot boat had gone. Glancy, at that point, had been taken to the captain and had told him that the three of us were hiding in one of the holds, at which point the skipper had dispatched groups of sailors to find us. The captain said that, if Glancy had been brought to him five minutes earlier, he would have had to turn back and deliver him up, and there's little doubt that he would have blown the gaff on us all. Instead, we were on the high seas, and the Swedes couldn't have been nicer to us. Once we were stripped of our boiler suits, we were left with reasonably clean clothes underneath, although our socks were taken away and washed for us while we showered and scrubbed ourselves as clean as we could.

13

Homeward Bound

The ship was heading for Malmö in southern Sweden, which couldn't have suited us better, but halfway across the Baltic we suddenly got a diversion call to go to Slite in Gotland. When that call came through, I was the only one of the fugitives at large because the crossing was rough and the others were hanging over the rail being sick or lying in their beds groaning. The captain sent for me and apologised about this diversion because it meant that he would have to hand us over to the military and not the civil authorities as Gotland was a military area and no civilian movement was allowed on it. After spending so long trying to get back to Britain, the thought of spending the rest of the war interned in Sweden – nice as that might have been – was a huge psychological setback.

As soon as we landed on Gotland, we were handed over to a Swedish official whose name, I remember, was Bertil Bondie. He treated us with undisguised suspicion and filled out all sorts of forms, but thankfully he also acceded to our request that the British vice consul on the island should be informed, and that proved to be our salvation. I can't really blame Bondie for his suspicion, because in the condition we were in we probably didn't look much like two captains in the British Army. However, the vice consul at Visby, the capital of the island of Gotland, was a wealthy and independent Swede who reacted very positively to the presence of the first four Brits to have set foot on his island since the outbreak of war. He immediately got in touch with the embassy and, through them, informed Bondie that he had carte blanche, financially and otherwise, to give us anything we wanted and that we were to be transported, as soon as it was convenient, to Visby and then on to the British Embassy in Stockholm.

What we wanted, quite clearly, was a decent meal and some clean clothes. We were taken to have hot baths in the Bondies' own house and then delivered to the local tailor, who must have had his windfall of the war because four hideously identical double-breasted dark suits were produced and roughly fitted to us, all made of a fabric that was a by-product of wood fibre. We were jokingly warned not to go out in the rain, otherwise the leaves would grow. But at least we were clean and looked passably civilian for our next moves in a neutral country. From there we went to a restaurant, where we were presented with four pint glasses of milk, which was probably the first fresh milk I had seen since leaving the United Kingdom before the expedition to Egypt years earlier.

Later that day we dined with the Bondies at their house and, in the evening, were fetched by the vice consul, Mr Bierkanda, and taken to his luxurious house in Visby, which is known in Sweden as the 'City of Roses' and of which he was inordinately proud. Next day we set out on a ferry with him as he had business to do in Stockholm, and after we reached the mainland we caught a train to the capital, where we were met by a British military attaché. Over the next few days we enjoyed the greatest possible hospitality, although we perhaps only later appreciated that we were lucky to have arrived in Sweden just as Swedish sentiment was changing. The Swedes were officially neutral, but their natural trade was across the Baltic and they had firmly believed that Germany would win – indeed, virtually had won. But in 1943, after El Alamein, after the Allied invasion of Italy and after the huge Nazi setbacks in Russia, they had realised that the pendulum had swung and now knew we would win. Had that sentiment not been widespread, we would not have got out of the place. The British ambassador was also extremely generous in his hospitality. Colin and I dined there and were shown a film in his private cinema, with a large number of Swedish guests. This neatly illustrated the change in their sentiment because it was Charlie Chaplin's spoof film of Hitler called *The Great Dictator*, a provocative movie that certainly couldn't have been shown in Sweden a year or even six months before.

We were occasionally allowed to go out on our own but were told not to make ourselves conspicuous and not to speak English audibly to anybody else. With the two of us dressed in identical dark suits and wide-brimmed, grey, Swedish felt hats, which made us look like Chicago gangsters, it was difficult not to feel conspicuous.

One day we went off to lunch at a restaurant, had our glasses of milk and studied the Swedish menu without a word to the waiter. The menu was divided into three sections, and we chose a dish from each. The waiter came back, we pointed to our dishes and he looked somewhat surprised and uttered a long tirade of Swedish, which we heard out and replied to with, 'Ja, Ja,' in our best Swedish imitation, after which he went away shaking his head. We soon discovered why when he brought us the first course, which was cauliflower, followed by a second course of cauliflower done in a different way, and then a third course, which was cauliflower in a white cheese sauce. We had, of course, thought that the three parts were starter, main course and 'pud', but in fact they were three separate menus and we had simply picked the middle, or vegetable dish, out of each of them. No wonder he showed some astonishment, but he went away satisfied with a handsome tip from the money the embassy had generously provided us with, which I later found was deducted from our pay.

Much as we enjoyed the hospitality in Stockholm, by now we were desperate to get back to Britain, an aim that seemed to be thwarted time and again. This time the embassy flight, an unarmed Liberator that would hazardously cross Norway and fly into Leuchars, in Scotland, was cancelled, meaning another lengthy wait. Eventually, on 4 November, we climbed aboard a plane bound for Scotland. The pilot took all sorts of evasive action at high altitude over Norway before heading for Leuchars, in Fife, only for fog to force a late change of plan and a diversion to Kinloss on the Moray Firth. As we came down to Kinloss, my folded fist was in the air, and as the wheels touched the runway I turned to Colin, who was sitting on the other side of the narrow fuselage, just in time to see him raise his hand in salute.

Two years to the day after I had been captured in Egypt, I was home. How I had missed Scotland.

14

Joining the Jedburghs

Despite the stresses and strains of travelling through occupied Europe from East Prussia back to Britain, by the time our plane from Stockholm touched down in Kinloss I was feeling refreshed and ready to re-enter the fray. That turned out to be fortunate because my masters considered that I had enjoyed plenty of rest and recuperation in Sweden and plans were already in place for me.

Within days I was instructed to report to a place called Milton Hall, near Peterborough, in Cambridgeshire. On arrival I found an enormous English country house that had been the family home of the Fitzwilliams since the 16th century but which had been commandeered for the duration of the war. In the grounds there were several rows of Nissen huts, and it was clear that they had the capacity to accommodate a great number of people. The mansion itself was given over to a whole series of lecture rooms, the headquarters and the instructing staff's accommodation, so I was allocated to one of the Nissen huts.

When I'd been told to report to Milton Hall, I was given no details about what I'd be doing there, but I soon discovered that I was to be a part of the Jedburgh group, which were three-man units that were to be dropped into occupied Europe to act as a high-profile focus for the local Resistance. The name was apparently chosen at random from the Ministry of Defence's secret war code book, but I liked it: not only did it remind me of home, but the Borders town of Jedburgh was home to the sorts of rugged scrappers I'd like to be sent into battle with.

The reality was even more appealing: a unique fighting force that contained Brits, Americans, French and a smattering of Dutch, and which turned out to be one of the few inter-Allied operations of the war in which everybody worked closely together and cooperated without any duplication and with an absolutely unified sense of purpose.

The advantages of being part of an international grouping were apparent from the very beginning, especially when it came to the grub. That may sound very prosaic now, but in the midst of war you tend to concentrate on the necessities of life, which inevitably boil down to shelter, defence and food. The British basic military ration was not at all bad and certainly met all our dietary requirements, but no one pretended that it had much culinary merit. The French were supposedly dependent on us for rations but somehow managed to get hold of quite a regular supply of half-decent wine, while the superior American rations didn't consist of just the dreaded tins of Spam but included luxuries like chocolate and coffee that were about as accessible to your average Brit as champagne and caviar. When the various rations were mixed together, the overall effect worked extremely well, even if it occasionally entailed sitting next to a large American while he tucked into a breakfast of fried bacon and eggs mixed in with waffles and syrup. Still, I suppose that they all end up together in the end.

Our time at Milton Hall was also pleasantly sociable, and if we ranged far and wide on exercises, we did the same in search of pleasure, frequently taking the train down to London for a night out before rushing back in time for morning parade. We often cut it fine, and I vividly recall one occasion when I ended up in the cab of an early-morning goods train alongside the driver and fireman before getting a taxi at Peterborough and grabbing an hour's sleep before going on parade.

Yet the combat to come was never far from our minds, especially for those people who had never seen active service, which at that stage was most of those at Milton Hall. A small number of the French officers had been in action, while a few Americans had taken part in Operation Torch, the invasion of North Africa, in 1942. Some of the American Jedburghs later had extremely distinguished careers, such as William Egan Colby, who became director of the CIA, and Colonel Aaron Bank, who was the founder of the US Special Forces. Even among us Brits there were very few who had been under fire, and looking back I suppose the fact that I was already blooded, having won a Military Cross for escaping from Torun, bestowed upon me a certain prestige.

Such was the collective curiosity about our future that one Saturday morning three of us set off in high spirits to find a blind soothsayer who was rumoured to live in the nearby village of North Luffenham. It didn't take us long to locate him, but what had started out as a big joke became a lot more serious when he beckoned each of us in turn into his study. I went last and didn't know what to expect, but he told me that after the first handshake he didn't want to have any physical contact with me at all. Instead, he asked me for something that I wore intimately and constantly about me. So I handed over the slim wallet in which I kept my identity card and money. He felt this carefully, sighed and then suddenly said, 'Thank God for that.' Obviously I was curious, and in response to my questions he said, 'Well, don't tell the others – I haven't told them – but the three of you are going into action, and you will be the only one who comes back.' Spookily, he was proved to be absolutely correct.

The process of forging us into combat-ready troops included all sorts of instruction, a great deal of which – such as night work, demolitions, unarmed combat and shooting with enemy weapons – simply recapped my original Commando training. However, we also had a great deal of tuition in new areas, such as coding, targets for demolition and the most efficient way to deal with individual targets. The course was intensive and lasted from January to the end of March, when we were considered to be fully trained. At that point the members of the Jedburgh course were divided into multinational teams of three, with, for instance, an American as the senior officer, a French number two and a British radio operator. The radio operators were either sergeants or promoted to the rank of sergeant and had already been at an intensive radio training course for some months. A large proportion of them came from the Royal Tank Regiment, whose radio training was probably the best in the British Army. My team consisted of myself in charge – for which I was promoted to major – and under me a French lieutenant, Michel de Bourbon, and a British radio operator, Sergeant Arthur Brown. Naturally, over the subsequent long months we became very close to each other and, unusually among the teams, we have all remained alive and close friends.

The Jedburghs were quite different from any of the previous infiltrations of intelligence operators into occupied Europe. Before we came along, all the other agents had been essentially clandestine, worn civilian clothes and been kitted out with identity cards. Their job had been to contact Resistance groups and try to foment sabotage, but, rather than take part in operations against the enemy, their task was to liaise with the Resistance and to gather intelligence for their handlers back in Britain. The agents dropped into Europe had enjoyed mixed fortunes and were beset by a sad degree of error and betrayal.

The Jedburghs' role was entirely different: we were there to act specifically as high-profile harbingers of war. We were to be dropped into Europe as the vanguard of the Allied armies, as proof that an invasion was imminent. Rather than hide, our job was to be as visible as possible, to provoke the enemy and to give some succour to the Resistance and to any citizens of occupied Europe who were thinking of making a stand against the Germans. Whether it was in the months before D-Day or while the battle was still raging in Normandy, our presence in France and elsewhere was also designed to act as a signal to hostile groups among the population that might be hoping to take advantage of any power vacuum, basically saying, 'Look out, we're coming.' Indeed, that proved a vital part of our role and one that helped to shape the map of Western Europe after the defeat of Germany.

Such considerations were, however, for the future, and in the meantime we busied ourselves with preparations for our deployment. Several teams went up to RAF Ringway near Manchester for a parachute course that lasted 24 hours, during which we did some theory and then practised free-falling onto mats in a gym to learn how to roll on impact. Finally, we went up to 600 feet in a hot-air balloon for our first real jump. When you go up in a balloon, it is much more frightening than a plane because you have nothing else to think about but the height, the dead silence and the gradually receding ground before you jump by sitting on the edge of the balloon basket and pushing yourself off. There was no slipstream to open your parachute quickly, so it seemed quite a long time before you felt the jerk on your parachute harness as the chute itself opened and steadied you before you winged your way slowly earthwards. As you approached the earth, it seemed to be coming at you suddenly, but we all landed successfully before unharnessing and rolling the parachute into a manageable ball that could be hidden or taken with you.

The second balloon jump was at night, which was basically the same, except you couldn't see the ground until the very last moment. Finally, we jumped at night from a Whitley aircraft, which, after jumping from a balloon, seemed easy: the noise of the engines and the howling wind as the hole in the floor was opened meant we were keen to get out, while the slipstream opened your parachute almost immediately and you floated serenely down in the darkness to a safe landing.

Now that we were fully qualified, we and several other teams were transported to North Africa aboard the SS *Oriana*. Well protected by escort vessels and overhead aircraft, we passed in considerable comfort through the Bay of Biscay and the Straits of Gibraltar before disembarking at Oran. From there we travelled 200 miles eastwards to our training camp near Algiers for some final team-building and fitness exercises in the Atlas Mountains. I remember one particular exercise, high in the mountains on a glorious spring day, when we came to the aptly named Valley of the Monkeys, where locals caught the monkeys to sell by putting out a jam jar with a few peanuts in it, whereupon the monkey would grab them but be unable to remove his fist and would be trapped. It reminded me that the simplest methods are often the best.

That arduous exercise in the Atlas Mountains gave me a valuable insight into my second-in-command, Michel. I started one walk at too fast a pace and tried to jolly the team along in a way that clearly upset Michel, who put on an expression of total determination and headed into the hills at maximum pace to show that he could get ahead and stay ahead of me. Many years later, I upset his granddaughter, and she did exactly the same thing.

Michel was, and remains, an exceptional person. A member of the French royal family whose full name is Michel de Bourbon-Parme, as a boy he narrowly escaped to America when France was overrun, joining the American Army at 18 before transferring to the French Army when he arrived back in Britain for special service. After the war, he fought gallantly with the French Army in Indochina in the ghastly precursor to the Vietnam War before he was captured at Hue, only to then escape with great difficulty after terrible privations and trek back to the French lines. He has always been a man of great courage and determination, whose unbreakable good humour and general calm can transform into epic spates of Gallic volatility at any moment, even if most of those occasions are chosen for effect. When I first met him, he was just 20, as was our radio operator Arthur Brown.

Arthur had just left school when he joined the Army, but he was clearly very able, which is why he ran the whole customs and excise operation for the Port of London after the war. Arthur was a devout

Roman Catholic, and one of my more difficult tasks when we first got
our departing orders was to find at short notice a Roman Catholic
military chaplain to take what could have been his final confession. My
obligation to Michel was slightly different. His sister, who later married
the ex-king of Romania, was in the Women's Services in Algiers, and
it was my pleasure and duty to take her out to the cinema and dinner
on the same evening.

The Jedburghs were designed to complement the work of the
Commandos, whom Churchill had formed to 'set Europe ablaze'. But
while Commando raids formed a constant threat to the enormous coastline
of Europe, they had a negligible effect on the interior of the continent,
where a whole range of local Resistance movements had adapted to the
huge variety of conditions that existed across Europe. At one extreme
you had wooded, hilly, barely inhabited countries like Yugoslavia, where
first Drazha Mikhailovich and then Josip Tito were able to set up, in
effect, a continuous guerrilla war with occasional pitched battles, using
quite large numbers of personnel. At the other extreme were heavily
populated countries like the Netherlands and Belgium, where clandestine
operations were virtually all you could achieve and the numbers involved
were necessarily small.

There were, of course, some major Resistance operations that did
have a dramatic effect on the course of the war, such as the heavy-water
attacks in Norway, which delayed Hitler's search for an atomic weapon;
the blowing of the Gorgopotamos Bridge in Greece, which seriously
delayed resupply of the German forces; and the delays that stopped
divisions like the Das Reich from attacking the Normandy beachhead
from their bases in southern France. As the war wore on and the Resistance
became increasingly well organised and more able to conduct small but
continual operations, the cumulative effect of the Commando raids and
the Resistance on the Germans in countries like Yugoslavia and Greece
was to tie up an estimated 54 divisions that might otherwise have been
usefully employed elsewhere. In some regions the Jedburghs were to play
a crucial role in bolstering the Resistance's resolve and firepower.

That said, while some of the Axis troops who were engaged in internal
security were fighting units having a rest from the rigours of the Russian
front or battling the Desert Rats in North Africa, most were second-rate
troops, including a large number of conscripts or volunteers from the

occupied countries – we came across everything from Mongols and Finns to the supposedly neutral Spaniards and dyed-in-the-wool Italian fascists. They were nevertheless armed troops who were not available for front-line duties fighting the Allies and the Russians. My own experience was that the huge delays and frustrations caused by the sabotage of factories, railways and power supplies also had a cumulative morale-sapping effect on the occupiers.

By the time I joined the Jedburghs, the writing was on the wall for the Germans and their allies, so many of the Resistance movements were already looking ahead to the post-war balance of power. This applied particularly to the left-wing and communist groups such as Tito in Yugoslavia, who had persuaded the Allied governments to abandon Mikhailovich, the monarchist leader, and to support his Red Star communist movement. A similar scenario was rapidly unfolding in Greece, where the 60,000 communist fighters of the Greek People's Liberation Army (ELAS) were openly at war with the non-communist partisans and trying to arm themselves for a decisive *coup d'état* after the war – an outcome that was prevented only by Churchill's ordering General Scobie's force to resist them in 1944, thus saving Greece from a communist future. The same applied in Italy, where the openly communist Garibaldi guerrillas allied themselves with Tito's partisans and tried to take over the whole north-east corner of the country.

It was against this confused backdrop that, shortly before we went abroad, I was sent down to the Hyde Park headquarters of the French government in exile to pick up my authority to operate in France from General de Gaulle or, to be exact, from Colonel the Baron Constant, his chief of staff. I was very surprised to be ushered into the great man's presence. 'I hear you're going to France,' de Gaulle said as I nodded my head in acknowledgement, before adding, 'I won't wish you luck. I disapprove of your mission and that of your colleagues. No one should be going into France without my command, and everyone in France must be under the command of General Kœnig, whom I have nominated for the purpose.'

More than a little taken aback, I replied – I hope politely – 'Sir, I'm aware of General Kœnig's appointment, but you will realise I am somewhat down the chain, and I must take my orders from my direct superiors. This is the military pattern, as you know.'

He nodded and turned away, saying, 'In the circumstances I will not personally sign your authorisation, though it will be in my name. Colonel the Baron Constant will sign it for you. Good luck.' So Colonel Constant signed on the dotted line, which was the password I carried with me to impress the French – except it didn't. It was rarely used and, with one notable exception, had no effect when I did try to employ it.

We have all heard just how difficult relations were between the British and Americans and General de Gaulle, and having met him and studied his demeanour at close quarters, I can quite understand why Churchill once said, 'The greatest cross I have ever had to bear was the Cross of Lorraine.' Yet I'm loath to speak ill of a most extraordinary man who was perhaps the outstanding continental European of his generation. Here was a man who came to England as a relatively junior officer, a brigadier, but who established himself by sheer force of action and personality as leader of the Free French, fought off later attempts by the Americans to replace him with Henri Giraud and, somehow, at the end of the war made France – a country that had been dishonoured, defeated, occupied and humbled – into a country that has had a seat at the UN's top table ever since. This was an amazing feat.

But if de Gaulle was at the head of the government in exile, the facts on the ground were very different. In particular, in occupied France there was a strong communist movement called the *Francs-tireurs et partisans* (FTP), which was the most disciplined, and in many areas the most effective, of the Resistance units, and after the war they almost toppled de Gaulle. More generally, the Resistance in France suffered from a whole range of personal, regional and political factors that made unified action fiendishly difficult.

Although such considerations were of central importance to our survival, we were entirely unbriefed on them. We had been given whole files of information about German policing, including the tale about the unfortunate British secret agent arrested because he looked the wrong way for traffic, yet nobody thought to mention that the French Resistance was deeply riven with infighting and hopelessly disunified.

Nor did we know of the ambiguity of feeling about the war among the French population, particularly in the south, where there was a degree of loyalty to the Vichy leader Marshal Philippe Pétain, a great hero of the First World War seen as a man of honour who would defend the interests of his people. More generally, there was a fear that the peace of sorts that the occupied French had come to know after the cataclysm of the blitzkrieg would be disrupted should the occupiers be antagonised in any way. The Germans played on this fear by the periodic execution of hostages as a reprisal for acts of sabotage by the partisans. So, when the railway between Bordeaux and Toulouse was blown up near Agen, 20 hostages were strung up on meat hooks on the poles alongside the railway and left there to die as an example of what would happen should German displeasure be provoked again.

The result was that by 1944 there were very few real Resistance fighters. There were many young men living rough and hiding in the more remote areas, particularly in the scrub of south-eastern France – the name '*Maquis*' means 'thicket' – but initially they were there simply to avoid the laws that would have sent them to Germany as forced labour. Only later did they morph into an organised Resistance. The normal population, however, was just keen to go about its ordinary business and not get involved, and I have always found it extremely difficult to blame the passivity of people who had livelihoods to protect, families to nourish and homes to keep.

Turning the other cheek is one thing, but actively conspiring against your own countrymen when they are doing their patriotic duty is quite another. There was also a substantial minority who were sufficiently afraid that the smooth continuity of their lives was about to be disgracefully interrupted by partisans and freedom fighters, and were so worried that their own lives might be harmed or the Germans so irritated that reprisals would be taken against them, that they were prepared to take action on behalf of the occupying forces. This minority were prepared to give the Germans information, to betray their countrymen and to infiltrate Resistance units in order to destroy the very people who were fighting for France. Those were the ones whom we could not forgive. The difficulty for people like me was that we knew nothing of this before we landed. We had absolutely no idea that the biggest danger we would face was this section of the French population rather than the more predictable actions of the occupying German forces. Back at Milton Hall, the thought that there was a constant risk of infiltration and betrayal hadn't even crossed our minds.

Edgebrook, the Edinburgh house I grew up in, was an incredibly happy and sociable place, with my brother Phil's rugby pals, including Eric Liddell, often in residence.

A portrait of the young man as a pupil at Edinburgh Academy, aged seven.

As a boy, I spent every day of the holidays exploring the wilderness around my beloved Newtonmore. Here I cradle two tiny birds I've found on the Glenbanchor Estate.

I was only just into my teens when I was diagnosed with osteomyelitis, an infection of the bone, which meant painful operations and years off games. I soon became quicker on crutches than most boys are on two legs.

Fooling around with my eldest brother, Jim, on Orkney, where he was a doctor. Jim and I enjoyed a particularly close bond, and I looked forward to my regular visits.

At Loch Insh, above Newtonmore, with the mighty peak of A' Chailleach rising in the background. It was the summer of 1937, and I was 16 – those carefree days were not to last.

While taking the long way round to Suez, we stopped at Cape Town and were hosted by local families. Here I am in the home of Mrs Moore, the indomitable editor of *Cape Argus*.

I saw my first action fighting against the Vichy French at the Battle of the Litani River as part of 11th Scottish Commando. Here I am shortly before that battle, in El-Geneifa, on the Suez Canal, sporting the tam-o'-shanter with our distinctive black hackle. This photo was taken by Geoffrey Keyes VC, who died in the ill-fated Rommel Raid.

Here I am (front row, fifth from left) in Egypt with 11th Scottish Commando. Egypt was the base from which we moved into Palestine and then into Syria, where the Battle of the Litani River was my first taste of action.

The forbidding medieval Italian castle of Gavi, where I was imprisoned, was used to incarcerate the most dangerous Allied prisoners. No one ever successfully escaped from this damp, freezing citadel.

From left: Glancy, Colin Armstrong, me and Hutson. After we had escaped from our prison camp in Poland and stowed aboard a boat to Sweden, we found ourselves stranded in Stockholm and wearing four identical suits made from a by-product of wood fibre. After the war I found the cost of my hideous suit had been deducted from my pay.

When my three-man Jedburgh unit 'Quinine' was dropped into France in 1944, my team was completed by young Frenchman Michel de Bourbon (left) and our radio operator, Sergeant Arthur Brown (right).

Whether in France or Italy, we could not have functioned as an effective guerrilla unit without radio operator Arthur Brown's ability to communicate with London.

Nino, whose real name was Ezio Bruno Londero, was my companion on almost every mission I went on in Italy. We are still friends, and I am godfather to his son, Lucio, also pictured.

In Udine, General Sir Richard McCreery, commander of the British Eighth Army whose victory at Po had just ended the war in Italy, and I (second and third from left) inspect local fighters with leaders of bitter rivals the non-communist Osoppo and the pro-Slovene Garibaldi.

My elder brother Phil was a legendary rugby player before the war, and after it he was a brigadier working on the reconstruction of Austria. We met up in 1944 at the Hotel Eden in Rome, a palace of luxury after the months I had spent in open country in France after D-Day.

This is the 880-yards Centipedes race in which I finished first and my friend and rival Roger Bannister came third, the highlight of my athletics career.

Back at Speyville in Newtonmore with my brother Phil, his son Ewan and my mother.

The Macpherson family assembled at Creag Dhu, in Newtonmore. Back row, from left: my elder son, Angus, who followed me into the Army, me and my younger son, Duncan, now a successful barrister in London. Front row, from left: my wife, Jean, and my daughter, Ishbel, who now lives in Devon after a rewarding banking career in the City.

15

'Chef, There's a French Officer, and He's Brought His Wife'

On 3 June 1944 we were warned that we would be dropped into Europe the following evening and were given our final briefings, in which we were provided with detailed information about the area we would be working in and given maps. We were to land on a dropping zone that had been used since 1942 by the intelligence services for periodic infiltration and were given one name, Bernard Cournil, who would be our initial contact. Apart from our code name of Quinine, that was all the information we were given. Our brief was to assess how many Resistance fighters there were in the area, to offer them weapons and explosives training, to encourage active action against the enemy and, finally, to prepare as large and efficient a fighting force as possible for the big liberation struggle to come.

So, on 4 June we got dressed in full uniform, piled into our aeroplane and strapped our parachutes onto our backs. The parachutes had a ripcord for emergency use but were all attached to a static line, which was in turn attached to the plane and would automatically open our chutes for us almost as soon as we jumped. We were on board a Halifax, a four-engine propeller bomber that was able to throttle down to a reasonable hundred and thirty miles an hour, which allowed us to jump without the wind actually blowing our heads off. We aimed to jump from about 700 feet, which was high enough for our parachutes to open and for us to steady ourselves before we hit the ground.

We had learnt in the briefings shortly before our departure that we were headed for an area on the border between the departments of Cantal and Lot in the Massif Central, in south-central France. We had barely had time to look at the maps – which told us that we would be operating around the town of Aurillac and ranging throughout an area bordered to the west by Brive and Cahors, to the north by Clermont-Ferrand, to the south by the northern approaches to Toulouse and to the east by the town of Saint-Flour – and we certainly had no idea of the sort of terrain we would be expected to operate in. In fact, the most memorable aspect of our preparation was the almost entire absence of any useful information: we had no specific targets, no knowledge of the region in which we were to land and no idea of the probable movement of German forces through our area.

So, as we flew through the night, uncomfortably cooped up in the noisy rear of the bomber, we had plenty of time to contemplate what lay ahead. We sat just in front of the tail gunner, with the rest of the crew up front, but we were fortunate that the sergeant dispatcher, whose main job was to ensure we jumped promptly when the time came (and who had orders to heave us forcibly over the edge if we didn't) shuttled backwards and forwards, keeping us abreast of our location and the time to our jump zone. Halfway to our destination, he came back to tell us the pilot had just heard that the Allied forces had entered Rome. That, however, was the end of the good news: half an hour past the time at which we had been due to jump, the pilot informed us that he had been unable to identify the landing ground, so he was aborting the operation and heading back to Blida Airport in Algiers. The sense of anticlimax was intense, as were the feelings of frustration and impatience as we waited for three long days in Algiers before finally, on the evening of 8 June, we were summoned to the airport again for a second shot.

We had a Polish crew, which augured well. Our Polish allies could be impetuous, but they were also fiercely determined, and we felt sure there would be no turning back this time. So it was that, at two o'clock in the morning under an extremely bright moon, we floated down towards the dropping zone, exactly as planned. I had dropped first and was on my own at the edge of the field, but Michel came second and landed smack-bang among our hosts. I followed the sound of voices as he announced his presence, and just as I arrived I heard an excited young Frenchman saying to his boss, 'Chef, Chef, there's a French officer and he's brought his wife.' I smiled to myself, but their mistaking me for a woman wearing a skirt was, I thought, an easy error to make because I was wearing my Cameron Highlander's uniform, with a battledress top and kilt and over that my jumping smock, which fastened between the legs and made a very comfortable cushion out of the kilt.

Bernard Cournil was soon up to speed with who we all were. He was a splendid, large, jovial fellow of great courage and initiative. He had done a marvellous job since late 1942 in organising that airfield as a dropping zone in the paddock of a small farmer called Puech, who was the archetypal French peasant – taciturn, almost toothless, as strong as one of his own bulls and enormously reliable to his friends. We had been dropped with nine bulky cylindrical containers that were stuffed with supplies and had to be retrieved and manhandled onto four ox-drawn carts that Puech had brought along for the purpose. We then trundled off in the moonlight, hiding the containers in the darkest, leafiest corner of an almost impenetrably thick evergreen forest on Puech's land. It was a few hours later, at dawn, after a brief sleep, that we were finally to discover exactly where we were and precisely who our companions were.

The adrenalin flowed pretty freely, yet, while it was exciting to have arrived safely, to be alive and to have made our contact, the outlook was otherwise completely disheartening. Bernard had done great things in organising the drop zone and in putting in place the infrastructure to cope with any agents or supplies that were dropped in, but to describe this as an active Resistance unit in any real sense would have stretched credulity to breaking point. Bernard had seven men to call on, and none particularly impressed me.

The elder statesman of the unit was a small, elderly Jewish dentist whom everyone called 'Tonton', or uncle. He was ostensibly in charge of supplies, but he certainly wasn't doing a very good job of it, because the only thing there was a lot of was scarcity. Then there was Bernard's brother Joseph, who was responsible for transport. He had so far mustered a single two-ton truck in which a tall, cylindrical charcoal boiler at the back of the cab produced the fuel to drive the engine. It is genuinely difficult to imagine a vehicle less suited to covert guerrilla operations: it produced a deafening amount of noise and choking fumes and was really very slow indeed. As well as Tonton, Bernard and Bernard's brother Joseph, there was a cousin of Bernard who allegedly knew his way round everything and could wangle supplies, other than food, of one sort or another. He certainly fancied himself as a wheeler-dealer but, again, had achieved very little – he ended up running a restaurant in the market district of Paris, which I visited with some highly astonished Australian friends just after the war. The remaining four were young boys who had run away to hide but had been recruited by Bernard to do rather more active work. They had a few Sten guns and a little ammunition between them, but they had yet to carry out a single aggressive operation – nor did they look as if they had the morale to do so.

It was immediately apparent to me that, unless things changed radically, we weren't going to be causing the Germans any discomfort at all. I decided that we needed to raise morale as quickly as possible and that we could do this by hitting their traffic, their electrical supplies and their railways as soon as possible – and hitting them hard. We certainly had the means to do so: in the containers that had dropped with us there were Sten guns, rifles, ammunition, a bazooka, a small two-inch mortar with ammunition and a couple of smoke bombs, a crate of grenades and, finally, the Army's favourite light machine gun, a Bren gun. We had also brought in enough explosive to blow up half of southern France. As well as large quantities of plastic explosive, which came in quarter-pound cellophane packets, smelt of almonds and gave you a headache if you moulded it in your hands for too long, there was a parcel containing half-pound slabs of gun cotton. These were enormously valuable because they fitted exactly between the top and bottom of a railway line, could be taped on very quickly and had just the right amount of force to break the line. They had a hole in the middle into which you inserted the primer, which in turn had a hole in the middle where you inserted the detonator, to which you attached the fuse to produce your ready-made instrument of destruction. But if we were well equipped, we didn't know our territory and we hadn't got a fighting force.

Conscious of the need to inject some spirit and fight, I decided to take immediate action. Over breakfast, which consisted of a cup of the acorn coffee known as *café national*, I asked Bernard whether he knew of a worthwhile railway line nearby with an unguarded bridge. He consulted with his brother Joseph and, after much humming and hawing over the map, pointed out an important branch line about seven or eight miles away. As the bridge was unguarded, I decided to do this blind: we would simply prepare our charges in advance, take the lorry as close to the bridge as possible, make a quick sweep after dark to check the coast was clear, lay the charges on the bridge, set them off and depart.

I spent a large part of that day preparing the charges in portable sacks, which we would then dig into the gravel under the railway tracks on the bridge, connecting them together with a detonator and cord that had a three-minute delay. It worked perfectly, in fact far better than some of the better-prepared operations that came later, but that's the way of the world. We got down there shortly before midnight and parked our desperately noisy gasogene lorry in some trees. We reconnoitred the bridge, and when we found it unguarded we got the youngsters to fetch the explosives. These were laid and the fuse lit as we trotted back to the lorry. Just as we turned back onto the road, we heard a very satisfactory bang behind us. The effect upon all the Frenchmen was startling, but particularly the youngsters; from that moment on they were enthusiastic participants eager to strike a blow against the Germans at every opportunity. We had started.

In the days that followed, we were, of course, in constant contact with Britain. We had been given our codes and signalling instructions before we left, and the daily schedules were of immense importance. Even if you could only make contact and were immediately cut off again, it established the continuity of contact that in turn meant you could listen to messages without fear of interception – it was only with sending that the dreaded direction-finding vehicles could discover and then pinpoint you. The main code we used was something called a one-time pad, of which we had a copy and the base had a copy, and your letters, corresponding to the letters of the alphabet, were in a complete jumble, with no two consecutive messages being the same. It was totally random, which meant it really was unbreakable, even more so than the Enigma code. We had a fallback in case the pad should be lost or stolen, which depended upon a poem that we had to memorise but which, sadly, I can no longer remember. Again the letters of the first three or four lines of the poem would combine with the alphabet to give us a one-off code to fill in the gap if things had gone wrong.

The main radio was called a B2, which had the nickname of the 'Jed Set' and was a suitcase set designed to work off a battery or the mains. In extremis, the battery could be charged by a bicycle-chain pedal attachment where you expended an enormous amount of energy to produce a tiny amount of electricity. We also had the backup of a very small receiving set with which we could get Morse-coded messages from the base and which was also invaluable because it could pick up the BBC *London News*.

On this wavelength we were given codes for messages that gave us the time and location of parachute drops of arms, supplies and, occasionally, agents. Our code was '*De la chouette au merle blanc*', which means 'From the owl to the white blackbird', and when we were listening to the daily messages this would attract our attention very quickly because it meant we were about to be told whether a planned drop was coming and whether it was an important or small one. For example, the message, '*Un ami très riche arrivera ce soir*' – 'A very rich friend is coming this evening' – would tell us to expect a drop of a substantial number of loaded containers of arms and equipment. Or the message might be a negative one to indicate that a drop was no longer happening or that '*Plusieurs amis arriveront*' – 'Several friends will be arriving' – which meant either that there was more than one aircraft or that the drop would include agents as well as containers.

If most drops were announced beforehand, we received an unannounced and unexpected visit shortly after dawn on the day after our first raid, just as we were waking up. This was the morning after Arthur had managed to check in with base for the first time. Our visitor was a highly polished French officer wearing the rank of captain and the boots and breeches of a cavalryman. He had come to tell me that the various French Resistance groups to the south of us had, following the landings in Normandy, decided to rise up and make a redoubt in the area of Mont Mouchet. Their plan was to defy the Germans and to detain their troops. The French officer asked whether I would come down and take charge of the large number of Resistance fighters who had assembled for this task or, at least, ensure that there was a further parachute drop of weapons and ammunition.

I was absolutely horrified and told him quite plainly that this was totally against my training and understanding of guerrilla warfare. As soon as clandestine fighters openly engage the enemy, they simply make themselves a target for regular occupying forces – who are far better trained and better equipped – and the most likely outcome for the French would be that they would all be captured and locked up. The other option was that they would be slaughtered, so there was no way I was going to help. He was not best pleased and said he would report me to de Gaulle's headquarters in London and to General Kœnig, who was the nominal superior for the French forces of the interior.

I was unmoved by his huffiness and threats, which was a good thing because events turned out exactly as I had predicted. A small number of German combat troops simply surrounded the area and walked in against the gallant but totally ineffectual Resistance. Happily, most of the fighters got away, but the Germans still captured a large amount of arms, ammunition and equipment that had been painstakingly dropped at considerable risk of life so that the Resistance could carry out clandestine operations – not open warfare.

It was a valuable lesson, and I'm just glad it wasn't more hard-earned.

16

The Das Reich Are Coming

Context is all, and our spat with the captain soon appeared a trivial aside as one of the most fearsome fighting forces in the Second World War came into view. The unhappy captain had barely had time to take himself off in a Gallic huff when events took a turn for the worse as two young Frenchmen roared into the yard at breakneck speed on a motorbike. It was clear even before they had dismounted that they were shaken and frightened. No wonder: they'd risked coming through unfamiliar enemy territory in broad daylight, a desperate feat that showed just how urgently they needed to find us.

Once they had explained why they had come, we understood completely. They had hightailed it to us from Bretenoux to tell us that a German armoured heavy division was snaking its way along the Figeac–Tulle road, had recently passed through the town and was making its way up the *route nationale* from the south, heading towards Normandy. If so, it was a clear threat to the D-Day beachhead, which was still being bitterly contested.

The young Frenchmen believed we should do everything in our power to delay them, and I agreed. I'm glad now that I knew little about the identity of the troops and tanks that made up the column, that I'd never heard of the Das Reich Division or the 2nd Motorised SS Infantry Division, a corps of battle-hardened troops whose mettle had been forged amid the savagery of the Eastern Front. They'd brought the ruthless tactics of the Russian campaign with them, hanging civilians from lamp posts every time Resistance fighters had the temerity to try to slow their progress, most notoriously at the village of Tulle. All we knew was that they were a threat that had to be halted and, if that was impossible, slowed for as long as possible.

Michel and I quickly discussed our situation and decided that we should split up. I would go with Bernard, Joseph would drive our lorry and we'd take the four young boys and as much explosive as we could carry. One of the Bretenoux boys would come with us, so we would know where to hide our vehicle close to the main road, while his pal was dispatched on his motorbike to tell the fighters in Bretenoux to carry on with their plan to hold the Germans for as long as possible on the river crossing. We would lay booby traps and ambushes for them further down the road and try to get as close to the column as we could.

We didn't know it then, but the Battle of the Bretenoux River Crossing was one of the most important and bloodiest operations ever carried out by the Resistance. Of the 29 lightly armed Bretenoux villagers who held that river crossing against the Das Reich armoured division, 27 were killed or severely wounded. Yet, by holding up one of Germany's most formidable fighting units, they saved countless lives in Normandy and beyond, which is why the battle is seen as one of the key events of the D-Day invasion.

It was important to get a look at the target before nightfall so that we knew what we were facing. I knew that the column wouldn't move after dark, so that meant we were able to move through the night. After we had loaded up, our guide directed us through a web of tiny country lanes to a small farm, where our lorry was hidden in a barn.

This was the perfect base for our little crew, and as the light began to fade I was able to move through the thick screen of trees and bushes that flanked the road, getting close enough to see that this was a major convoy of vehicles. As well as trucks and partly armoured half-track trucks, there were tanks and armoured cars stretching out as far as we could see down the road. They were, for now, crawling up the highway, delayed by the Battle of the Bridge at Bretenoux.

My group didn't have enough firepower to engage the Das Reich, so I came to the conclusion that throughout the night we should prepare a whole series of dummy ambushes to slow down the Germans. In the end I prepared three of these while the column was at a halt overnight and grouped close together in defended laagers with gaps in between.

In the first of those gaps we scraped our only anti-tank mine into the ground and covered it with dust, but not before strapping a chunk of plastic explosive to it to provide some extra oomph. Just before dawn, as the German vehicles sprang into life, we brought down two large trees, one on each side of the road, so that their branches intertwined and their trunks blocked the road. These trees were certainly too big to be moved by anything other than a tracked vehicle.

About two-thirds of a mile further up the road, in another gap, we had toppled two trees to create an almost identical obstacle. This time, however, instead of a mine we put in the branches an improvised booby trap made of two grenades with their pins out, in the hope that they would come looking for a mine on the ground and forget to look up. As soon as there was any real movement in the branches, the levers would spring and activate the detonators.

Then, further up, in another gap, I marked two more trees to be exploded later but didn't bring them down. Instead we waited by that last set of trees, with two of our boys with Sten guns on the side where we had hidden the vehicle. The boy from Bretenoux was with us in case we needed him to act as the liaison with the Bretenoux fighters.

As dawn broke, the explosion that brought down the trees was masked by the almighty noise of every engine in the column starting up and the whole caravan moving off. They soon came to our first obstruction, halted, went to look at it and then decided that the lead vehicle – a half-track packed with infantry – should try to push it out of the way. When it couldn't do it, because it simply didn't have the muscle, they signalled for a heavy vehicle. A tank support vehicle with a mine-sweeping blade in front trundled into view and was in the process of pushing the heavy trees aside when the mine and explosives blew up under one of its tracks, causing it to slew across the road and rendering the road completely impassable.

When they had cleared the road and eventually rolled on, they soon found the second blockage, which looked identical to the first. This time they sensibly stopped in front of it, at which stage our two men at the back opened up with their Sten guns into the troop-carrying vehicles – just one magazine each – and then scrambled into the bushes and back to our vehicle, where they waited for us. The Germans, spooked by the mine from the first obstacle, sent forward a squad of engineers to look for mines. Hearing all this from a distance, we'll never know if they looked up, but what we did know for sure was that one of them must have disturbed the branches, because we heard the sound of the grenades falling to the floor and detonating, followed by angry shouts and screams.

By the time they reached our third obstacle, they led with the heavy vehicle at the front of the column. As they had already come under fire, they took no chances, deploying troops to sweep the edges of the ambush, at which point we blew the third lot of trees and made our way back, leaving the young fighter from Bretenoux, at his discretion, to fire his Sten gun before getting back to his own group. Sadly, he was our only casualty; somebody must have spotted him, and he was killed by a burst of fire from the leading vehicle. Despite that, it was still a successful operation. The Das Reich was the only major column that we ever confronted face to face, and we were not well equipped for the job.

Although we were flushed with the success of our brush with the Das Reich, when we got back to our camp in the wood more prosaic concerns began to intrude. It was obvious to me that something had to be done to improve our food supply, so we targeted the unescorted German supply lorries that shuttled between two small towns in the neighbourhood. Our two looting parties registered what can only be described as ineffectual successes, with the first set of raiders obliterating the lorry's engine with an anti-tank rifle, only to find just two very large tins of chestnut purée in the rear. The second party shot out the tyres of their target lorry with a light machine gun before killing the driver and escort, only to find that their reward was four sacks of sugar. Our diet the next day was very strange, although the French were never likely to put up with that culinary state of affairs for too long. Within 24 hours Joseph and Bernard Cournil had enlisted the help of local bakers and farmers so that we were soon tucking into ham, eggs and bread.

If we were well fed, our lack of transport was a serious problem. So I was pleased when Joseph managed to acquire a tiny Peugeot 202, which served us very well for a couple of weeks. Like most cars of that period, it had dreadful tyres, which meant that we had to carry two spares on the roof as well as the spare at the back of the car; they would blow out at such inconvenient moments that our speed in changing tyres became almost Formula One class. We also had to watch where we drove because many of the smaller roads in France were so dusty that you advertised your presence with a great white plume following your car.

The car was invaluable for familiarising ourselves with the neighbourhood and recceing railway lines and other objectives that might be vulnerable. Once mobile, we would be out on the railway somewhere laying the gun-cotton slabs on the rails and blowing a series of holes that would take some repairing. If you blew the rail while a train was passing, it was a bonus, but the real aim was to have the rail constantly out of action, with repairing gangs busy in one place after another.

Our success rate was such that a steady stream of recruits began to appear. However, infiltration by collaborators was a constant threat, so they were all carefully vetted by Bernard. We also took delivery of two French officers sent by headquarters. Oheix and Daladier, whose code names were André and Dundee, were two extremely loyal and efficient young lieutenants whose task was to train our recruits while Michel de Bourbon was away blowing up railway lines.

We managed to blow up several important road bridges, but when it came to the heavily guarded railway viaduct at the Pont du Garabit, we enlisted the help of the communist FTP. They were commanded by a political commissar known only by the code name 'Georges', a remarkable man who ran indoctrination classes for all his recruits and kept detailed dossiers on their family life, upbringing and foibles. We viewed each other with barely concealed suspicion, even if I recognised in him a really active force against the common enemy, while he saw me as a potential pointer to the right type of operation and a supplier of equipment.

Our mutual suspicion was heightened by a parachute drop at the beginning of July that nearly had disastrous consequences. We had identified a good landing place close to their headquarters near the town of Cahors but had barely given the confirmation for the drop to go ahead when we found German troops occupying the two crossroads at each end of the designated drop zone, having clearly been tipped off by a collaborator. The equipment was too important for us to abandon the drop, because we were almost out of explosives and ammunition, so we switched the drop to a kitchen garden and small vineyard three miles away, where we could set up the lights without being seen, except from the air. Even then it was touch and go, the Germans arriving while we were looking for the last container. The eventual success of that operation also won me significant kudos within the communist FTP, and after that their cooperation increased markedly.

In fact, 'Georges' – whose real name was Robert Noireau – and I later became firm friends and remained so until he died in 1999, well into his 80s. He had a remarkable life, going back to his building firm in

Boulogne after the war to find himself unable to make a living thanks to the communist administration and trade unions. This did a lot to change his views, and he made the bold decision in the late '40s to set up as a building contractor in the West African colony of Senegal. It can't have been easy, but he won several post-war government contracts, making a good deal of money and returning to buy a charming estate called Parisis, near Mouchy, to the north of Paris, where he raised wild ducks for shooting on his ponds, did a little gardening and farming and generally lived the life of a patrician country gentleman. Nevertheless, he maintained not only the friendship but the trust of many leading communists, and to dine at his table with René Andrieu, the leading communist and editor of the hard-line communist newspaper *L'Humanité*, was a surreal experience.

At the time that Georges and I were operating in tandem, one of my key jobs was to muster and train a fighting force for the forthcoming liberation battle. That meant travelling the countryside to contact the small groups that existed here and there, so I was fortunate that I was able to upgrade my vehicle when we captured two of the French police's rather smart front-wheel-drive Citroën cars. Having decent transport was more about survival than luxury: I regularly had to scoot to avoid German troop movements or static positions, and on at least two occasions I almost ran into a German roadblock before skidding to a halt and going back the way I had come.

On another occasion I was heading south of Cahors on my way to a meeting with a group that was said to be fairly active. We were in the Peugeot 202, which was being driven by Denis Cournil, Bernard's cousin, when we turned off into a maze of unmarked third-grade roads and into a thick wood, as arranged. Instead of the waiting contact, we suddenly found ourselves in the middle of what looked like a very capably planned ambush. There was a blockage on the road, signs of movement in the trees and what appeared to be black uniforms beyond the blockage. Denis rammed the car into reverse, stopping deep in the foliage, at which stage we took to our feet in the certain knowledge that we were already being pursued.

By sheer bad luck, that day we were moving our own hideaway, so I had my satchel with maps and codes with me. Unobserved even by Denis, I quickly stashed it in a hollow tree, which turned out to be a sensible course of action because we were immediately surrounded by Sten gun-toting figures in black bomber jackets and hats. Mercifully, this happened to be the Resistance unit we were looking for, although I was amazed to see them so uniformly equipped. They turned out to be a hugely successful group that I used a great deal, particularly for rail sabotage and then, later, to help me gain entrance to the guarded German garrison town of Cahors via its famous Roman bridge.

Cahors, which is famous for its black wine, was a particular centre for our activities. One of my favourite tricks was to use local children to scatter little nails that punctured the tyres on German trucks. One evening, a report came to me of a garage on the edge of the town where there were a dozen German trucks and an underground store of petrol. The black bomber group and I planned an operation there, employing the children as couriers and using one of their men who was a native of the town, which allowed him free civilian entry into Cahors. The garage was guarded at night, but there was a way of getting into it through a lavatory window, so I equipped him with 12 primers, complete with a detonator and a time fuse set for 30 minutes. All he had to do was to open the petrol tank of each vehicle, drop in the time fuse and primer and squeeze the capsule at the end of the fuse to set the 30 minutes running. Blowing up the petrol in the middle of French-inhabited houses was out of the question, so instead he opened the lid of the petrol tank and left a hosepipe running water into it. His last task was to set off a smoke bomb in the garage and, on his way out, to fire a couple of shots to alert people. This worked perfectly: the smoke billowed out, the shots were heard and the German drivers tumbled out of their barracks and drove their vehicles out of the garage. The charges went off as the trucks reached the outskirts of town, resulting in carnage and leaving a ring of burnt-out German transport vehicles circling the town – a very satisfactory result.

That Cahors bomber wasn't the only French civilian to risk his life in the fight against the Germans. Shortly after that first contact with the black bomber gang in the wood, we ran into a very tight German security cordon on our way home and sought shelter with the local infant school teacher, Simone Courtiau. She hid Denis and me in the store of her school – which was just as well because the Germans came to the village and scoured every house but ignored the school. Simone is still alive, and after having kept in contact once a year, to my absolute astonishment she turned up at the Newtonmore Highland Games in 2000 when I was chieftain of the games, coming to my tent and reintroducing herself after a break of 56 years. It was an emotional moment.

Not all Frenchmen and women were as patriotic as Simone, and nor did contacts with other groups always go as smoothly as with the black bombers. One group that contacted me gave me a rendezvous at a particular map reference where they said I would find a row of abandoned buildings. My driver Martial and I decided to go there early in the morning before the rendezvous at three o'clock that afternoon. The moment we got there, I had a bad feeling about the place. There were five relatively new brick-built houses in a row in the middle of the countryside, totally abandoned and not in very good shape. They were in a clearing beside a small road and surrounded by woods.

We decided to look around and found another small track about a quarter of a mile away where we could stash the car. At three o'clock I got Martial to drop me, and I walked up the road to the clearing and into one of the houses, concealing myself so that I had a good view and leaving the back door open for a quick getaway. At five past three I heard the sound of motorcycles and knew that we were in trouble. The Germans used motorcycles, particularly a motorcycle and sidecar with a machine gun mounted on the sidecar, and there were several coming from both directions. I made myself extremely scarce indeed and got safely to the car.

This was certainly not the only occasion on which French traitors had infiltrated the *Maquis* in our area in an effort to trap me. By that time I was fairly well known, not least because of the kilt, and the Germans had notices out with a 300,000 franc price on my head, which was a very large sum of money in those days. I was described as 'A bandit masquerading as a Scottish officer, and extremely dangerous to the citizens of France.'

On another occasion, I was given a rendezvous by the FTP at the inn in a little town called Saint-Céré. We were in a backroom having our discussions over a very nice glass of wine when the barmaid rushed in and said, 'The Germans are here.' We vamoosed, with great stealth and speed, through the back door and successfully made our escape. Unfortunately, three of the FTP were not so fortunate: they were in the front bar and ran up the slope away from the café and were gunned down in the street.

Another risky occupation was acting as a courier. General Kœnig, who was endeavouring to organise the disparate groups of the French Resistance, had a network of couriers who travelled across the whole country. I had local ones, for the most part young boys or girls who had legitimate occupations and could travel around on their bicycles. The national couriers were based mostly in Paris, and I have still not discovered their main purpose, although they certainly brought news of other groups. I got to know two national couriers: the main one was Colonel Rebattet, who came under the code name of 'Cheval' and became a friend after the war; the other was the author and later minister in the French government André Malraux, whom I met by rendezvous at Sousceyrac, where we stood in the middle of the bridge on a sunny afternoon – to me a quite ridiculous exposure – while he discussed broadly the philosophy of the Resistance. I have no idea what practical purpose he was serving, and nor did his communist allies.

Travelling about gave other occasional unprepared opportunities. Once, when heading back to base from a small night-time operation on the railways, we were stopped by a local contact who told us to be careful because the road we were on was used regularly by the Germans, adding that the local commandant in his staff car was expected shortly. As it happened, he had stopped us on one of the unmanned rural level crossings, which had a very heavy wooden pole that lowered itself across the road when a train was coming. This seemed like a perfect opportunity, so I had a look at the bar, which was held in its upright position by a steel wire that served to lower it slowly down, but if the wire wasn't there it would fall very sharply. I quickly fixed a small piece of plastic explosive with a detonator to this wire and attached it to the battery of our car, hidden beside the old railway house at the edge of the level crossing. Shortly afterwards we heard the approach of a motorcycle and sidecar, followed 50 yards afterwards by an open staff car with a senior officer in the back. The moment the motorbike passed, I blew the fuse with most satisfactory results: down came the pole, with the staff car hitting it at around 50 miles an hour, ripping off the whole top and decapitating the commandant and his driver. The motorcycle and sidecar immediately swung round and, with its machine gun poised, cautiously approached the scene of what was clearly a disaster. We were ready for that, though. Denis Cournil was in the ditch with his Sten gun, and when they stopped bang opposite him he had the easiest of targets and duly dispatched the three Germans. Another satisfactory morning.

We were constantly moving from one hiding place to another. As well as the risk of being betrayed by the locals, there was an ever-present worry about our frequent movements being noted or, even more likely, Arthur's regular signals being picked up by the German direction-finding vehicles, or DFs. These were extremely efficient, particularly in urban areas, as many of our intelligence agents found to their cost. It was more difficult for the DFs in the rural areas because the distances and open spaces made triangulation difficult, but they could narrow it down if radio operators didn't take the precaution of very short bursts of sending and moving frequently. This meant a constant search for places from which to broadcast, with the invaluable Bernard Cournil invariably finding somewhere suitable. Even then, Arthur had to realign his equipment constantly, particularly his aerial, to be sure of making contact.

Michel, of course, was always busy on missions, but Arthur was often fed up because he felt he was being left out of things, always left behind, always guarded and told not to wander out of the perimeter of wherever we were ensconced. It was only late in our mission that I was able to convince him that he was the most valuable asset that we, as a team, had. As a British officer parachuted into a Resistance situation – a foreigner among patriotic Frenchmen – your only authority was your own personality, which I had tried to reinforce with my kilt and a degree of flamboyance. Our ability to communicate directly with Allied headquarters in London gave us a great power that had to be preserved, along with the radio operator, at all costs.

One of our main targets was electrical power. A huge number of power lines ran through the Massif Central, all carrying electrical power not just to the enormous Michelin factory at Clermont-Ferrand but up to the great industrial areas of central France and the north. Blowing up pylons became a source of enormous pleasure, with the sparks that flew when two pylons collided reminding me of the fireworks we'd always have on Guy Fawkes Night back in Scotland. We blew lines of pylons whenever we happened to be passing an area, but our most impressive single haul was on 14 July, the same day that the Americans made a special daytime demonstration of a huge number of aeroplanes parachuting arms into central France. If this was more of a propaganda coup than a military success, our way of celebrating Bastille Day – to traverse the whole breadth of our area at night, blowing up pylons as we went – was an unqualified success.

We would blow two adjacent pylons to ensure that the whole line came down properly. Pylons are a sort of Meccano erection and are very susceptible to well-placed demolition. The plastic explosive would be placed at the angles of each upright, as far as I could reach from the ground, so that the pylons would fall inwards towards each other. If you merely placed the explosives in a straight line it was likely that the pylon would simply settle down on the ground at a lower level and that the lines would continue to flow. When you blew two pylons together, it made for a splendid firework display, the pylons toppling with a dramatic crunching noise while the cables blew out sparks in every direction as they shorted and slapped against the pylons. We blew eight different lines of pylons that night; all in all, a very fitting way to mark 14 July.

It was a long night, though. We had to travel considerable distances, and it was first light before we had finished the last one, which was far later than we would normally be out. We were soon reminded why we wouldn't usually move at that time of day when we ran into a German patrol on its way out as we returned home. They must have been a bit bleary-eyed because they met us at a crossroads but didn't react very quickly, giving us enough time to accelerate away as they fired after us. We weren't afraid of pursuit, because our car was far faster than theirs, and we were able to use full headlights, while the German convoys had their tiny blackout lighting.

We were speeding away from the crossroads at full throttle as dawn broke when suddenly there was an ominous clunk from the engine and we realised that the petrol tank must have been hit. We ran dry almost immediately but still had just enough fuel to turn up a track into the woods and bring the vehicle to a standstill. The car was well hidden from the road, but there would be German patrols out looking for us by now, and we were a long way from home. When I pinpointed our position on the map with the torch and the growing light, Martial said, 'I have a cousin, a nun in a convent, about two kilometres up the road.' Perfect.

'Let's go,' I said.

By the time we got to the convent, it was broad daylight, which was perhaps fortunate for us. We rang the bell and, through a grille, requested sanctuary. After scuttling off to consult the Mother Superior, the young sister quickly returned and let us in. Within moments we were in front of this imposing woman, telling her our story and explaining that we needed to hide until our car could be repaired. After a moment's thought, she said, 'I have a sister here whose brother is a garagiste in the next village. I think he could probably help.' So the nun was dispatched – on her works of charity, of course – to see her brother, who thankfully had a crashed front-wheel-drive Citroën in his workshop. That night he came up to the convent, and after Martial showed him where our car was hidden he replaced the petrol tank by torchlight and we were off. It remains my proud boast that I must be one of the few men who have spent an innocent night in a convent.

We felt that we were making real progress in annoying the Germans, but it was still a delight when, after just less than two months in the field, we received a message from headquarters that read, 'Congratulations in becoming, in six weeks, one of the best-known names in the Resistance.' This praise was not destined to last long. About a month later we were told to expect ten Americans from the Office of Strategic Services (OSS), whom we were to hide until they could find something useful to do. I was running very short of explosives and, in umbrage, sent out a coded message saying that I would rather have ten containers of explosive. I received back a message that said, simply, 'Do not be insubordinate.'

The OSS team duly arrived under command of a very senior officer who, as a colonel, outranked me but who had been told to take heed of what I said and seemed happy to do so. As they were immaculate but very green, not having been in any operation before, our priority was to find them an out-of-the-way location where there was no risk of their endangering our operations. After we had hidden them for a few days, Bernard Cournil once again achieved the impossible, finding a suitably remote and spacious barn, sorting out a vehicle and arranging for a local farmer to bring them supplies each day. That was the last I saw of them, but unfortunately it was not the last I heard of them. I don't know what, if any, other operations they did, but at the moment of liberation, after we had taken over the railway line and were running our own troop train for members of the Resistance to be ferried to the fighting in the north, they blew one of the bridges on the line.

17

Bluffing for Victory

The war had swung decisively in our favour; we knew it, the French knew it and so did most of the Germans. An important part of my role ahead of D-Day was to be as visible as possible so that I could act as a focus for any Frenchmen who wanted to fight against the Germans when the time came. It's safe to say that there weren't many men wandering around the Lot wearing a kilt, so I certainly stood out, which helped word of my presence to spread.

The ladies of the local village decided that my car ought to be distinguished from the others, so the garage owner welded two little poles onto the front mudguard and the ladies produced a silk Union Jack for one side and a silk French flag, complete with Cross of Lorraine, for the other, both surrounded by little gold-tasselled fringes. Very smart it looked, too. From then on, I flew these everywhere I went, and they saved my life on at least one occasion.

By this time, in late July, the Germans were changing their troops in garrison towns so that there was a gap between the time the outgoing troops left and their incoming replacements arrived. The plan was to ensure that the two sets of troops wouldn't both be caught in the town if there were an air raid or even a passing fighter-bomber strafing the streets, but it also provided me with an opportunity for exactly the sort of high-profile provocation for which I had been dropped into France. I decided I would make a morale-raising visit to the town of Decazeville – from which the first French prime minister of the post-war period, Paul Ramadier, emerged, beard and all, just after the war – where there was also a substantial petrol-filling point for the Germans that I felt needed to be dealt with.

When I got to Decazeville, shortly after one German garrison had left and, I reckoned, about two hours before the next one appeared, we were taken to see the huge petrol tank. Blowing it up wasn't an option, because it would have taken half the town with it, so instead I shot it nine times with my pistol. That was clearly risky, but time was short, and in any event the petrol did not explode, instead gushing out all over the place. At this stage of the war it wasn't enough just to sabotage things; I had to be seen to have done so with impunity. So, after puncturing the Germans' fuel supply, I and Mayor Ramadier, who wore his sash for the occasion, while I was in full uniform, ambled across the town square in full view of the whole population and sat down at a table outside a café to take a glass or two of wine.

I'd hardly had time to take a sip when my attempt at nonchalance fell rather flat. Suddenly, long before the next batch of Germans was due to arrive, there was a commotion at the far end of the street that ran through the square. Martial and I, who were luckily sitting facing that way, saw to our horror the unmistakeable silhouette of an armoured car about 300 yards away and instantly scampered harum-scarum towards our own car, which was fortunately pointing in the right direction and left in gear.

The Germans could see us quite clearly, but as we were driving exactly the same sort of black Citroën used by the Gestapo, and one which had two pennants fluttering from its front bumper, they momentarily hesitated, presumably believing us to be senior officers from their own side. However, it didn't take them long to realise their mistake, and before we had even turned the corner of the street ahead two armoured cars set off in hot pursuit. We weren't particularly concerned because we were several corners ahead and would be able to outpace them easily on the long straight. Yet still they rumbled after us, even as we pulled further away up a long hill and into a small side road that continued uphill. This little road looped towards the bridge over the River Lot at Port d'Agrès, at one point bringing us above the cutting through which the armoured cars would have to travel if they wished to keep up their pursuit.

While Martial drove our getaway car, I had been making preparations in case something went wrong and we were forced to stop and fight. By the time we were looking down into the cutting, I had constructed a home-made gammon grenade, which consisted of one and a half pounds of plastic explosive and a primer stuffed into a plastic container resembling a lady's shower cap, which was pulled tight with strings. As the first armoured car trundled below, I dropped the gammon grenade into the turret, knocking it out completely. When the second armoured car saw what had happened, it sensibly turned tail and headed back towards Decazeville.

We soon reached and crossed the bridge at Port d'Agrès, which was a big concrete construction supported on a rather elegant single arch across the river. The Germans would have known full well that we would cross the river heading northwards, and after we had brazenly attacked one of their main garrison towns the possibility of a pursuit in force was high, as were the prospects of reprisals across the river. I summoned Michel down from our base, telling him to bring a load of explosives, and I proceeded to mine the bridge. This took a fair time because every concrete support had to be mined and at least two explosion points lined up, in case one failed. We finished just as it was getting dark, and I put Reynaud, a local engineer who had previously been in charge of building roads in the area, in charge, telling him to blow the bridge if there were any signs of the Germans trying to cross.

It was at exactly that point that we suddenly saw lights on the far side. The Germans had regrouped, and at least two armoured cars appeared at the far end of the bridge, firing at any movement as they approached. Amazingly, although there were a number of interested spectators as well as helpers there, nobody was hit by the machine-gun fire that rattled across the bridge, with everyone immediately taking cover. The tension was high because we would have had to blow the bridge if they had made any serious attempt to cross it. They eventually thought better of it, which made sense: not only were they probably unnerved by the dark, but they could see figures on the other side and knew that the bridge might well be mined. For the second time that day they turned and retreated to Decazeville.

Although the Germans never attempted to cross the bridge, Reynaud still blew it up long after such an act was necessary. I assumed that he was ensuring there was sufficient work for him to do when he regained his post as the local engineer after the war.

Meanwhile, Martial and I drove northwards, heading towards our base at the time but deciding to take a detour via his uncle's house in the little town of Maurs. I've no idea how word spread so quickly among those small towns, but by the time we turned up his uncle already had a bottle of champagne on ice. He looked surprised to see us in such fine fettle and said, 'You've had a very turbulent day, but you are so calm!' I looked at him in astonishment because, in those days, it was simply another day at the office. That was one of those moments when I stopped and briefly considered my extraordinary life.

I thought of the last time I had been in the area, a few days earlier, when Michel and I had visited a nearby town called Capdenac, which was basically a railway junction with engine sheds. We had broken into the yard, overcome the civilian guards and tied them up and then proceeded to blow away the right-hand cylinder of every steam locomotive, a highly effective way of not only immobilising them but also ensuring that they couldn't be repaired by cannibalisation. It was a good, neat operation.

After the Operation Dragoon landings of 15 August 1944, when a force of almost 200,000 mainly American and French troops opened a second front in France by landing in the south of the country along the coast between Marseilles and Cannes, we all knew that it was only a matter of time before the Germans began to withdraw from their garrison towns in the south and south-west of France to consolidate their defensive lines nearer the German border. I quickly decided that my strategy should be to do everything I could to deny the retreating Germans passage through the Massif Central. In the densely wooded mountain roads there would be plenty of cover to hide them from attacks by the RAF and US Air Force, but if they were forced to bypass the mountains and use the main roads up the east and west of the mountains they would be in open country and very vulnerable.

Although it wasn't an entirely popular course of action with all the French, I began to blow up a whole series of bridges over the main river crossings that protected the south side of the Massif, leaving only the Port d'Agrès bridge and one light bridge further west that wouldn't take heavy tank vehicles, knowing all the time that the heavy bridge at Port d'Agrès was mined and ready for demolition. The furthest south-east I went was to Saint-Flour one Sunday, where I stymied a rumoured German withdrawal northwards by blowing a bridge and, for good measure, blocking the road completely by blowing up two electric pylons just north of it. As a result, I was known by those who didn't sympathise with the Allied cause as 'that lunatic Scotsman who keeps blowing up bridges'.

As far as France was concerned, we were quickly beginning to reach the endgame. General Patton's US Army was moving south from the Channel beachhead, heading down the Loire Valley and threatening to cut off all German retreat from southern France. At the same time, the forces from Operation Dragoon were coming up the Rhône Valley and threatening to cut off the same troops. The first major development in our area was the German decision to remove the garrison from the departmental capital of Aurillac, at which stage the Resistance troops from the neighbouring department of Corrèze appeared on the north side of the town. The Corrèze fighters were led by a Colonel Mortier – who was unveiled as General Fayard after the war – with his number two being Lieutenant Colonel Schmuckel of the Chasseurs, the elite light infantry regiment. With them as liaison was Major Freddie Cardozo of the British Army, who became and remains an extremely close friend of mine. He had been dropped into the Corrèze by the Special Operations Executive (SOE) as liaison to the Mortier–Schmuckel group, who were basically officers from the French Army and their Resistance group.

Mortier and I had been in contact for some time, and as soon as he had moved south we set about trying to blockade the German garrison inside the main road tunnel at Le Lioran, on the way to Clermont-Ferrand. The plan was to trap the column, which was a mixture of troops on foot, vehicles and horse-drawn wagons, in the tunnel and force them to surrender. The large contingent of Resistance troops from the Corrèze would block the north-eastern exit from the tunnel, while my lot dealt with the south-western end. The confrontation started at about ten o'clock in the morning when we blockaded one end, while at the other end a few soldiers escaped on foot. The trapped Germans put up a heavy mortar bombardment over our positions, but we sustained very few casualties and our blockade held.

As night fell, those Germans who had broken out at the northern end withdrew to the safety of the tunnel, while Mortier withdrew his blockade to what he must have thought was a safe distance. However, he made the dreadful mistake of not leaving any sentries, so that virtually the whole German column was able to break out during the night. When we arrived in the morning, we found a token force of defenders, who immediately surrendered. So, too, did the rump of the column just miles further up the road.

Just as that crisis abated, I received a message that the German garrison at Sarrans was mining a big dam, which would have flooded a huge area of fertile and inhabited country. Martial and I shot off towards Sarrans, where a young officer called Christian was waiting for us, his thick black beard making him look more like a pirate than a former naval officer. He also had only one man with him, but the four of us reckoned we had to try bluffing the hundred-strong German garrison into surrendering. Christian and I drove up the steep hill, walking the final bit with a very large white flag before demanding to see the German officer in command.

Before heading up that hill, we put on a small show of force – which we didn't have. We used our plastic explosives to make two explosions that we hoped would sound like mortar fire, and then we wrapped wet handkerchiefs inside the metal hand grips of Martial's and Christian's Sten guns, which produced a percussive, menacing noise that sounded like heavy machine-gun fire. We explained to the German officer that we had the only exit road covered and that we could call up the RAF against him. Although he had twelve Bofors anti-aircraft guns, they were of fairly light calibre, and he looked unsure of himself, asking for one hour to consider his response. As we withdrew to await his answer, André turned up with about 20 of his men in a truck to bolster our numbers.

An hour later we managed to pressurise the German officer into surrendering, provided we could guarantee him the safety accorded to prisoners of war. Half an hour after that, and with the help of Mortier's recently arrived troops, our new prisoners were taken by truck to Aurillac football stadium before becoming regular prisoners of war. They had indeed mined the dam, although we quickly removed the detonators from the charges and even managed to get some of the Bofors guns he had immobilised working again. By cannibalising them, we got four guns on the road, which became the main support artillery for the ragtag Resistance army that soon began moving north.

With the Germans leaving the south, the French Army sent a Colonel Schneider and a couple of middle-ranking officers to Toulouse to coordinate the Resistance during the process of liberation. Michel and I went down to meet the colonel, a rather elderly man who was deaf as a post but full of goodwill. He was totally unimpressed by my letter of authority from General de Gaulle but seemed extremely grateful for any assistance we could give, which included putting the wonderfully efficient Commissar Georges from the Lot in charge of transport.

Resistance of the 11th Hour, as they were soon christened, poured in from every direction, with many brandishing Sten guns that seemed to have come from the famous American daylight drop of 14 July. A large force was soon assembled, but its goodwill was matched by an almost total absence of training and discipline. I'll never know how he did it, but Commissar Georges somehow got this disorganised rabble moving up the road, where they joined up with my people and those of Colonel Mortier. Whatever its fighting deficiencies, ours was a large force whose obvious role was to try to fill the gap between the Americans who were advancing eastwards along the Loire and the French and Americans who were moving northwards up the Rhône. Our key objective was to stop the large force of German troops who were retreating from Bordeaux and clearly hoping to break through that gap before it was closed.

We chose to make our stand at an area called Le Bec d'Allier, which is the point at which the River Allier, a large tributary of the Loire, meets the Loire itself. The Allier had to be crossed by any German force moving eastwards up the valley, and ours was a particularly strong position because there was only one bridge. This was at a place called Decize, which is in the heart of France, halfway between Paris and Lyon, and which I immediately mined but left intact because it would be our only route of advance if we had to go westwards. Once our troops were in place, I drove off to the Rhône Valley to contact the French Army, who were badly uninformed about our movements and knew little about what was going on in the centre. I had a typically lavish lunch with General de Monsabert, the commander of the French Army B, in his headquarters. It was also highly profitable: once I'd apprised him of the situation, which was that our lightly armed and inexperienced troops could not withstand a determined attack, he provided a squadron of Sherman tank chasers and a company of Foreign Legion to stiffen our position.

Even then, we were woefully outgunned. Our intelligence, which proved correct, was that the advance guard of the German Army, under the control of the former commander of Biarritz, Major General Erich Elster, had 7,000 hardened fighting troops who could go through our inexperienced irregulars like a knife through butter. The German rearguard, numbering around 15,000 men, was far more numerous but was made up almost exclusively of third-line garrison troops with primitive, often horse-drawn, transport. They would give us no trouble, but those 7,000 front-line troops would have had us on toast.

The Germans, who were fighting their way back home from the Spanish border, weren't sure of our strength, and when they came to the water there was a good bit of skirmishing along the riverbank as they tried to probe with boat and raft parties. Late that evening I was racking my brains, trying to think how we could withstand such a superior force, when I was summoned to the local telephone exchange, where, of all things, a perfectly normal landline call came to me from Captain Arthur Cox, another Jedburgh who was in an area in the middle Loire. He had tracked me down, perhaps through radio contact with London, to give me the news that he had been approached by the Americans, who were asking for an attempt to be made to get the surrender of the Germans under Elster. Since leaving Biarritz, his column had grown to include 6,000 regular *Wehrmacht* troops and 7,000 marines originally stationed in the Bay of Biscay, plus a range of various soldiers, sailors and airmen. By the time they reached us, they had also accumulated 400 civilian cars, 500 trucks and 1,000 horse-drawn vehicles, a motley collection of men that stretched back almost 30 miles along the road and was constantly strafed by the 9th US Air Force. No wonder he was willing to consider surrendering.

The Americans had already dispatched a party to take over the prisoners if the Germans could be persuaded to surrender, but Cox warned me that the Germans were prevaricating, possibly in the hope that their crack advance guard would have enough time to make one determined attack. I told him that they had already had one go and had nearly knocked out one of our tanks – actually blowing the tank commander out of his hatch, where he was standing up, but missing the tank itself – and that another attack was probably imminent.

Cox said that he had already persuaded Elster and his staff officers to come to a meeting the following morning but that he felt reinforcements were needed from our side to drive the point home that they couldn't get through. The rendezvous was set for a little village in Allied hands called Pont d'Arcay, which effectively meant driving through mile after mile of nervous and trigger-happy German soldiers. While I had no idea how on earth I would get there, I promised Cox that I'd make it.

Schneider and I conferred, and we soon alighted on a German Red Cross vehicle that we had recently captured, complete with a number of doctors. I thought this was the perfect vehicle for the job, especially if we went at night and took the masks off the headlights so that we were able to drive at top speed. Schneider provided a driver, and we decided that, as well as a German doctor, I should be accompanied by a French regular major called Sarazan. At eleven o'clock that evening the four of us drove over the bridge: all unarmed, as it was a Red Cross vehicle, all on a non-combatant white-flag mission.

For the first five miles we were horribly conscious of the lines of Germans on either side of us, and we waited for a reaction, but none came. Then, suddenly, all hell broke loose, with machine guns firing from both sides of the road. Our driver, who was already haring along at a decent pace, simply put his foot down harder, and we went straight through, totally unscathed. I'm convinced the combination of raw speed and our dazzling headlights saved us. After that we sat back, happy just to be alive and looking forward to the moment we could rendezvous with Elster, when, without warning, exactly the same thing happened again. This time we were coming up to a bridge over the road, so for a few moments the fire came at us from three sides, until we passed under the bridge and were shielded from view. We eventually arrived in the early hours of the morning at the little schoolhouse of Pont d'Arcay, and there, in typical French fashion, we laid our plans for the morning over a meal and a good deal of very palatable Loire wine.

The following morning we took our seats on one side of a long table in the main schoolroom, and exactly on the appointed hour in came General Elster and his second-in-command, who was a black-uniformed full colonel, plus an aide and an interpreter. The negotiations were conducted in French and revolved around the surrender document we had prepared. We knew that Elster had two concerns: one, could he legitimately say to his superiors that he had no option but to surrender; and two, were his troops going to be safe if they surrendered to what they had been brought up to believe was a barbarian, lunatic French Resistance?

My job was to convince the Germans that they could not get through. I think the unexpectedness of seeing an officer in full Highland uniform – on this occasion complete with my hat – lent credibility to the fact that my brigade was on the other side of the river waiting for him. I was able to say, in all honesty, that we had tanks and, thanks to the four cannibalised Bofors guns we had dragged along, that we also had artillery.

I was even able to say that we had the support of French regular troops, as embodied by Major Sarazan at my side. The clincher, however, came when I told him that I was in full contact with London by radio and could at any time call up the RAF to blow his people out of sight on the unprotected roads of the Loire Valley. In truth, the only thing I could whistle up was Dixie, but Elster had no way of knowing that and it was a bluff that may have saved thousands of lives.

The German general accepted the inevitable but continued to fret about his own protection and that of his troops. We eventually agreed that he would order an immediate ceasefire, with his troops laying down their arms but retaining them and not moving from their existing locations until they were handed over to the safe custody of the Americans. We had hardly finished these negotiations and got his signature when up came Lieutenant Samuel Magill of the 329th Infantry, who was the American lieutenant with whom they had talked a couple of days before. He was accompanied by American Lieutenant Colonel Jules French, who saluted politely and said he would be very pleased indeed to take immediate responsibility for all 23,000 Germans.

On the way out I exchanged some words with the black-uniformed colonel. I had a sneaking suspicion that, although he looked like a tough and seasoned soldier, he was probably quite glad at the outcome and appreciated the inevitable end of the war. We spoke reasonably cordially. He handed over to me his Luger pistol – which, alas, I no longer have – and the staff flag, a metal pennant from his rather smart Mercedes staff car. I also kept a copy of the surrender document, which was delivered to the War Office in my final report. There were a few other parties of Germans trying to make their way through the gap, which we had to deal with, particularly at the key road junction of Autun, but the surrender of Elster's 23,000 men brought the liberation of France a huge step closer.

Around that time, for some reason, I found myself going through the delightful town of Dijon, and this coincided with a visit from the famous French general Jean de Lattre Tassigny. He and I stood together on the balcony of the town hall in the main square while he made a speech, and we waved and received the plaudits of an enthusiastic and liberated crowd. He was an amazing character, a decorated veteran of the First World War who commanded the French 14th Infantry Division at the outbreak of the Second World War when they defeated the Germans at the Battle of Rethel. He briefly commanded the Vichy forces in Tunisia before turning against the Germans and distinguishing himself fighting against them, eventually leading the 300,000-strong French Army that took major German cities like Karlsruhe and Stuttgart and representing France at Germany's unconditional surrender in Berlin in 1945.

From Dijon I went back to Clermont-Ferrand and the final stages of the liberation. If that was a day that was notable partly for being the only time that I successfully used de Gaulle's letter of authorisation, it was even more memorable for being a day that I dodged death by a matter of inches. Martial and I were driving down the hill to Clermont when there was an almighty bang as some stray German fired an armour-piercing shell straight into the engine of our Citroën. I have no idea how Martial kept the car on the road, but our speed took us round the corner and out of our would-be assassin's gunsights very quickly. When we pulled to a stop, there was a whacking great hole in the casing of the engine, and it was clear the car would never go again.

I desperately needed another car quickly, because I wanted to get to Vichy to see if I could provide any assistance in hastening the departure of the quisling French government of Marshal Philippe Pétain. I eventually got a car, but the delay perhaps saved me from an awful dilemma. By the time I got to Vichy, Pétain was long gone, but the puppet regime's prime minister, Pierre Laval, was so recently departed in a heavily armoured Mercedes saloon that we gave chase. Just a few miles further on we found the Mercedes broken down and heard he had gone on in a much faster car. He was wanted by a war crimes tribunal, and had we captured him I would have had difficulty in knowing what to do with him. I couldn't have put him in any sort of safe custody, because the French mood at that time was such that he would have been torn to pieces. Not that he survived into a benign old age: for his role in signing orders allowing foreign Jews to be sent to the concentration camps from French soil, not to mention the small matter of high treason, he was executed by firing squad after the war.

With the despicable Vichy regime at an end and France liberated, this chapter of my war was drawing to a close. Shortly after I left Vichy, Patton's army coming south from Normandy and the Franco–American army coming up the Rhône from the south joined together and the gap was closed. In the pivot of that gap, at the town of Besançon, the Resistance fighters came forward to join the regular French Army and be given proper uniforms, a process that was already under way when I arrived in the town. They weren't going to leave without saying goodbye, though, and I was incredibly touched when I was given a full parade of my ex-forces as a send-off. For both Michel and me it was a highly emotional occasion as I had the *Croix de guerre* pinned on my reluctant bosom and was kissed on both cheeks.

18

To Italy

By the end it must have appeared to outsiders that I was bulletproof. I was only 24, but I'd already bluffed my way to the capture of 23,000 German soldiers, survived endless gunfights, ambushes and skirmishes and blown up several bridges and dozens of pylons. I felt at home in this environment, energised by the carnage around me.

I realised just how dangerously fatalistic and blasé I had become about my own survival on the drive from Special Forces Headquarters at Avignon to the airstrip at Marignane, outside Marseilles, which was where the French chapter of my life drew to an end and the Italian adventure began to unfold. We had been told to report for a flight that evening, but instead of moseying down the road, breathing in the sights and sounds of one of the world's most beautiful regions, Arthur and I decided that it would be fun to see how quickly we could get to the airport. Within moments we were thrashing the nuts and bolts off our little black Citroën as we hammered along the small, dusty lanes of southern France at breakneck speed.

I almost came to grief when I overtook a French officer who took umbrage at the perceived insult and immediately gave chase. Neither the Frenchman nor I was ever going to give way, so we were soon embroiled in a hare-brained race down narrow, potholed roads, weaving in and out of each other as though we were racing drivers at Brooklands rather than two testosterone-fuelled army wallahs suffering from a temporary common-sense deficit. In those days, as soon as you got off the major roads in France, it was like driving through a dust bowl, and we must have been quite a sight, our engines screaming as we raced side by side with plumes of white dust billowing in our wake. There was, though, no way I was giving ground; it simply didn't occur to me. Eventually, after several miles, as the two lanes merged into one and our cars were still neck and neck, my co-racer either lost his nerve or saw sense and slowed down just enough to allow me to sneak in front, my tyres spewing out so much dust that he had little option but to let me go. I was in high spirits, happy that my long drive had been enlivened. Arthur was just happy to be alive.

We bedded down for the night at Marignane and at dawn piled into a waiting plane. Even at this stage we were none the wiser about our eventual destination, but this was standard procedure and it didn't occur to us to bother asking where we were headed. Eventually, after a flight of three hours or so, we touched down at an airfield outside the town of Bari, just above the heel of Italy, before transferring to the appropriately named one-horse town of Monopoli, about 30 miles down the coast from Bari and the headquarters for that region's SOE.

At Monopoli, inevitably, despite the urgency of our summons and our arrival at breakneck speed, no one was ready for us. When we were finally seen, we weren't allowed to know which mission we were to take over; all we knew was that the British officer there was in the process of being withdrawn via Yugoslavia and that we were to take his place. Unusually, there was to be no handover between us, partly I think because of the difficulty of coordinating a meeting, partly because our relations with the partisan groups who were leading him out weren't always easy.

As we had some time to kill, Arthur caught up with various signals affairs and took some local leave. I was given permission to head to Rome and was driven there a couple of days later by Ronnie Grierson, an officer I had come across during my SOE training but whom I really got to know at Monopoli. He was a remarkable multilingual man from an Austrian–Jewish family that had come to Britain when Ronnie was a child. Although he changed his name to Grierson to join the British army, he never made any bones about his origins. He is a most completely anglicised and delightful man who remains a close friend and sometime business associate.

At Rome he dropped me at the Hotel Eden, a palace of luxury after the months I had spent in open country in France after D-Day. The hotel was the headquarters of the Allied Commission for Austria, which was preparing for victory and occupation there, and my elder brother Phil was a brigadier in charge of the embryonic finance commission that would oversee the rebuilding of Austria after the war. He was obviously a very big noise in the hotel, so finding me accommodation was no problem. I checked in and went up to my room carrying my small grip, and the first thing I saw was the lacy pantaloons on the behind of an exquisitely attractive Italian maid dressed in the traditional short black dress and white apron. It turned out that this entrancing glimpse was the closest I was to get to a lady who subsequently became a famous Italian film star – I have long since promised not to reveal her name because of the embarrassment of that first encounter, although you can probably guess her identity.

After months of privation I threw myself into life in Rome, touring the city's cultural hotspots and enjoying a busy social life. In fact my time there was so relaxing that I suddenly realised I was at risk of overstaying my leave. Due back the following day, I was really beginning to worry about how I would get to Bari when I went along to a party given by an RAF officer and, by chance, got talking to a pilot who was due to fly a transport plane full of senior officers to a conference there the following day. As he had no co-pilot, he happily offered to give me a lift in the cockpit, but when I turned up at the airport the following morning his plane – a Dakota DC3, the workhorse of the skies – was on the tarmac ready to go but with the pilot nowhere to be seen.

Just as I was beginning to despair, and moments before the plane was due to leave, along he came. He'd obviously stayed at the party long after I had left and looked a real state as he wove his way across the tarmac. He quickly pushed me into the cockpit, where I sat quietly watching him until shortly after take-off, when he turned to me and said, 'Tommy, I really have to have a sleep. Now, you drive this thing. It's just like a car. Here's the steering wheel' – and there was a sort of half steering wheel in front of me – 'and you stay at this height. You just follow this road through the Apennines, and when you see the sea, wake me up and I'll swing right-handed and land at Bari.'

It was as much as he could do to finish his spiel before he dropped off to sleep, and I found myself, for the first and last time in my life, flying an aeroplane full of senior officers – or flying a plane of any sort for that matter. It was no trouble to follow the road. I tried out the steering wheel: it turned left, it turned right, just like a car. And I found myself, on this brilliantly sunny, clear-skied Italian afternoon, carried away by the joys of flying and singing happily to myself, loud and clear. Almost unconsciously I leant back on the high notes and forward on the really good low notes, oblivious to the fact that the steering wheel moved downwards and upwards with me. Up at the front end of the plane, I had no idea of the effect that this wave-like motion was having on the top brass behind me. The pilot landed as if nothing had happened after I had awakened him on seeing the yellow sands of the Adriatic coast, and it was only when a collection of green-faced senior officers poured out of the plane that we realised what I had done. As our passengers left the plane, the pilot saluted, 'Sorry, sirs, there was a bit of turbulence on the flight, wasn't there?'

It was only once back in Bari that our mission was revealed and we were finally briefed on our area in the north-east of Italy, which was bordered by Venice to the west, the Austrian border to the north, the Adriatic to the south and the Yugoslav border to the east. We were to land on 31 October in the foothills of the Alps, north of the small town of Gemona, which was in turn north of both Trieste and Venice. We were told that our main targets were the road and railway running through Venice up to Austria through the Pontebba Pass, obviously an important route for military traffic, which it was our job to disrupt. We were also invited to do as much damage as possible to the road going up to Austria on the Yugoslav side, which passed through the old battle ground of Caporetto, where the Austrians had so severely defeated the Italians in the First World War, although this target was secondary to damaging the main Pontebba route.

Once again we were given no briefing at all on the divisions that existed among the Resistance forces. We were told that Tito's Yugoslav partisans were on our right flank over the border and that they were occupying a good deal of the attention of the German forces, and for that reason it was likely that German forces would be quite thick on the ground. Arthur was equipped with his new radio schedules, codes and programmes, and we were ready to go. But, as ever, delays intervened through a lack of aircraft and bad weather, so it was 4 November before we took off. It is amazing the way that date has haunted me. It was the date of my becoming a prisoner in 1941, the date of my return home in 1943 and the date of my dropping into northern Italy in 1944.

It was a memorable drop for many reasons. We were delivered to our destination – a field in the north-east of Italy with the code name of Beaverton, which was also the code name of our mission – by a Polish crew, and in many ways it was a perfectly normal jump, with the light going red and then green, the hole in the bottom of the RAF Halifax opening and the dispatcher saying, 'Go!' as we piled out of the plane. It was only then that I realised something was up: the Poles, obviously concerned about the altitude of the mountains, had dropped us extremely high. Given that my parachute opened just below the summit of Monte Canin, which is almost 10,000-feet high, my estimate is that they had dropped us at about 7,000 feet instead of 700 feet, as planned.

However, it was a beautiful, windless, starry night with a clear sky, and we floated down almost without being blown off course. Or at least I did: Arthur fell a little bit off the drop zone, and some of the containers went considerably further afield. However, we found quite a competent team on the ground – very different from our French arrival – and although we had to wait until after dawn to find some of the containers that had fallen in the rocky ground up the hillside, we eventually discovered everything. One container, which included our own personal effects, had broken open upon impact with a rock, so the frame of my rucksack was bent and the stock of my carbine broken. I fixed the rucksack myself, while the stock was fixed by an ingenious Italian who lined it up and put in brass strengtheners, which made it look extraordinarily handsome as well as being useful.

If the landing went without a hitch, what we found on the ground was a sorry state of affairs, pretty much as we had encountered in France. Once again we found ourselves confronted by a divided, demoralised Resistance that had got ahead of itself and paid for its presumption by being routed by the Germans. We found it incredible that the lessons from France – where, immediately after D-Day, the London-based Free French leadership of de Gaulle and General Kœnig summoned a mass of untrained and lightly equipped Resistance fighters to a mountainside redoubt to face down the Germans, only for them to be slaughtered in short order by experienced and hardened *Wehrmacht* veterans – were replicated in Italy, with equally disastrous results.

When the Allies were making slow progress up the length of Italy, everything had been peachy for the Resistance groups. There were rich harvests, and, with the trees leafy and concealing, supplies and movement presented no difficulty. Unfortunately, it all went to the heads of the local leaders of the groups, and they, sadly, with the connivance and encouragement of my predecessor in the region, decided to have an open uprising and 'liberate' a slew of villages between the River Tagliamento and the River Isonzo, on the Yugoslav border. They had the advantage of surprise and easily overcame the Germans stationed in the region; they even reigned in splendour for a week or two.

Then, inevitably, came the German reaction: they mustered a substantial mobile force backed up by the garrison troops on foot, surrounded the area and proceeded to rout all the partisans, seizing a lot of valuable equipment that had been dropped to them at great risk. The result was a huge number of desertions and a massive drop in morale. Not only that, but their precipitate and foolish actions led to the total destruction of several villages by the Germans, notably Attimis and Faedis, plus reprisals that led to the deaths of numerous hostages, many by public hangings from lamp posts. The whole fiasco was the total antithesis of the way in which to pursue an effective guerrilla campaign, and I found it somewhat ironic that on his return my predecessor, Major Hedley-Vincent, was then taken on the staff of the SOE Headquarters in Italy, promoted and decorated.

But not only did we find a disillusioned Resistance; it was also deeply divided. We had been dropped to a team of the non-communist Osoppo Resistance, who were recognisable by their green scarves, while their mortal foes, the communist Garibaldini, wore red scarves. We knew that much, yet we simply didn't appreciate the implications of this difference: that was to come later and was to be a painful lesson. It was clear from the outset that there was no love lost between the two groups.

We did, at least, have two British officers left from the previous mission, yet in truth they were of limited use. Taylor and Godwin, two junior Sapper officers who had been sent in as instructors in weaponry and explosives, did their best. Yet, despite their undoubted diligence and courage, Taylor's limited Italian and Godwin's inability to communicate at all meant they were almost completely ineffective and were quickly evacuated through Yugoslavia at the end of December. The radio operator from the previous mission, whose relations with the mission had not been smooth, couldn't wait to get out. He departed even before the officers, which left only Corporal Trent.

The last member of the party, Trent was an extraordinary character. No one really seemed to know the origin of this soldier, who was of indeterminate central-European race and spoke fluent but heavily accented English as well as a number of other languages, including Serbo-Croat. Despite the fact that I could speak pretty fluent Italian from my time in Gavi, he soon became my eyes and ears. We lost Trent in pretty unsatisfactory circumstances when, in late January, with the Yugoslavs going out of their way to make our lives difficult, we sent him and two bodyguards to set up a meeting between me and the senior officer of the Slovene corps of Tito's army, who were stationed in a command post on the Yugoslav–Italian border. We never saw him again. He made contact as arranged, but as the Slovenes marched him towards the rendezvous point they robbed and murdered Trent and one of his bodyguards. The second bodyguard sustained life-threatening wounds but still managed to fight his way free and report back to me. It wasn't the first time, nor would it be the last, that we were to be double-crossed by our Yugoslav 'allies'.

By the time of Trent's death we were ensconced in the Osoppo group's temporary headquarters, a small stone cottage in the woods between the Alpine foothills and the flat plain that runs down to Udine and Venice. In all, we had 20 armed Osoppo fighters, the vast majority of whom had fought with the Italian Army in the Greek campaign. Their leader was a captain whose code name was Bolla, a calm and splendid officer for whom I had a great regard. His second-in-command was an honest and enthusiastic but uncharismatic former schoolteacher called Aenese, who had been a reserve lieutenant in the Italian Army. The rest came from all sorts of backgrounds and from all over Italy. One, called Victor, had a really splendid tenor voice, and round the evening fire in the cottage he led some very soulful, moving singing while the candles shimmered around us in the semi-darkness – with all the windows covered and the room filling with smoke.

But we weren't there for gentle lullabies and quickly set to our task of severing the main road and rail arteries between Austria and Italy. The Pontebbana line, which came into Venice, was particularly vulnerable because the railway was electrified and the poles were easy to attack. We blew up so many that it was only a matter of weeks before they had to abandon the use of electric trains and turn instead to steam locomotives, so we decided to put those out of commission too.

This was a trickier proposition because the locos were kept in the marshalling yard in Udine, with regular German patrols. While there was a good chance of getting in unobserved, moving around without being spotted would be extremely difficult. The most effective way to divert these patrols would be to have an air raid on the city, but it would be very tricky to arrange that, so I managed to organise a dummy air raid in which a plane would fly over the town and drop a couple of hand grenades out of the doors to make sure that the sirens sounded and the troops went to their shelters.

The attack was planned for the first week of December, and I trained a six-man squad led by a very courageous young man who had chosen the code name of 'Wolf'. I showed him how to attach the charges to the cylinders of the locomotives, how to get in, how to withdraw; they practised every manoeuvre time and again. We had a system of signals so that if the midnight plane was cancelled a red flare called a Very light would be fired at six o'clock from a hill visible in Udine, and if it was coming then the flare would be green.

After two postponements the green light went up, and as the plane droned overhead and the town's sirens were sounding, Wolf and his team broke into the yard. Yet, when the aircraft failed to drop anything and there were no diversionary explosions, the German patrols – alerted by the regular firing of flares at a fixed time – simply hunkered down in their bunkers. As the guards weren't moving, our raiders couldn't see them, and Wolf and three of his team walked straight into the front of a machine-gun post in the engine shed and were captured after a brief firefight. The remainder got away, but the saboteurs knew what to expect and Wolf and his companions were summarily executed on the spot.

19

A Dirty War

The risks run by saboteurs were never better demonstrated than in the case of Berto, an explosives expert with whom I would plan operations. Unlike in France, the distances and difficult terrain meant that it was impractical for me to be hands-on in the instruction of operatives, so Berto would train our fighters in the art of blowing up rails and electricity pylons with plastic explosives, accompanying them on their first foray and then dispatching them to predetermined spots.

The greatest threat to our operations – even greater than the highly accurate direction-finder vans with which the Germans tried to latch on to our radio broadcasts – were the collaborators who went to enormous lengths to infiltrate our group. Berto, unfortunately, was betrayed by one of his own countrymen when he was hiding in a safe house in one of the villages down on the plain just prior to an attack. Even worse, he was captured with his girlfriend, who had acted as our courier, taking messages to and from me and Berto as well as to the outlying parties.

Beaten and tortured, Berto broke when the Germans threatened to mete out the same punishment to his girlfriend. He agreed to show the Germans a major explosives dump that we had established not far from the target area, and with a startling degree of bravery he persuaded the German guards who were escorting him and his girlfriend to help him with the heavy lid. Berto knew that the dump was booby trapped – knew that when he lifted the lid the whole thing would blow – yet he drew the Germans in so close that when he lifted the lid they were all killed or maimed. Berto knew he and his girlfriend had moments to live and chose to meet death on his own terms.

The Germans were driven to apoplexy by our acts of sabotage, and after every night-time operation they would send up a Fieseler Storch spotter plane at first light to search for the culprits' tracks, particularly in the winter when tracks in the snow were clearly visible from the air. We tried to create so many cross-tracks that following our direction would be difficult, but there were many Italians who would have been happy to see the back of us, and that included the Garibaldi brigades and the Slovenes. One morning at dawn, even as we could hear a Storch droning in the distance, our watchman rushed in, shouting that in the valley below us on the one patch of open snow – a ten-acre meadow – was written the word 'Osoppo' in enormous letters, with an arrow pointing in our direction. We scrubbed it out using branches, finishing the job moments before the spotter plane came into view, but it gave us enough of a fright that I immediately moved my headquarters to a hideout further north in the hills from where I could attack a totally different sector of the line, leaving Bolla and his team in the southern area.

Travelling by day, the trip into the mountains over narrow and hazardous paths was tough, with whatever equipment we could not carry ourselves being loaded onto four overburdened mules. Just how overladen became obvious when one stumbled and fell, rolling down hundreds of feet and breaking its neck. The mule, as with everything else, was not wasted, and two men were left behind to skin it and cut the meat up into portable sections. I never got fond of mule meat or mule sausages, but it's certainly better than an endless diet of deadly dull maize-meal polenta.

Our destination was a small collection of derelict cottages above the tiny village of Musi that were used periodically by shepherds for summer grazing. Arthur and I were accompanied by a ten-strong team commanded by a quietly confident ex-Italian Army sergeant called Sardi and including a young man of twenty called Nino, whose real name was Ezio Bruno Londero. Nino was my companion, guide and bodyguard on almost every mission that I went on – we are still friends, and I am godfather to his son, Lucio. The other man allocated to us was code named Siena, after his home town, and he was an elderly but immensely tough man who was slow-moving in thought and deed. Hugely loyal, he cooked for us, made the fires, produced hot shaving water and generally helped make life tolerable.

Nino was my partner in crime, and together we plotted a spectacular operation in the town of Pordenone, across the Tagliamento River, where a substantial factory was making textiles for the German Army. Nino made contact with the manager, who very reluctantly agreed to leave the doors unlocked at the back of the factory on three successive nights. This was standard procedure because the risk of betrayal was huge, so we would always send an advance party the first night to spring any trap and to find out what machinery was involved so that we could prepare the charges. Nino led that reconnaissance and was part of the hugely successfully attack the following night.

We had been forced to move to our mountain redoubt by the activities of either the Garibaldi team or the Slovenes, so, while I wasn't particularly bothered by political niceties, before we moved to our alpine meadow it seemed a sensible precaution to make contact with the red-scarved Garibaldi team. Up until the summer they had seemed reasonably cooperative and had been active against the Germans. But I had failed to appreciate just how ideologically driven they were, and just how far they would go to realise their political ambitions. Just how far included murder, collaboration and even trying to gift large tracts of their own country to a neighbouring state.

During the winter, the Osoppo cut down their numbers because of the difficulties of supply and movement but continued hitting the Germans wherever they could. The Garibaldi, by contrast, simply hibernated, although we later discovered that they used the quiet period for intensive contacts with the Slovene 9th Corps of Tito's army, just across the Yugoslav border. The 9th Corps used to send out regular patrols in the border areas to intimidate villagers into declaring themselves Yugoslav, to forcibly requisition food and to become graffiti experts, writing on all the walls of border villages the slogan '*Sloboda narodu, smrt fašizmu*', which meant 'Long live liberty, death to fascism.'

This was really like a dog lifting its leg round its territory: they were already thinking past the war to the peace, marking out what they considered to be Yugoslav territory. In the event, only the arrival of British troops in Trieste shortly before the Yugoslavs rolled into town, plus our willingness to defend the border, stopped the Yugoslavs claiming a huge slice of Italy. We later found out that the Garibaldi partisans had even signed a formal written treaty with the Yugoslavs, whereby the province of Veneto, effectively the whole north-eastern corner of Italy, would become a part of the Federal Republic of Yugoslavia provided the

Garibaldi bigwigs could run it. They were, as I made clear when I named them in my final report on this mission, traitors to Italy.

In late 1944 and early 1945 we didn't appreciate how low the Garibaldi zealots were prepared to sink. Had we known, then we might have been able to stop a massacre that had many parallels with Glencoe. Early in February 1945 a party of Garibaldi and a couple of Slovenes arrived at Bolla's headquarters, my former base, in bad weather and asked for shelter for the night. But they weren't looking for a bed; they were looking for me. During the course of a convivial evening in which the Garibaldi broke bread and drank wine with their hosts, they scoured the place and immediate surroundings for me, believing me to be in the area. When they couldn't find me and Bolla denied we were around, the Garibaldi and their Slovene friends slaughtered the majority of the Osoppo, whose hospitality they had so happily accepted. Bolla and Aenese were tortured before being killed: Aenese had all his teeth ripped out, and Bolla's mangled corpse bore the hallmarks of the most savage treatment. No wonder the Garibaldi ringleaders were tried and convicted in Milan in 1951 and served lengthy – and well-deserved – terms of imprisonment.

Throughout this period we were constantly blowing things up, derailing trains and generally making a huge nuisance of ourselves. We knew the night paths through the mountains and forests and did a brisk business couriering escaped prisoners to the Yugoslavs and on to safety. Usually the Germans wouldn't venture into the mountains at night, but, on one occasion, when we were coming back from blowing up a bridge on the eastern route through Caporetto, Nino and I stumbled on a German patrol. They had been shooting a couple of hostages in reprisal when we ran into them just as they emerged from the local inn. They opened fire at once, but we threw ourselves off the steep path, leaping into the undergrowth, Nino's fall broken by a bush while I wrenched my foot and ankle between two big stones. We walked with difficulty for a couple of miles, then thought it safe enough to spend the night in the inn, where the local wise woman made an extremely smelly poultice of onions and olive oil while the entire female population of this tiny village stood at the end of the bed desperately trying to look up my kilt.

Apart from the predatory village women there was always the danger of the Germans coming back, so the following morning I was taken in a cart to another inn, off the road but a little closer to the Austrian border. I convalesced there for three days before Nino turned up with an extraordinary country character called Vonn – huge, strong, bearded, a poacher by trade before the war – and a mule. If I don't much like eating mule, I like riding on them even less, and this one was particularly bad, with its bony spine covered only in sacking that chafed my thighs as we went downhill. When we eventually got to our hideout, I had to be helped to lie face down on the palliasse that served as our bed while poor Arthur anointed my backside, which had been flayed through my kilt.

During the severe winter weather we not only reduced our party to seven or eight active members, but with spring possibly coming early we decided that it was too dangerous to remain in the alpine meadow, so we constructed two log huts in a very thick wood further down the valley. Days after we moved, the only house down the track hung a sheet on their balcony to dry, our warning of danger. Shortly afterwards, a company strength of Germans came up the path, passing below us and heading for the alpine meadow, led by an unfortunate girl who had been one of our team before we reduced the numbers. She had been arrested, cross-questioned and had cracked, leading the company to exactly where we had been. I presumed that none of our crew would be there; sadly I was wrong, the Germans arriving to find two Osoppo fighters staying overnight on the way back from a mission. One was Vonn, the huntsman, who used all his stalking craft to escape up the hill; the other was caught in one of the huts, locked into it and burnt alive.

Episodes such as this served to constantly bolster my desire to make life as difficult as possible for the Germans. One place I was desperate to hit but never managed to – not least because it was where I had been recaptured on my escape attempt in 1943 – was a narrow gap called Chiusaforte through which the road and railway both had to pass. It was guarded by a large number of troops, and if getting in was difficult the steep slopes made a getaway equally hard, so I decided that the only thing to do was harass them using my .303 sniper rifle with a peep sight, which was accurate up to 500 or 600 yards. So, although it wouldn't stop the traffic, I'd often pop down and shoot one – or, if possible, two – of the sentries on the key guarded points. These were small but annoying raids that intensified the requirement for guarding.

Riling the Germans was always guaranteed to bring a reaction, and as patrols intensified so did the risk of their finding tracks in the snow.

Because of this we split our operations. One group remained in the log cabins while another went to a newly built log cabin in woodland nearer the railway and linked with a group in the plain being run by a New Zealand corporal called Frank 'Franco' Gardener. The final group, including Arthur, the faithful Siena and me, went up into the mountains from where we could strike northwards to Chiusaforte and Pontebba.

We had made our headquarters in a cave high up at about 5,000 feet, but no sooner had we settled in than a platoon of Poles in German uniforms poured out of a ravine near our cave. In the ensuing firefight I ordered Arthur to immediately send the signal QUG – 'We are in imminent danger and transmission must close' – which was replied to straight away by the even greater priority signal QSQ – 'This is extraordinarily urgent, and you must take it under any circumstances.' So, as bullets ricocheted off the rocks and the Poles gradually closed off all our escape routes, Arthur solemnly received a very long coded message that started 'Please disseminate the following rumours to the nearest enemy.' It turned out to be a message from the Department of Psychological Warfare – how it managed to be given the sort of priority that meant we had to take it down while people were shooting at us, only they would know.

If we were fighting for our lives, with Arthur, Siena and me pouring fire down on the Poles and leaving several grey-coated bodies lying on the hillside, our attackers appeared to realise that there was no need for them to die in this alien corner of a foreign land. As if sensing for the first time that that was about to be their fate, they retreated at top speed, running harum-scarum down the mountainside and leaving us to melt back into the woods and head back to the log cabin.

20

The Turncoats' Comeuppance

The Poles were by no means the only non-Germans fighting as part of the *Wehrmacht* and SS. Towards the end of April a huge number of Russian troops in German uniform concentrated on the western side of the pass leading to Austria through Pontebba. They had been stationed as policing and garrison troops through the villages and had taken a major role in security and in chasing Resistance fighters, which they had done with considerable brutality. As well as taking and killing hostages, they had burnt several villages and, when forcibly billeted on local village families, had eaten all their hosts' precious food.

The Poles and Russians were just some of the 'volunteer' troops fighting for Germany despite the fact that they were from nations that had been overrun or armies that had been captured. In France we captured Mongolians whose passbooks contained a page for a '*Bordellbesuch*' – or brothel visit – to which they were entitled once a month as part of their service contract. In Italy we came across others, such as Spaniards and Finns, as well as assorted north Russian nationalities. One of the worst things I saw during the war was when a group of Finns exercising as mountain troops on skis in the snow were chasing two villagers who were in turn running through the snow to escape. The Finns came from above, skiing down the hill in the snowplough position and firing from the shoulder as they skied – a remarkable yet terrifying performance. One of the unfortunate villagers was hit in what seemed to be an outing entirely for sport.

The Russians, however, were the most numerous, the most feared and the most hated of all. One group based in the village of Ovaro and under the command of Major Nausiko had murdered a large number of villagers in reprisals for the actions of partisans. A war crimes tribunal later said that this group of Cossacks alone had killed 29 Ovaro villagers, including two priests and one woman, with the tribunal recording that all the corpses displayed 'horrible wounds in the head'.

As the Germans retreated, giving priority on the roads to 'real' German troops and their transport, the Russians had been forced to concentrate in a group of villages west of the main pass up on a plateau in the hills. Arthur got onto the radio and advised SOE Headquarters that, while they were lightly armed and not regarded as the best troops, the Russians still posed a threat to any of our men who were driving through the pass in soft vehicles in pursuit of a retreating enemy. We were told that, in such a case, the RAF would deal with them heavily.

That prospect inevitably horrified the villagers in the areas where the Russians had concentrated, who sent their mayor to beg me to attempt to get a surrender from the Russian commanders so that their villages would not be devastated by bombing. In reality it was unlikely that the RAF would bother with a major mission against these troops, who numbered about 20,000, but I thought the threat might be enough to persuade them to surrender. I sent a courier, with a very formal letter, back with the mayor into the mountains to request contact with the most senior Russians.

Instead, they sent a middle-ranking staff officer. I was as stern and threatening as possible, saying that not only would they be bombed but that we were arming the surrounding villages, which would rise against them and decimate them. Given the war crimes many of them had perpetrated, being left to the tender mercies of the local population was an absolutely desperate prospect for them, and the following day I received a delegation of two grizzled gentlemen, in the uniform of major generals, and a Georgian lady who introduced herself as the sovereign princess of this Cossack division.

They offered me a deal: if I protected them from the RAF and the Italians, they would surrender to British troops. I agreed, with the proviso that they must accept a total ceasefire and agree not to move at all from their present position until they were told to. When the time came, we sent a courier to the village with a formal message instructing them to come to a rendezvous, where British troops took them over. This all went smoothly: they quietly laid down their arms and were transferred to a prison camp in Austria.

This cadre of 20,000 Russians formed a substantial part of the group that was later, on the orders of the Foreign Office, handed over to the Soviets. In 1989 this was the subject of a famous libel case that resulted from Count Nikolai Tolstoy's attack on the senior British officer at that time, Brigadier Toby Low – who by the trial had become Lord Aldington – for his part in repatriating the Russians. Low, who sued Tolstoy and was awarded £1.5 million in damages, was a friend of mine until his death in 2000, and I am in no doubt that he acted honourably in this matter. That the Cossacks went back to their almost certain death is undoubted, but if a soldier in one army changes allegiance to another in the middle of the war and has the misfortune to lose out, he can have few complaints when he is returned for justice in his own country.

There were very few British prisoners of war, even those of a fascist persuasion, who acted in the same way, and I have no doubt that we would have viewed any such renegades in the same way as the Russians viewed the Cossack traitors. After all, we wasted little time before executing William Joyce, the voice of Lord Haw Haw, when he was arrested at the end of the war. These Cossacks had performed major brutalities, and they had deserted the army of an ally that we had shed blood and precious resources to support and who had been a major factor in defeating the Germans. They had to go back to where they belonged. There was also a risk that, had we not sent them back, some of the British troops being held by the Russians might have been detained indefinitely.

The Italians were certainly in no doubt that what we did was right. I was very touched in 1994 when the largest of the villages where the Russians had concentrated, and where the villagers had faced the imminent destruction of their homes, contacted me to say that they had erected a memorial in my name as a token of gratitude 50 years later.

21

Saving Trieste

Long before that episode with the Russians and shortly after our run-in with the Poles, the winter began to turn to spring. One of the first signs of the changing seasons was a pair of ravens who nested in a high rock right above our hideout. While one fed and tended their newly hatched chicks, the other would forage for food and soar in the air, watching for approaching danger. Somehow they seemed to get used to us and soon ignored us, but they croaked violently if anyone else approached the hill.

Protected by the woodland and the snow on the ground, we managed to survive a marked intensification of patrolling in the area, often with dogs. Whenever the dogs were out, my mind would involuntarily go back to one of the more absurd pieces of our training at Milton Hall, when some scientific boffins from Professor Zuckermann's department had produced some extraordinarily good gadgets but also come up with the most way-out ideas. We were warned that we might be pursued by dogs and were encouraged, as their latest secret weapon, to carry with us a bag of tennis balls to be rubbed on the behind of a bitch on heat and then thrown as we were chased by the dogs in order to distract them. I promise you this was a serious suggestion.

By now the Allies were making good progress through Italy, and we started to go down into the little local townships to establish contacts there for the phase of liberation that we knew, sooner or later, would come. I would hold meetings with Verdi, who was notionally the head of all the Osoppo in the area, and organise arms drops for him so that his men would be in a position to harry the retreating Germans. I also – and this was unspoken but implicitly understood between us – wanted him to be in a position to stop the Slovenes coming over the border and

179

combining with their Garibaldi friends to simply annex the Veneto for Yugoslavia. We also continued to arm Franco's little group, which was doing an excellent job of sabotaging roads, bridges and railway lines, and we derailed as many locomotives as we could.

The unmistakeable signs that we were preparing for the end of hostilities in this part of the world were confirmed when I received instructions from our headquarters, which had now moved from Bari to the city of Siena, to meet up with the future civilian government of Udine, which was the capital of the province of Friuli. A rendezvous was set up at the town of Gemona, halfway between us and Udine, with me staying with Cily de Carli, the sister of Sergio, one of our liaison officers who couriered between our different detachments. She had a nice house on the edge of the town, with a little garden, a terrace on which she set up a ping-pong table and a garden with fruit trees. Most importantly, though, she had billeted on her a German Army medical doctor who was extremely inclined to mind his own business and wait for the war to end – handy, because we knew the German Army, police and Gestapo would be unlikely to come looking for me in such proximity to one of their own.

Not that everything went smoothly. On the way to one of our meetings, the air-raid alarms went off just after we had started walking down a narrow lane with high walls on each side. At the end of the lane was an air-raid shelter where Italian fascist troops tended to go in times of emergency: it was too good an opportunity to waste. We waited until we saw them rush in, and then I simply opened the door, chucked in a grenade and turned to run. Just after the explosion, however, a young Italian officer who was obviously late getting there came running towards the shelter and, seeing me, drew his tiny pistol and fired it, hitting me on the webbing of my rucksack, with the bullet ricocheting through the notebook in my pocket and breaking the skin without causing serious injury. I survived; he did not.

By this stage our thoughts were turning from the Germans and the Italian fascists to the Slovenes and the Garibaldi communist partisans. The same considerations were dominating the plans of the civilians, who were ready to take over once the Germans left, as I found during my meetings with the future mayor of Udine and designated prefect of the province, in the de Carli house. We were convinced that the Germans would leave sometime in May and knew that our main task would be to prevent looting or the settling of old scores. This was where Verdi's heavily armed Osoppo from the plain would come in. If there was a battle, then the civilian government would simply take to the cellars until the Allies appeared.

In the meantime we were still trying to make the German retreat, which was pretty orderly, as difficult as possible. The best way to do that was to blow up the main bridge over the Noncello River, which their troops were using, but HQ seemed to think it was a job that would be better done from the air. Yet, after two attempts – a dawn raid by RAF bombers followed the next day by South African Kittyhawks – the bridge was still standing, with German traffic flooding across it.

Franco, the Kiwi corporal, and I got in as close as we could, saw that there were two unexploded bombs in the ground near the surface, one right up against one of the pillars of the bridge, and decided to take matters into our own hands. Our plan was simple: that night we would start a firefight, attacking the German positions from a reasonably safe distance, and while the guards were distracted two of our men would go in under cover of darkness and place an explosive charge against the unexploded bombs. The Germans reacted with an unexpectedly furious response, and there was a little bit more of a firefight than we had expected, with two of our men being slightly wounded, but as we withdrew we heard the satisfying dull thud of an explosion, then watched as the bridge sagged and fell to the ground. It would never be used again.

We were all leading charmed lives, but taking proper precautions could – and did – save our lives on many occasions. I was, for instance, going down into town increasingly regularly and was still staying at Cily's house, where I felt very comfortable. Then one day, for no apparent reason, the German Army medical captain came in while we were playing ping-pong on the balcony and asked for our identity cards. There was a horribly pregnant pause: I had a convincing but fake identity card. I can't even remember what my name was supposed to be, although I do know that my mother was called Irma Gambarini, from Gemona, and that I was excused military service or work in Germany because of war wounds. He even checked for the wounds, and I breathed a sigh of relief when he was fooled by my schoolboy osteomyelitis wounds – I knew only too well what would have happened had he not been. He retired to his room, either satisfied or discreet.

As it became increasingly clear that the Germans were preparing for a hurried departure from Trieste, so our arrangements became ever more urgent and, at times, ridiculously elaborate. At one stage I even got a message from some department concerned with post-war economies, which urged us to stop any German attempts to cut down mulberry trees on the grounds that they were the staple diet of the silkworms that formed one of the big industries in the area. Just how these bureaucrats thought I might achieve this they didn't explain.

Other cries for help were more pressing, such as an urgent call from the Bishop of Trieste, who had been informed that he was in danger of being invaded in his palace and held hostage by the Slovene 9th Corps, which we all expected to sweep into the area as part of the Yugoslav plan to annex the Veneto. We sent a group of Verdi's men to the bishop's house; he was so grateful that he wined and dined them with the best of his kitchen and cellar for several days, until the first New Zealand troops turned up and dislodged the Slovenes, who had tried to take control of policing as soon as the Germans left.

The situation was even more difficult in Udine, where the Gestapo were absolutely determined to execute all the hostages and anyone in their jails who had helped the Allies. We found out that their plan was to send out firing squads on the day they left, so the night before we broke into the main jail, opened the gates and got virtually all the prisoners out. There was also a threat to the city's archbishop, this time from the Germans, who, on the day that they were set to leave, sent a large force of soldiers to the archbishop's palace in Udine. We simply didn't have the firepower to oppose a direct attack, so took to sniping at them in the streets, slowing them to the point where the archbishop was able to slip away and hide as the Germans left the city. The archbishop, Monsignor Nogara, was so grateful that after the war the Pope, at his archbishop's behest, bestowed on me a papal knighthood and the Star of Bethlehem for saving the bishop's life and stopping the Slovenes annexing the Veneto.

Twenty miles north of Udine, in the city of Gemona where the road crosses the Tagliamento River, the last major obstacle before the Alps, the Germans were slower to move and were obviously planning to hold the city and its bridges in a rearguard action. Yet none of their troops could have relished being left behind, especially in the dog days of the war when there was going to be only one outcome. So, as the rest of their countrymen streamed up the Pontebbana road and left the Gemona garrison isolated and alone, I dressed in full uniform – kilt, sgian dubh, the whole kit and caboodle – and drove into town. There, in the city hall, without a shot being fired, I took the surrender of the German major who was commanding the small garrison, a hugely satisfying moment given that this was the same fellow whose troops had been hunting me all over the country for the past six months.

Within hours of taking the garrison's surrender on 1 May, I was having a wash and brush-up in the de Carli house when news arrived that British armour had finally been spotted. Shaved and refreshed, I immediately rushed down to the town square, where, rather than armour, I found two armoured cars of the Lancer Regiment, which had been sent to reconnoitre the situation. I quickly explained that the Germans were leaving a moving rearguard going up the narrow Pontebba Pass and that the most difficult place to pass them would be Chiusaforte but that there might also be resistance just north of Gemona in another narrow place on the road. I had already sent a strong force of 50 men from the Osoppo resistance around the back of a small hill so that they would emerge under reasonable cover along the Germans' flank, ready to pour fire into the retreating column. They were, however, under orders to wait until I gave them the word because I wanted to see how the battle developed.

Just then two Panther tanks, heavy and menacing with long guns, the younger sisters of the Tigers, emerged from the mouth of the pass north of Gemona. The armoured cars knew that they were no match for the German tanks and simply turned tail and departed with full speed. One of them broke down even before it had left the town, its young officer taking the breechblock off its gun so that it was unusable, while the other hightailed it in the opposite direction. My heart really sank for the first time in Italy: after the euphoria of seeing British troops arrive, to see them run while the German heavy armour advanced slowly but inexorably towards Gemona was gut-wrenching. The war was virtually over, and people I had come to know and love were about to have their homes flattened, because that was clearly what was going to happen. The whole thing was hideously unfair. So I did the only thing I could, sending a signals party to tell the Osoppo fighters to open fire, to make as much noise as they could and to create as big a diversion as they could.

The tanks immediately stopped in their tracks, turning back towards the ambush, and the town was saved.

The next day the serious forward troops of the Eighth Army appeared. I wouldn't have blamed them for not rushing northwards, because the pass at Chiusaforte, if defended, would have been one hell of a battle. It turned out that they, like us, had learnt the night before, shortly after the Panther tanks had turned around, that the German forces in Italy had capitulated. We found that out by listening to the BBC on Arthur's favourite little toy, a tiny radio receiver that worked on torch batteries – highly advanced for those days – which had been our fall-back for receiving messages whenever our main radio malfunctioned. It's difficult to explain just how important the BBC had been to us. It provided our only real link to the outside world and allowed us to boost the morale of the Italians who surrounded us as we listened to 'Lili Marlene' on the BBC European broadcast news each evening.

The capitulation of the Germans saw us follow the plan that we had prepared for the armistice and the inevitable clashes with the Slovenes and Garibaldi militia. By midday on the day after the announcement Nino and Sergio had arrived in the local capital of Udine, requisitioned a large house called the Palazzo Rubini for us to base ourselves from and found us a butler, a serving girl and a cook so that, after months of privation, we were extraordinarily well looked after. I headed over to meet the head of the Eighth Army, General McCreary, who had just established a tented and caravanned camp nearby. They were already dealing with threats and rumoured armed incursions from the Slovenes, and given my knowledge of the area General McCreary decided that I should stay with him and let the Special Forces Headquarters in Siena know.

So I was straight back into the hills to lead patrols of the border area. We arrived in the nick of time, walking into a firefight between invading Slovene troops and Italian villagers blasting away with shotguns, rifles and whatever they could lay their hands on. This was a village that forded a stream where one half was Italian and the other half Slovene, but once they realised that we were in the area both sides were happy to sign an agreement to keep to their own side of the river, which amazingly they adhered to. Nevertheless, there was still sufficient uncertainty for three villages based on the little hill of Monteaperta – Cornappo, Sambo and Debellis – to come to me and formally request to be adopted as a British colony.

The Slovene incursions were all led by people who claimed to be colonels and were covered with Yugoslav army badges and red stars to prove it. Our chief of staff roared with laughter when I told him this, saying, 'You must outrank them.' So he dug out a pair of red tabs and gave them to me to put on my summer-uniform shirt. 'Wear these,' he instructed. 'Take your badges of rank off, and tell the Slovenes you're a brigadier general.' It worked, too.

Although it was fairly hairy up in the hills, we all expected Trieste, the border city that had once been part of the Austro-Hungarian Empire but had become part of Italy after the First World War, to be the most likely flashpoint. Fortunately, the arrival of large numbers of Allied troops had headed off any trouble, and by the time I arrived there was little to do but eat and drink. My first task was to brief the general of that division, General Allan Adair, who was based in the magnificent castle of Duino, where we shared an amazingly good lunch. Then I called on the city's bishop, who insisted on giving me a dozen of the best bottles of wine from his huge cellar to take back to my Udine palazzo.

I was back in Udine and tucking into my vintage haul with Nino and Sergio when my brother Phil unexpectedly called in for a night on his way to become brigadier in charge of finances for Austria, where he was to establish himself in the magnificent Habsburg palace of Schönbrunn, in Vienna. Sergio was absolutely astonished that we didn't fall into each other's arms but 'only shook hands, sat down and started to talk'. Nut brown and completely fluent in Italian, I may have been able to pass for an Italian, but I hadn't acquired all the local characteristics.

Phil had captained Scotland's Grand Slam-winning rugby team of 1925 and was something of a legend back in Edinburgh. It was great to catch up with him as we headed in my ancient jeep for a day's outing with some friends to a lovely and remote place in the foothills of the Alps. The sun was shining, and as we swam in a small lake I remember thinking it was a perfect interlude and wondering what would happen to me now that I had to resume real life after the end of the war. Just at that point it started to pour down, and I had some more immediate considerations to deal with. We were at the bottom of a very steep slope, which the jeep had comfortably driven down when the ground was dry and hard, but there was no way my clapped-out vehicle was going to make it back up the quagmire, and it took a couple of hours of hacking off branches before we could get enough grip to get back up that hill and back to Udine.

With the border situation stabilised and under control, my halcyon interlude couldn't last, but in the end I was there for almost a month. I had sent Arthur, who was exhausted, on leave and was horrified when he was shipped out to the Far East, although, mercifully, the war was over before he was in action. As I was still very busy writing reports and making daily reconnaissances for the Eighth Army, they sent me an experienced major to be my second-in-command, and, to my absolute delight, this turned out to be my great friend from France, Freddie Cardozo.

I spent the next period at the SOE Headquarters in Siena, writing reports and sightseeing in that magnificent town before it was once again overrun by tourists. During that time I was lucky enough to witness the first post-war *Palio*, the world's most extraordinary horse race where each ward of the city produces a horse ridden by a jockey who wears a hard hat, carries a solid whip and makes three circuits around a sanded track in the centre of the town. Winning wasn't enough: the main idea seemed to be to win by jostling and hitting the other jockeys off their respective mounts, a fantastically violent affair that virtually guaranteed casualties. But we were fairly inured to such trivial injuries by then.

The one real scare of my time in Siena came when I was informed that I had been earmarked for Special Operations in the Far East, where they thought my experience would come in handy. The war in Europe was my war, a war in which I'd flown too close to the wind on too many occasions, and I viewed the prospect of more active service with barely disguised horror. However, before I had managed to protest that I had never fought in the jungle and had none of the necessary language skills, the two atom bombs were dropped and, on 28 August, the Japanese announced their unconditional surrender.

My last posting saw me sent back to Special Operations Headquarters in Siena for a debriefing. My detailed report was not, however, universally well received, mainly because the local head of station in north-eastern Italy, an Oxford don called Hewitt, wasn't happy at my trenchant criticism of the situation that I had found on my arrival and of the briefing that I had been given. Nor were those communist chiefs who had been prepared to kill their fellow countrymen for an alliance with the Slovenes to give themselves power over that border province particularly pleased when I revealed their names and wartime aliases.

Hewitt and the communist traitors weren't the only ones who didn't like the cut of my jib. The Yugoslav leader General Tito had been sure that he would be able to annex the Veneto when the Germans left, yet in the end he made no territorial gains at all, a disaster that he placed at the door of 'the Scottish Major'. I hadn't realised just how much my activities with the non-communist partisans or my efforts to keep Trieste and Udine as part of Italy had annoyed him, but I later found out that he had put a death sentence on my head. I never found out how much the reward for my demise was, but years later, when I was working as a timber merchant and at a dinner in Dubrovnik, Tito heard that I was in the building and summoned me to a personal hearing. He was welcoming, enquiring and interested in my war experiences, while I'd had enough Dutch courage to find him jovial and engaging. Either way, we got it all sorted out. Somewhere in a drawer I have a napkin with my hand-written 'pardon' on it in Serbo-Croat. Or at least I think it's my pardon . . .

22

The Dreaming Spires

After I had escaped from the prisoner-of-war camp at Torun in Poland and made my way back to Britain via Sweden, I had expected to be given a cushy desk job. Instead, I had been told that I was 'volunteering' to join the Jedburghs, which presaged my years as a guerrilla fighter in France and then Italy. After the fall of Italy I almost found myself sent out to the crucible of the Far East campaign against the Japanese, a prospect that, while only fleetingly threatened, was particularly horrifying. Luckily, the events in north-east Italy were to be my last serious spell of active duty, even if I didn't know it at the time. With hindsight, life was about to get safer and, in many ways, happier.

After the end of our Italian campaign, Freddie Cardozo and I drove southwards in an old jeep to report to Headquarters at Siena before taking some leave. We had planned to visit my brother Archie, who was commanding a field hospital in the pretty town of Rimini on the Adriatic coast. As we approached the coast in the twilight, we could still see headlights moving on the road below us but found that a large bridge across a valley in our path had been demolished. The only way across was via a sharp turning down to the valley below and up again, but the path was so narrow that the jeep's wheels slipped off the road and we rolled down the hill, ending up undamaged but upside down. We were just deciding what to do when, out of nowhere, a farmer appeared with two oxen and rapidly got the jeep the right way up. Being a jeep, it started first time. He then produced an axe, and we simply chopped off the wooden bodywork, so we were back to having an open jeep.

We eventually found our way to Rimini just in time to play in a cricket match on matting arranged by Archie against a local regiment of South Africans. Amid the debris of wartime Italy it all seemed like a somewhat incongruous activity. There were, however, already signs that life was returning to normal. For instance, after arriving in Rimini I had three rather fascinating operatic experiences, the first of which was an open-air performance to celebrate the return of peace to Italy's troubled north-eastern region. It was a deliberately political gesture: the opera was held north of Trieste on the River Isonzo, which the Yugoslavs were claiming as the minimum border to which they had a right, although they wanted much more territory. The audience for the opera was on the west side of the river on a slight incline while the singers were on the east shore of the river, which made a magnificent effect under a bright moonlight sky, with the sound carrying brilliantly across the water.

My next operatic experience was in Rome, where I was taken to see *Aida* at the Baths of Caracalla. It was an absolutely sensational setting, with huge walls forming the back of the stage, the music resonating right through the open-air auditorium and, within the triumph scene, trumpeters picked out by floodlights right on top of the walls, with elephants and horses marching across the stage as the hero led his triumphal procession. From there I went to Naples, where I was invited to the gala opening of the Teatro Real, at which King Umberto of Italy, who had recently taken over from his abdicated father, was present. He was in the box next to ours, but the evening was instead memorable for the performances of *Cavalleria Rusticana* and *Pagliacci*, with the latter featuring a long prologue by baritone Tito Gobbi, a new boy whose voice was so magnificent that he received three encores and almost eclipsed the operatic legend, tenor Beniamino Gigli, who also sang that night.

Although that was a blissful interlude, by now it was September and I was desperate to get home and take up my university place at Trinity, Oxford, if possible. In those days there was a system of early release for people with priority needs, which included starting university, but the problem was getting home. Aeroplanes were for very senior politicians, and any ships were crowded with priority personnel. Fortunately, a good friend of mine found an excellent reason for me to go home. The FANYs – the First Aid Nursing Yeomanry, who had done so much of the coding work for SOE and staff work at various headquarters – were sending 28 of their ladies back on a liner leaving Naples for Liverpool but didn't have a suitably ranked conducting officer, so I found my last serious wartime job was accompanying a group of extremely efficient women on their journey home. Far from needing a chaperone, they instead looked after me extremely well, mending my battered kit and sewing on medal ribbons so that I was as presentable as possible when I arrived home.

At Liverpool docks nobody was allowed to disembark until the following day. Fortunately, a senior FANY officer came on board and took over my 28 ladies, while I and another Scottish officer from the same regiment managed to persuade the commander of troops on board that we had to catch the midnight train from Liverpool. After changing on the windy platform at Preston, we took a train to Inverness so we could report to the Cameron regimental depot at Strathpeffer. I recall waking in the Scottish Lowlands, fresh from what was considered one of the most beautiful areas of Italy – with its mountains, pinewoods and green-and-blue background – and looking out and knowing at once that, on a sunny late-September morning, there is nothing in Europe to rival the vivid colours of our own country.

At Inverness we found an Army transport heading to Strathpeffer. The officer-in-charge was Colonel Myers, a very good soldier known for his brusque manner. He wasn't impressed by my immediate request for some leave to visit my nearby home and started the conversation by looking at my decorations and saying, 'What's all that egg froth on your chest?' I gave a polite reply, which disguised a great deal of impoliteness, and he smiled and dropped it and signed my leave pass right away.

As I left the camp in the front seat of the fifteen-hundredweight lorry that was the workhorse of the Army, I saw, to my amazement, Pryde and Fowler, two stalwarts from my Scottish Commando troop, playing football by the side of the road. They saw me too and turned round with a broad grin and a crashing salute. We didn't have time to stop, which I've regretted ever since, because at their own expense and in their own time they had turned up on my mother's doorstep while I was a prisoner to give their latest account of me, which she appreciated enormously. This time it was me turning up on my parents' doorstep, which came as a complete surprise to them because none of my letters had reached them. It was, though, a very pleasant shock.

My first task was to contact Trinity College in Oxford, who immediately accepted my attendance from 4 October, which was just a fortnight away. On arrival in Oxford I found I had been allocated rooms in the inner quadrangle of that lovely college, looking out across the courtyard into very well-kept gardens with their extensive lawns. Even now I can remember all those who had rooms around me. Opposite was James Ramsden, from the north-east of England. A scion of an old brewing family and one of the most brilliant people of our generation, he became minister of war in the first post-war Conservative government. Below me was Stephen McWatters, who became headmaster of Clifton College in Bristol. On the same level were Duke Hussey, who lost a leg in the war and, like me, developed osteomyelitis but later became managing director of *The Times* newspaper and governor of the BBC; plus Richard Hornby, who became a prominent MP and minister after a successful career in the advertising industry. Those friendships endured as long as they lived.

I had gone up to Oxford to study Classics, but after such a long break from my studies and a fiendishly demanding course under the redoubtable Ronald Syme, I went to the all-powerful bursar Philip Langdon and told him that I couldn't see myself doing Classics with any possibility of success. He sat back in his deep chair, with his pipe puffing, and finally said, 'What do you actually want to do at university, Macpherson?'

Almost without hesitation, I said, 'Actually, sir, I want to play rugby football.'

'Ah!' he said. 'Splendid. In that case you'd better read PPE [Politics, Philosophy and Economics], all of which subjects are more or less at least written in English.'

After two weeks of undue diligence, I discovered that my lectures, which were optional, were largely a waste of time and that I'd be better off doing background reading at my own pace and of my own choosing. It was, however, fun going to lectures in totally different subjects by such distinguished people as Dr McCallum, a Canadian and the leading psephologist of that generation, and the celebrated historian A.L. Rowse. Our work was mainly concentrated around the weekly tutorials when we would hand over our essays.

My small first-floor room at Trinity was pleasant enough in the summer, but with no heating except for a tiny fireplace it was extremely cold and damp in the winter, with condensation running down the walls in the spring term despite the fire blazing away in the hearth. Each staircase had a manservant, known as a scout, to keep the rooms tidy, make our beds and, as there was no running water, bring up a ewer of water for the basin in the bedroom so that we could wash and shave. If I wanted a bath, I had to put on my dressing gown and slippers and walk through the courtyard to the college bathhouse. This was fine for me, but some people had a very long trek indeed, so many of them left their baths until the late afternoon after sport, when the bathhouse became a busy and raucous place.

We ate in college virtually every night, mainly because there were rules governing the minimum number of times you dined in but also because we couldn't afford to go into town to eat. I would occasionally splash out one shilling and sixpence on a breakfast treat at a café in Market Close that seemed untouched by the horrors of rationing, but mostly dinner was in college, where undergraduates wore their gowns. The high table was occupied by gowned dons, and we were all overseen by a splendid butler called Cadman, who only recently retired. As a scholar I periodically had to read the lesson in chapel at the services that were held on Sunday mornings and each evening of the week, while the senior scholar said the Latin grace before each meal. I had a long scholar's gown, as opposed to commoners' gowns, which came to just below the waist. We all wore gowns for tutorials, and it wouldn't have crossed our minds not to wear a collar and tie, although sports jacket or blazer and flannels were more common than a suit.

I found philosophy sessions absolute rubbish but quite fun. I would use obscure or ambiguous vocabulary and bad logic to reach conclusions that were logically indefensible but which, from the moral philosopher's standpoint, seemed marvellous. I enjoyed economics, although I rapidly came to the conclusion that nobody had written anything particularly sensible since Adam Smith and that the contemporary – meaning socialist – writers simply did not understand the practical applications of their theories. My tutor, Robert Hall, and his even more left-leaning wife, Margaret, were economic advisers to Clement Attlee's Labour government, and I enjoyed these sessions. There was no doubting Hall's intellectual brilliance, and, as we fundamentally disagreed, our sessions sharpened the mind. After my finals, when I took first-class honours, Hall sent for me and said, 'Well, I consider you were remarkably lucky.'

The politics component of PPE, which meant political history and analysis, was the most enjoyable aspect of my studies. My tutor was a pretty undistinguished young man called Williams, but, while my other tutorials were solo, this one was shared with Tony Crosland, who had a pin-sharp mind and went on to become an extremely distinguished Labour cabinet minister in spite of thoroughly enjoying all the good things of life. We spent much of our time studying the 19th century, and, as Gladstone was one of Crosland's heroes, I automatically championed Disraeli, so most of our time was spent arguing and ignoring the tutor's occasional and plaintive attempts to interrupt.

Socially, we had a fantastic time. Perhaps because there were strikes in virtually every public service, including the coal mines in that particularly cold winter, London society was making frantic efforts to rebuild its old traditions and lift the gloom that had settled on the capital. The London hostesses wanted to revive the society debutante programmes of the pre-war years, so the older single men at Oxford were deluged with invitations. In fact, in my time there I don't think I spent an entire weekend in Oxford: our Saturday rugby matches were often played away in London, so I would disappear until late Sunday night. Looking back, we young men were so in demand that we didn't behave very well. We were very lax about replying to invitations and just tended to show up if we were able to do so, turning up to the first of the night's two parties as late as half past ten in the evening and missing dinner completely. If we did deign to show our faces, we didn't spend much, if any, time talking to the fluttery 17-year-old debutantes, instead concentrating on drinking as much champagne as we could and chatting with the dowagers who were supposed to be there to chaperone their young darlings.

From the experiences of my sons, Angus and Duncan, in the '70s and '80s, I know that there is a good deal of continuity in the way the university operates, but there are also some marked differences. Immediately after the war there was a large proportion of ex-servicemen experiencing adult civilian life for the first time and determined to enjoy themselves. They were also immensely committed because they felt, during the long war, that life had been passing them by, so they wanted to get stuck into business or professional life as soon as possible and needed a good degree behind them to do so. They consequently took work so seriously that standards, at least in the arts subjects, were extremely high. Not long ago I took the senior classical tutor of Trinity my college scholarship entrance exam papers in Latin and Greek; after looking at them, he said that not one of his brightest pupils today would be able to tackle them, even after the completion of their degree. The workload was so heavy that we all worked through our holidays, the only possible exception being a week-long sports tour at Christmas or in the summer. There was never any question of taking a job or travelling abroad for the whole vacation.

We lived in a fairly spartan way, not just because of the fairly primitive college arrangements on the heating and hot water front but because rationing was in full swing and things were tougher than they had been in the worst stages of the war. Nobody had enough money to go to a pub more than perhaps once a week, and the idea of dining out in a restaurant seemed preposterous. When I was elected to the prestigious and largely sporting elite of Vincent's Club – with its famous dark-blue tie and the crown upon it – we sometimes dined in the club, but that was so affordable that it was no strain on the budget.

Undergraduates always wore a collar and tie and a suit, tweed jacket or blazer, and none of my friends, except Ossie Newton-Thompson, had a car, so travelling by train and bus was the norm. Once or twice a term, when I was particularly broke, I would sign on to be a temporary waiter with a city caterer, travelling up to London in the late afternoon and coming back on the last train. As I had my own tails – which were made in 1908, inherited from a great-uncle and which I still use – my only expense was the rail fare of 7s. 6d., as opposed to payment of £3 a night, a substantial sum in those days.

Like me, most Oxford undergraduates had been overseas for some time with the military and were not in the country when the 1945 election was held. We were shocked on our return to Britain by the attitude that was being created in the country, directly and indirectly, by the Labour government. Many of the armed forces were still abroad in the various occupying armies, and so the people at home were mainly those who had spent the war working in industry and the support services. Those of us who had been overseas fighting were very surprised to learn on our return of the number of strikes there had been during the war, and we were even more shocked to encounter the degree of spite and malice in some of the more vocal Labour ministers.

Aneurin Bevan, who was burnt in effigy in a prison camp in Italy after some of his parliamentary attacks on Churchill were reported in the Italian press, declared that voters who supported the Tory opposition were 'lower than vermin', adding, 'we are the masters now.' He has gone down in history as a quasi-saint for putting through the legislation that created the National Health Service, but this was based on the Beveridge Report and other studies that had been initiated by the wartime government, just as the education reforms were based on the Butler studies of the same government. As class warfare intensified, income tax rocketed up to 82 per cent, with the various surtaxes meaning that a good number of people were paying income tax at 98 per cent. There was not generally a good spirit in the country, and we were bewildered that, having spent six years fighting for the institutions of Britain, we were being told by our government that these institutions were ripe for dismantling. Strikes were very prevalent in heavy industry of all sorts. One of the leading trade unionists of a subsequent period, Hugh Scanlon, who later became Lord Scanlon, said towards the end of his career that he had only just begun to realise what harm he and his ilk had done to the country. Ernest Bevin, however, was highly thought of. He had been a great contributor to the Churchill cabinet, and he was now foreign minister. At an early Durham Miners' Gala after the war he made an impassioned plea that, if they could deliver him 200,000 tons of coal per annum, he and Britain would walk tall in the world. Coal was king in those days, but the miners never did deliver the required volume.

Bevin was nevertheless a great man, and I was immensely impressed on the one occasion I met him, through a namesake, Tom Macpherson. Just before the war Tom had worked with my uncle, Ian Strathcarron, my father and my brother Niall to prepare the way for the founding of the Clan Macpherson Association, which has been a remarkable success in knitting together the clan and in preserving items of immense historical interest in our museum in Newtonmore.

Tom was a private soldier and then a corporal in the First World War, rising from humble origins. He used his gratuity to buy a patch of land near Brechin that was inexpensive because it was covered with bracken and then used the land as security to buy a herd of pigs. He had heard, rightly, that pigs, used intensively, would rootle out the bracken roots and leave the ground in a much more desirable state. He had foreseen that there were going to be food problems in Britain in 1920–1 when he sold off his pigs handsomely and gained some experience in the imported food trade, particularly with hams. He soon built up such a sizeable business empire, which included his own finance house, that by the beginning of the war he was a man of considerable means.

During the war, because of his import-export experience and his business competence, he was appointed regional port controller for Glasgow. It must have been an extremely busy job, with all the convoys coming and going along the Clyde and an immense amount of loading and unloading to be organised. He worked alongside Bevin in his ministerial capacity, and towards the end of the war Bevin approached Tom and asked, 'Why don't you stand for parliament?'

Tom allegedly looked up in absolute astonishment, having never been a political animal, and said, 'Ernest, what party?' The answer soon came, and Tom was elected in 1945 to represent Romford in Essex, doing such a good job that he held the seat in 1950 despite the many Labour losses. Shortly after the election Attlee approached Tom and asked him to accept a peerage and so force a by-election, with former foreign secretary Geoffrey de Freitas standing for the seat after losing his own in 1950. This was how Tom became the 1st Baron Macpherson of Drumochter, although ironically de Freitas was defeated in the subsequent by-election. Tom's family had spent a considerable amount of time as evacuees during the war in Newtonmore, and on my periodic leave I got to know his son Gordon, who was about ten years younger than me. We remained good friends until his death, and I'm happy to say I was able to help Gordon return to the Highlands when he bought Kyllachy House near Tomatin on the River Findhorn, where he remained a happy and generous friend and host until he died in 2008.

If I was not going to London for a party at the weekends, on Sundays I would frequently visit my brother Phil's house at Aston Sandford, near Aylesbury, catching the bus from Oxford to Thame and then walking the remaining three miles. On one of those expeditions I took with me a young Oxford undergraduate called Patty Lindsay, whose family had bought Cluny Castle, the ancestral seat of the Clan Macpherson, in 1943, when it was sold because the owners were deep in debt. When I took Patty to Aston Sandford, we were caught out in the rain and walked almost all of the three miles in a downpour. She had had her hair specially arranged for the occasion, and, by the time we got there, we both looked like drowned rats, but she gamely plodded on and never reproached me for it then or since.

The house at Aston Sandford also holds another happy memory for me. After the finals at Oxford there is one last hurdle called a viva, a verbal test in which three learned examiners fire questions at you to test your in-depth knowledge of the subject. I had asked for my viva to be postponed by two or three days because I was due to run in the finals of the AAA British Athletic Championships at White City on that Friday and Saturday, an unusual request which I knew might annoy the examiners. My request was granted, so I ran in the mile and performed reasonably well before heading up for the rest of the weekend to Aston Sandford, from where I would catch the bus on Monday to be in Oxford in time for Monday afternoon's viva. On the Sunday night my brother entertained a party of very senior and distinguished bankers, economists and academics, and after dinner, over their port, they were discussing a theory applying to the complex world economics of the day. I did not fully understand every nuance, but I picked up enough jargon and detail so that when, completely by chance, a similar question was asked in my viva, I was able to give an answer that, I'm quite sure, tipped the scales and enabled me to get the first that so depressed my economics tutor.

The award of that degree also brought to an end one of the most stable and enjoyable periods of my life, one in which I could immerse myself in the joys of sport and academia without the pressures of real life. From there on out, that luxury was lost to me.

23

An Oval World

An obsession with sport has been one of the defining characteristics of my life. Whether it's rugby, athletics, cricket, hockey, shinty, golf, tennis or skiing, if it involves running, catching, kicking or jumping, then I'll almost certainly have tried it at some stage. Even now I'm still the life-president of the Achilles Club, for athletes who have represented Oxford and Cambridge. Sport is hard-wired into my bones.

As a child I displayed the same sporting competitiveness as my siblings, and with an older brother like Phil we all had a formidable role model to look up to. Although the illness osteomyelitis blighted my schooldays, I still harboured sporting dreams that were only temporarily put on hold by the war. I did play one game of rugby in the Army in 1939, when I joined up, and then another in Alexandria in 1941. When I arrived at Oxford, it was with a determination to work hard but to play even harder. Rugby, hockey and athletics were to be my new battlefields.

At the end of my first week I was invited to play stand-off for an unofficial Oxford Greyhounds side against St Edward's School, Oxford, known as 'Teddies'. The Greyhounds were officially the university's second string, but this game was always regarded as one of the try-out matches. I had clearly been selected because there were fewer new rugby players available than usual and on the back of my prep school and family reputation, because I hadn't played serious rugby since I was 15, with the exception of the occasional wartime game. It was at that match that I first met Ossie Newton-Thompson, from South Africa, who was also at Trinity and had just come up from a wartime flying career in the South African Air Force. He was a fantastic player who was to win two caps for England in 1947, but, more important than being my scrum-half, he became my closest friend. We obviously passed muster that day because we were both elevated to the university squad and picked for the warm-up match against lowly ranked Old Millhillians.

Cars were a rarity at Oxford at that time, and as Archie had nursed my old Ford through several wartime repairs he not unreasonably thought he should have the use of it in the immediate post-war period. I didn't mind because the train was a far more convenient way of reaching my two regular destinations, London and Scotland. Besides, Ossie had been given a majestic old Daimler by his two aunts, who were both called Miss Nettlefold and lived together near Baker Street tube station.

That grand old car transported us to Mill Hill in some style on a wet and soggy afternoon, but it was downhill all the way once we arrived. Although we won, it was soon clear to me that we were a pretty undistinguished side. I played all right, kicking every conversion with a heavy, misshapen, old leather ball, until I stood back a bit from the final kick and tore the top of the thigh muscle in my right leg. It was incredibly sore, but I was damned if I was going to let anyone know. Immediately after the game I consulted a doctor friend of mine, who said, 'You have two choices: either you let it be – it will slow you up but probably won't do any harm until much later in life – or you can have a very lengthy operation.' Such an operation, followed by a lengthy period on crutches, would have stopped my rugby career dead and so was out of the question, which is why I still have a peculiar bulge in my upper thigh.

Ossie and I were a good half-back pairing, but we also hit it off extremely well. He was a year younger than me and had spent most of the war fighting in the Middle East. The Newton-Thompsons had been in South Africa for well over a century, which was an incredibly long time for an English-speaking family. His father was a judge and so well respected for his fairness and totally fluent Afrikaans that he had been invited to make the keynote speech at the Voortrekker Monument, so sacred to the Afrikaners. His widow was the mayor of Cape Town, and they lived in a lovely house in the shadow of Newlands cricket and rugby ground, where I had the great pleasure of staying before she died.

Ossie was a young pilot when he married his wife, Helen, and the strain of his wartime absences and his decision to take up a Rhodes scholarship in Oxford immediately the war ended put a tremendous stress on his marriage, which was eventually dissolved. This was constantly on Ossie's mind throughout his time at Oxford, not least when we shared rooms together in our second year. Fortunately, they were eventually reconciled and remarried, with Helen coming over to Oxford and their marriage turning out to be a long and happy one.

Their lives weren't without heartache, however. Ossie and Helen had two daughters and a son, Andrew, who was the apple of their eye. Aged 18 and doing his military service, Andrew showed the Newton-Thompson desire to excel at everything when he won a fitness test that involved running cross-country in the South African heat, no doubt carrying packs of equipment. But it was more than his body could take, and shortly after that run he collapsed and died. This was an enormous tragedy that left a permanent scar on both Ossie and Helen. Gallantly, they decided to augment their family – the girls were grown up by that time – and although they dearly wished for a son, the two girls they had after Andrew's death are lovely and deeply loved by their parents. Lindy, their youngest, became my godchild and when she was in Britain was very much under my eye.

Ossie, a barrister, went into politics and became deputy leader of South Africa's United Party, the only viable opposition at that time to the nationalists. Popular and respected, during the 1974 general election campaign he addressed countless opposition rallies, criss-crossing the country in his little plane. On 3 April 1974, however, as he was leaving Windhoek, a storm came out of nowhere and a flurry of dust cut straight across the runway, blowing into his engine and stalling it. Ossie died immediately his plane hit the ground. He remains a huge loss to his family and friends, among whom I am proud to count myself.

After my rugby debut against Mill Hill, my performances as stand-off improved steadily until halfway through the term, when the previous year's stand-off, a West Countryman called Tommy Cuff, reappeared. Unfortunately, this was just in time for the game against the all-conquering New Zealand tourists of that year, which meant that I was selected in the centre, a position I had never played in before. I did not have a good game, and to make matters worse I also managed to injure both thumbs and was heavily strapped up for the rest of term. As a result I wasn't invited to play against Cambridge in the Varsity match, although I did have the satisfaction of playing for the Greyhounds against the university and making a considerable mess of my opposite number, one Tommy Cuff.

The following winter's rugby followed a depressingly familiar pattern, as I was concussed in the first game. That meant a fortnight off, which is quite a lot in an eight-week term. During that time my place was taken by New Zealander Martin Donnelly, who was a tremendous athlete, a very fine international cricketer – whom I watched make a century at The Oval in 1937, when he was 19 – and a talented rugby player. I thought he would make a better centre than stand-off, and the England selectors agreed with me by picking him against Ireland in 1947. But, because Oxford insisted on picking him at stand-off, to my intense annoyance I missed out on my second Varsity match.

If my rugby career at Oxford wasn't following the script, there were at least several enjoyable distractions. In the autumn of 1945, when I was not playing for the university, I responded to an invitation from London Scottish to join them and play for their first XV. Because of my university commitments, I was only rarely able to play for the Exiles, but mainly because of the captaincy of Keith Geddes I greatly enjoyed my games with them. A former pupil of Loretto School in Edinburgh, Keith was one of the best full-backs I ever played with and a very good captain. From January 1946 to the end of 1947 my rugby was also constantly interrupted by my athletics commitments, but from 1948 onwards I played regularly. My official role was as captain of the Seconds, but I played the vast majority of my games for the Firsts, although my versatility meant that I was treated as a utility player and featured in every position in the backs, from scrum-half to full-back. Back in those days teams were numbered the other way round, so that the full-back wore the No. 1 jersey, which meant that, as my preferred position was at stand-off, my shirt usually had a 6 on its back.

London Scottish had a vast number of players who were irregularly available because they were either schoolmasters who couldn't get away in term time or on international duty, so there were always gaps to be filled. I also struggled to fill them, because early in my working career we were in the office on Saturday mornings and it was only by special arrangement that I could leave early for away games. Even home games were a rush: I would leave the office when business closed at half past twelve and would rush along to Broad Street to take the slow train that circles north London to Richmond, eating a meat pie and a bit of chocolate on the train to prepare me for the game. Saturday working stopped during the 1950s, so it became easier to fit in with every game, home or away.

I loved playing for the club until I hung up my boots in 1955, although conditions weren't always so salubrious in those days. I still remember a game against Bath when we arrived shortly after the ground had been flooded to find a small dead fish on the waterlogged centre line and had to jump into the sulphurous and historic Roman baths in our full kit after the match because their primitive clubhouse had no showers. However, there were ample compensations, such as the camaraderie and the fact that for much of my time with the club I played in an all-international back line that at various stages included such marvellous players as the brothers Logie and Rab Bruce Lockhart, centres Donald Sloan and the South African-born Kim Elgie, wings Doug Smith and Ian Swan, and the great Ken Marshall or Stewart Wilson at full-back.

Finding myself playing stand-off in such celebrated company each week, I did occasionally feel intensely frustrated that I was never selected to play for Scotland. Every one of my contemporaries in the London Scottish back division was capped, yet, despite the fact that I was creating the openings for them, the call never came. The nearest I got was a letter telling me that I was a non-travelling reserve for two games. Perhaps I would have seen this as a source of pride and achievement rather than frustration had I not been the baby brother of the great GPS Macpherson. I was always very conscious of the burden of Phil's reputation upon me.

Still, if I suffered from inopportune injuries at Oxford and was frustrated that my form with London Scottish didn't see me emulate my much-idolised elder brother, there was at least a huge amount of light relief through a series of tours that took us to mainland Europe. My annual income of £300 – my two scholarships making £160 and my father giving me £140 – was fairly average for a post-war undergraduate, and, while it didn't allow for great luxuries, there was just enough left over for the overseas rugby and athletics tours that were run on a shoestring in those days. I'm still not sure how we did it, because finances were so tight that tracksuits were simply not available to the likes of us, but we would warm up for games or races wearing our oldest pair of flannel trousers and a couple of sweaters.

At Easter 1946 I toured as the Oxford stand-off when we were invited to go down to Biarritz for the town's formal reopening after the war years as a spa and holiday destination of distinction. The wife of the British ambassador to France was the famous actress Lady Diana Cooper, who took part in the tremendous festivities, which included a most splendid party at the casino. We had been deprived of bright lights and luxuries, and the endless stream of pink champagne with which we were feted by our French hosts was a total novelty to all of us. We all felt dreadful the next morning, but at least we could take solace from the fact that our chaperones had been our opposite numbers, who had also indulged mightily. Or so we thought until, during the endless 'Marseillaise', we stole a glance at our opponents and, to our horror and subsequent amusement, didn't recognise a single face. Our 15 'opponents' from the previous night had disappeared, leaving us to face their daisy-fresh replacements. We were technically quite a good side, so we scored a lot of points in the first half, but as the booze began to take its toll we faded badly and were eventually overhauled. But it was great fun and a good lesson to us all.

From there we went into the real heartland of French rugby in Pau and Tarbes and enjoyed hard but successful games and magnificent banquets afterwards. As our interpreter, I had to translate lots of sentimental post-war stuff from our hosts, which was nevertheless well received. The next tour was a university one in December 1946, when we played in Paris, and my contacts there meant that I was delegated to exchange the squad's money on the black market, which gave a much better price than the open market. Our money was changed by Denis Cournil – the cousin of my wartime confrère Bernard – who was operating a splendid restaurant in Les Halles. That evening my brother-in-law Jim Mackintosh had asked me to look after the Australian high commissioner to London and his wife. They were great friends of his but didn't know Paris, so I took them to Denis's restaurant. Denis, however, had alerted almost every other Resistance person in Paris who had known me, and the Australians were astonished by a steady flow of rather rough-looking citizens who all rushed up and embraced me with warm kisses on each cheek.

After Paris we took the overnight sitting-up train to Nantes. We arrived to find the ground frozen solid and didn't expect to play, but our hosts had financed our tour and couldn't afford not to have a game. Most of us were extremely careful not to tackle or to hit the ground in the game that followed, which was unsurprisingly very high scoring. The one exception was our captain and scrum-half, Ossie Newton-Thompson, who hurled himself about so recklessly that by the time we reached half-time he was covered top-to-toe in his own blood. It was only in the interval that we discovered Nantes had an extra player, who had been running late and had changed in the taxi before simply joining in when he arrived. No wonder we struggled to score before the break, although we ran in a couple of tries soon into the second half and won comfortably.

These tours of Europe were a marvellous institution, and because much of the continent was still militarily occupied at that time a lot of the organisational onus fell on me, with my military and continental contacts. The tours to Germany between 1948 and 1950, when I was allowed to play because I was the organiser, were memorable. That particularly applied to the tour to Germany in 1948, when we took a strong side and played first in the West before flying into Berlin during the blockade by the Russians, who were trying to force the Allies to quit the German capital. What became known as the Berlin Airlift was a dramatic episode that lasted for almost a year, during which all goods and people had to be flown into the city's three airports, which were a riot of activity twenty-four hours a day. We flew in from a military airport in Holland in an old twin-engine propeller York aircraft, which was totally bare apart from some sacking on the floor that we sat on. It was used for transporting coal and salt, which meant that the fuselage had rotted away in places; as the pilot explained, this meant we couldn't go higher than 2,000 feet, otherwise we might implode with the pressure.

Berlin was amazing. We came down in the British military airport of Gatow and were able to observe the extraordinary organisation of aircraft coming in every two minutes without any of the sophisticated equipment that guides them today. Myriad Berliners scurried about like ants, unloading the precious supplies without which the city would have starved. It was an amazing achievement, and the government of the day showed great fortitude in insisting that Berlin had to be held. The atmosphere in the city was fascinating. I was staying with the Black Watch brigadier commanding troops in Berlin, Brigadier Russell, and what I found was akin to what I imagine Vienna must have been like at the time of the Napoleonic post-war congress in 1814, where there was a famously glittering social life. Every evening the French, Americans or

British were giving parties – at least two or three a night – from which we could choose. Perhaps the social scene was just to show that there was no spirit of defeatism, that we were not going to go away; or perhaps it was just to counterbalance the tension that pervaded the city.

Either way, we had a very big turnout of appreciative Berliners for the match against the British Army at the Olympic Stadium, which was in the British sector. It was a privilege to be playing there after hearing all about the excitement of Jesse Owens's wins in the 1936 Olympics from our old friend and doctor Robert Kennedy, who had been one of the British high jumpers at that Games. He got into the finals with a jump of six feet two inches, which was very good at that time. Today, the top women in the world routinely jump higher, and seven feet two inches would not guarantee a place in the men's Olympic high-jump final.

The following spring we took the Oxford team to Italy. By 1949 I was working in the timber firm of William Mallinson and Sons, but they were very good at releasing me for sport and finding ways of getting round the regulations of the company – in fact, that's the main reason I stayed there in those early years. Mallinson and Sons sent me out to Milan in the company of Arnold, a wizened little white-haired man who was an expert at veneers. He could look at a dirty log arrived from Africa and say exactly how it could be cut and what the veneer would look like in its manufactured state. I learnt a great deal from him as we did some inspection and buying in Milan before I joined the team there, having arranged the programme for them.

The first game was in Genoa, the second in Milan and the third in Rome, where we faced the full Italian side, perhaps the first match they had played against a British team. We played in the Lazio football stadium, which was a daunting experience because the stands were encased in rabbit-wire netting to prevent missiles being thrown at the players, but we managed to win a hard-fought struggle of a match. That game was the only time that I kicked a left-footed drop goal in a first-class match, a decision forced upon me by a horribly wayward pass from my erratic scrum-half, a fellow Scotsman called Jimmy Galbraith who won a Blue that year. As it was an international match we had a neutral referee, who turned out to be an old friend of mine from France, Serge Saulnier. Serge could be quite temperamental and decided that the Italian touch judge was cheating, so he reprimanded him once, reprimanded him twice and then sent him off and demanded a replacement – an act that was surely unprecedented.

While in Rome the squad were invited to have a private audience with the Pope, and as manager and interpreter I did the introductions. It was fascinating to be taken through the Sistine Chapel and the Holy Father's private apartments to meet the Pope, especially as he was shortly to become a highly controversial figure for his alleged favouritism to the Nazi cause during the war. Almost as memorable, if in an entirely different way, was an incident later that night after the excellent banquet thrown for us by the Italian rugby federation. At the end of the night their forwards carried little Mr Olivetti, the managing director of the eponymous company and the president of the federation, down the street on their shoulders. Unfortunately, one of the Italians was diverted by a pretty girl in a doorway and absent-mindedly moved aside, dropping Mr Olivetti sharply on the street, where he broke a rib.

I played rugby as often as work allowed, and it would take me all over the world. In my final year at Oxford we toured the south of France, playing the fearsome town sides of Marseilles and Toulon, where the concept of '*rugby de la cloche*' – or never being beaten within the sound of the church bells of your home town – translated itself into ferociously hard games.

As well as Oxford and London Scottish, I also experienced some Army rugby after the war when I joined the Territorial SAS. That allowed me to play for the Territorial Army until I left the regiment, just before I got married, in 1952, and for the last two or three years I captained the TA against the Army and others. One occasion that really sticks in my mind is when I and a fellow Oxford scrum-half called Derek Ashcroft were pitted against Evan Hardy and Dennis Shuttleworth of the Yorkshire Regiment, who were at that time England's first choice half-backs. I'm happy to say we didn't come out at all badly.

In 1955 my first-class rugby career came to an end after successive seasons of great enjoyment – almost increasing enjoyment, as I played more consistently and probably better in the later years than in the earlier ones. At least I went out on a high, with my last game turning out to be against the London Irish side in which a young wing called Tony O'Reilly, who went on to become one of the greatest Ireland and British Lions players of all time, made his debut. Tony was later to become a good friend with whom I would mix business and pleasure at his delightful home in Castlemartin, County Kildare. One regret I have is that I never played against his closest colleague and another great Irish player, Jim McCarthy, whom I knew through the timber trade in Dublin and who became, and remains, an extremely good friend of mine.

When my regular rugby stopped, it was largely because of an unusual injury. I had hurt my shoulder against London Irish and a few days later woke up after spending a night on the sleeper from Scotland to find my upper back and neck were in agony. I could barely be carted off home in a taxi, and over the next few days the pain became almost unbearable. Although it eventually subsided after some extremely unpleasant physio from a specialist at St Thomas' Hospital, I decided that my rugby days had drawn to a close.

That wasn't quite the end of the story, however. At the end of the decade I was down at London Scottish and was dragged out of the bar as an emergency measure to play for the Seconds against London Irish, taking great care not to tackle anyone and to pass the ball as quickly as possible. I obviously wasn't quite as hopeless as I felt and was part of a group of over-35-year-old veterans dispatched to play in the Chiltern Sevens. We might have been oldies, but with players like Logie Bruce Lockhart we were also goodies, and after an appalling start, where we won only 3–0 by a penalty goal – which is strictly not kosher for Sevens – we romped away with the tournament, much to everyone's amazement and horror. This time, though, enough was enough: I remain an obsessive watcher of the game to this day, but with my 40th birthday hoving into view my playing days were finally over.

24

Achilles Heel

Although rugby was a large part of my sporting life, I never let it dominate me to the exclusion of all other sporting pursuits. We were left in little doubt of sport's place in our firmament at Oxford, where it was strictly confined to the afternoons, mainly between two and four. We would make our way to Iffley Road for rugby in the winter and hockey in the spring, but we were always back at our desks by five and working until dinner. Sport was, nevertheless, taken very seriously and was of a high standard, partly because so many undergraduates had returned to complete their studies after the war and were in their mid or late 20s. There was, for instance, no doubt at all that the 1946–7 Oxford University side skippered by Ossie Newton-Thompson was the best XV in Britain.

Although we trained very hard, the ethos was enormously amateur and friendly, and it was considered quite normal for people to play multiple sports. There were numerous double Blues back then, and no one thought it odd that I would play rugby for the university on Saturday, hockey on Monday and run in the relays against Cambridge on Thursday. I was to maintain this approach throughout my life, and in 1955, when I finally gave up rugby, I took up hockey with Mid Surrey, who played on the same ground as London Scottish in Richmond. I spent three years in their red-and-white shirts, enjoying myself as a reasonably prolific centre-forward and even managing to be selected to play for the Anglo-Scots. Such diversity wasn't helpful in my campaign to get a rugby Blue, however, because the Varsity athletics meetings were in March, so from January onwards I moved from the rugby field to the running track and spent less and less time on rugby.

I was a fairly talented runner, winning the mile in 4 mins 40 secs at

Fettes, a record that stood for 50 years, but if I had led a charmed life during the war, when it came to the sports arena I had an injury and illness jinx. In the 1946 match against Cambridge I was the first-string miler only to get a heavy cold and get beaten by my second string. The following year, after Roger Bannister and I had been training together in his first year as a medical student – and he was already showing enormous potential with his huge lung capacity – I caught measles in Scotland just days before the Varsity athletics match and arrived looking spotty and feverish before running very indifferently.

That summer I beat Roger over half a mile during one of the regular intermural races staged at Iffley Road and have always delighted in being able to say that I defeated the first four-minute miler. Later that summer I also ran against Sydney 'The Mighty Atom' Wooderson in Dublin and against Emile Zátopek in Paris, both amazing athletes. Wooderson had been at his best before the war as world-record holder before his mark was overtaken by New Zealander Jack Lovelock, another Achilles member, while Zátopek amazed us all at the 1948 Olympic Games in London with his 'rolling head' style, which was agony to look at because it seemed as though he was in pain. He assured me, however, that it didn't hurt at all. Zátopek was amazingly fit and ran like a machine, as he was to prove in the 1952 Olympics in Helsinki. He had already won two golds in those Games but had never competed in the marathon before and was running alongside the favourite, English world-record holder Jim Peters. This, thought the Czech, would give him a speed guidance, so halfway through the 26 miles he turned to an exhausted Peters and said, 'Shouldn't we be going a little faster?' before accelerating away and winning gold in a world-record time.

In 1946 and 1947, for two summers running, I won the mile at the Three Nations Student Internationals between England, Scotland and Ireland, even if I was in many ways an anomaly. In those days you ran for the nation of your university, and as I was at Oxford I ran for England. The first year I won quite easily, but in the second Student International, which was held in Aberdeen, I was up against a Manchester athlete of considerable stature, called Parker, who had defeated me in an earlier race. My victory produced the *Sunday Express* headline 'Scotsman wins for England' and one of the most memorable finishes of my athletics career, with the Oxford, Cambridge and Scottish spectators cheering me home over the last 100 yards while the red-brick spectators willed Parker to catch me. It sounds as if it was a very class-conscious society in those days; it wasn't – certainly not on the athletic field – but it was highly personalised.

As a result of that victory I was selected for the British team at the World University Games in Paris in 1947, but it was not a success. In my crowded 1,500-metre heat, won by Zátopek, there was an enormous amount of jostling, and on the second lap I was barged off the track, twisting my ankle on the concrete surround and aggravating an old injury.

From Paris my next stop was Trieste, where I had been invited to run in an Army athletics meeting. Irritatingly, after my debacle in the World University Games in Paris, and having had no training and lots of wine since then, I ran the fastest time of my life in what turned out to be my last serious race. My next stop was Udine, where I had been active in the war and where I joined up with Ezio Bruno Londero, who, under the code name Nino, had been my faithful messenger and bodyguard throughout most of my time in Italy. He and I decided to go for a mountain hike, as, for him, it was to be a last fling before his wedding. We went up to an extraordinary isolated valley on the north side of our old territory, where the dialect remains much closer to Magyar than it is to Italian, and from there climbed up until we reached the 9,000-foot summit of the Monte Canin glacier, reputedly the lowest in Europe. The weather was magnificent, and by the time we climbed back down we were so hot that we plunged into the marvellously deep rock pool by our inn, only to find that we couldn't get out. This quickly proved to be a big issue because the stream that fed the pool came straight off the glacier and was ice cold, but the rocks from which we had dived had an inward curve at the top and were totally slippery and impossible to climb. Nino got out by standing on my shoulders, and then, by hook or crook, he managed to pull me out, very cold and very glad to be clear of the water.

Back at home I was playing a lot of rugby and taking my athletics seriously, but not too seriously. I had the opportunity of being in the 1948 London Olympic squad as a miler, having been a finalist in the AAA's championship, but in the summer of 1948 I had begun to work as a part-time PA to Stuart Mallinson, the chairman of the company I had joined, while also continuing to work part-time as a trainee in various departments. It's difficult to appreciate in these days of full-time funding and driving Olympic ambition, but back in 1948 business and athletics at that level simply didn't go together.

I was, however, keen to be involved in an event that marked the first real revival of London from its wartime misery at a time when Britain was still at the height of its prestige and popularity in post-war Europe. So, when I was invited to help prepare some of the female athletes, which gave me an inside track into the splendid Games that took place at the White City, I jumped at the chance. One of the girls whom I helped – mainly because she trained at Iffley Road in Oxford – was June Gardner, whose silver medal in ladies' sprint hurdles was unfortunately completely overshadowed by the undoubted star of those Olympics, Fanny Blankers-Koen. The deeply charming Dutch housewife swept through the sprints, the hurdles and the relays, winning gold after gold. She came to personify those Games, although I also vividly remember the Jamaican 4x400-metre relay team, which was stuffed with outstanding performers and led by the lanky Arthur Wint, whose enormous stride seemed to devour the ground.

Although working for Stuart Mallinson meant that running in the Olympics was never a realistic proposition, my new boss's all-consuming interest in sport allowed me to make the most of that halcyon summer of sport in 1948. As well as the Olympics, it was an amazing summer for cricket, with Don Bradman leading the Australian team in England for the last time. Stuart Mallinson and I saw his Australia side score 740 runs in one day against Essex at Southend, but we also saw England's Trevor Bailey and Vic Watson bat almost right through the day to save the Lord's Test against the legendary attack of Ray Lindwall and Keith Miller. Jeff Thomson, in later years, was faster than both of them, but Lindwall and Miller were the most precise fast bowlers who have ever been paired. I had the interesting experience of standing in the nets at Oxford when they were preparing for their game in the Parks against the university and fended off a few balls from each of them as they did their warm-up.

Stuart Mallinson's catholic tastes in sport extended far beyond cricket. He took me to Wembley several times for the big games, including the two Amateur Cup finals to feature Pegasus, the Oxford–Cambridge combination. We also saw the famous 'Matthews Final' of 1953 in which Stanley Matthews and Stan Mortensen magicked Blackpool through, and two Scotland–England games. In the first of these England triumphed comfortably after an unfortunate Celtic goalkeeper let two in through his legs, with Matthews tormenting the unfortunate Clyde full-back Harry Haddock, who looked a fish out of water. Mallinson and I were also there when Scotland got their revenge, winning by a smaller score but with total dominance at Wembley. Rangers' maverick maestro Jim Baxter totally dominated the field and so hypnotised the English players that he was able to juggle the ball in 'keepie-uppie' fashion while everyone else simply looked on.

We were also regular visitors to Wimbledon and were there when the young Christine Truman, who was a regular guest and tennis player at Stuart Mallinson's home, reached the ladies' final. Stuart and I went a number of times to Wimbledon in the early years to see those great Australians, Rosewall, Hoad and Laver, and then later to witness Boris Becker's emergence as a young red-haired tyro of the game with immense power and agility.

Of all those outstanding performances, however, I yield to no one that the most remarkable player of any game I ever saw was my brother GPS, who so often completely dominated the field of whatever club or international match he was playing in. Nor was I alone, which is why he captained the Scotland–Ireland side in the first ever Scotland–Ireland v. England–Wales celebration game to commemorate the centenary of Rowland Hill and the Penny Post.

Throughout this time I was still playing and organising rugby and athletics tours. In 1950, for instance, I was able to set up an Achilles tour to Greece. Achilles is a club for past and present Oxford and Cambridge university athletes, and at that time we were able to turn out a strong side featuring future Olympic gold medallists in Chris Brasher and Roger Bannister. That team also included my great friend Derek Steele, who was asked by the Greek press which of the 400 metres and 800 metres he preferred, to which he replied, 'Whichever I'm not doing at the time.'

We ran in Greece against the two leading athletics clubs, the Panathenian and the Panhellenic, in the stadium that had been put up by the Greeks for the first modern Olympic Games in 1896. It was modelled on the ancient Peloponnesian Olympian arena, which meant that the straights were long and the curves at the two ends were very sharp indeed. You were in a hopeless position if you were a 200-metre sprinter and on the inside lane, which meant that you had to wait and attack when you eventually got to the straight. The arena, besides its shape, was structured like an ancient Greek arena, with stone terracing to sit upon going up all round the oval and weather-beaten statues adorning the top row of the seating area.

The Greeks were enthusiastic about our visit and asked me to place a wreath on the war memorial in Constitution Square, an act that took place in the presence of a surprising number of Athenians. When I was invited to visit the then head of government, who gloried in the rather difficult name of General Nikolaos Plastiras – pronounced 'plaster arse' – he gave us two enormous carved-plaster ancient-Greek reproduction things for our clubhouse. We handed them over for safe keeping to Norris McWhirter, who at that stage was a little-known 25-year-old former Trinity College and Scotland athlete but who would go on to become a Fleet Street sports journalist by the end of that year and then later founded the *Guinness Book of Records*. They were, thankfully, never seen again.

The Greek press gave us extensive coverage, concentrating on established stars, like Chris Brasher in the 5,000 metres. The real favourite of the crowds, however, was freakishly tall hurdler Ray Barkway, a great character with probably the finest and most elegant hurdling style I've ever seen. Unfortunately, he ran rather slowly; fortunately, his Greek opponents ran even more slowly.

Our ambassador to Greece was an Achilles runner called Gus Tatham, and he could not have been more hospitable or helpful. He also had a very attractive daughter who rustled up an extraordinary number of equally attractive ladies to enliven our social life. From Athens we went on to Rome to meet an Italian university team, only to find that they had been unable to raise a team. They still provided us with hotel rooms and even laid on some entertainment in our hotel lounge in the form of ladies of spectacularly easy virtue. I remember one of my colleagues approaching a dark beauty and chatting her up a bit until finally she gently explained that the first thing he could expect if he went further was a large bill. He departed rapidly, and I think that was the view of us all.

I still maintain my long-running association with the Achilles Club, and these days I am the president. Our main task has been always to help undergraduates with athletic improvement, coaching and competition, to help stage tours abroad and to organise their quadrennial series of matches with American Ivy League universities, which have been held for over 100 years. This Anglo–American series almost lapsed in the '50s because of a lack of cash at our end, and it has been an uphill struggle to maintain the funds to keep the competition going.

25

By Royal Appointment

My sporting and academic life at Oxford was a fantastic relief after the harshness of military life. It was a world I enjoyed and one I might have stayed in after I was unexpectedly given a chance to work temporarily as a tutor. Towards the end of my first term I was unexpectedly summoned to see Dr Elliott, the headmaster of Eton. I had no idea why this might be until shortly before the meeting when my university friend James Ramsden explained that he had also been approached by Elliott, who had been charged with finding a tutor for a member of the royal family. James had declined for family reasons and had suggested me instead.

I had an interesting if slightly alarming interview with Dr Elliott, who was certainly a formidable character. I apparently passed muster, though, because he not only put me forward for the task but also offered me a teaching job at Eton as soon as I came down. That wasn't an offer to be refused lightly, especially because when you're at university you view the end of short days and lengthy holidays with some alarm and the onset of personal responsibility with something approaching horror. I did, however, eventually decide to decline his kind offer.

The job for which I was proposed was to be in the Duchess of Kent's household and particularly to look after her eldest son, the then young Prince Edward, who would go on to become the Duke of Kent. It was a particularly important job because his father had been tragically killed in an air accident in Caithness during the war. I was initially sent for by the formidable Tommy Lascelles, the King's long-time secretary, in the tower at Windsor Castle. He passed me on to Captain Hamilton of the Royal Navy, who was the chief equerry in the household and who gave me a very full briefing of what would be expected in relation to the royal family. I learnt that, when not immediately required by the Duchess, I would become an extra equerry for general royal engagements. Only then, with their blessing, did I see the Duchess of Kent herself. She was, at that meeting over the teacups, extremely charming, as she was during the rest of my time in her household and subsequently. She was a lady of character and culture, with a very interesting collection of friends who regularly dined at their house, Coppins, in Buckinghamshire. Perhaps the most intimate of these was the conductor Malcolm Sargent, who was extremely good dinner-table company and could always bring a smile to the face of his hostess – which was not always an easy thing to do because she found widowhood a rather sad experience.

The children were great fun. Michael was the youngest and not really out of the nursery, while Edward and his sister, Alexandra, who were around eleven and ten respectively, were immensely enjoyable to be with. Edward had clearly been short of male company, and we very soon got on extremely well. I was to report to Birkhall – which was then the Queen's own house near Balmoral and which is where Prince Charles now stays – in the summer, when the royal family moved north. I recovered my old Ford car from my brother Archie and drove over there with, I hoped, all the right clothing. I knew that it was dinner jackets and black tie every night, but I had a considerable shortage of the stiff collars that were always worn in those days with a dinner jacket, so I sent a telegram to my Aunt Jill in London to see what she could do, because no such thing would be obtainable in deepest Inverness-shire. She, with her usual generosity and without the use of clothing coupons, somehow rustled up a dozen collars, which turned up in a handsome parcel on my arrival in Birkhall and were extremely welcome because I was placed next to Queen Mary at the first dinner.

The children loved my noisy open car, but it gave their mother a headache, so she avoided it as far as possible. We had great freedom on the Birkhall Estate and frequently went up to Loch Muick. There, on one occasion, quite a severe storm came out of nowhere when I had Edward and Alexandra out in a rowing boat up at the far end of the loch. Nobody dreamt of life jackets or anything like that in those days. As there was a good deal of splashing, and I didn't want movement, I made them both sit on the floor of the boat while I pulled manfully at the oars to get, against wind and rain, down to the far end to the landing stage. Years afterwards, when I joked with Princess Alexandra that I had seen her in her bath, she said, 'Ah, but when I was on the floor of the boat in Loch Muick I was able to look up your kilt, and that was the first one I had seen.'

After ten days or so Edward, with me looking after him, was invited to join the main royal party at Balmoral, and we spent about a fortnight there. During the day he went out with me and the shooting parties, and we sat in various butts of the good and the great during what was a splendidly sunny summer. The King, who was an extremely good shot, had his favourites at lunch, which was served, quite simply, in picnic style. It was not at all grand, but, curiously enough, there was always a crested menu, and it was invariably headed with 'Mousse Grouse', for which the King had his standard joke of 'Moosse Groosse' each time it appeared. The Queen's brother, David Bowes-Lyon, was there during that period, and we got on well, as he knew my brother Phil from the banking world. I sat in his butt many times, and he was certainly one of the best grouse shots I have ever seen.

Edward and I were encouraged to potter about on a secluded piece of the Balmoral moor to train him to the gun. He had a nice double-barrelled .410, and he was a natural with it, learning very rapidly. I remember the excitement of the first bird he got. I remember, too, a near contretemps when I saw a curled-up adder just in front of him and I pointed to it with the muzzle of my gun. His reaction was that I was about to be attacked, and, to save me, he shot the adder at point-blank range and very nearly took my foot off.

The following Christmas followed a somewhat similar pattern in that Edward and I were invited, over the New Year and early January, to Sandringham, which was even more a family party. It was a very cold January, but everyone went out every day and enjoyed it greatly. I recall particularly Princess Alice, the last relic of Queen Victoria's family, and her husband, the Earl of Athlone, who was an absolute caricature of a Victorian club gentleman, almost straight out of a Spy cartoon but one of the nicest and kindest people you could possibly meet. He often helped outsiders like me navigate life at Court, acting as an intermediary where necessary.

I was always very aware of quite how well turned out everyone was, especially as I was struggling to re-establish a wardrobe. I remember walking back from Sandringham Church with Edward Ford, who was assistant private secretary and later became private secretary to the King and subsequently the Queen. He was immaculately turned out in a tweed suit, whereas I had managed to get myself a length of very nice tweed but hadn't had time to get to our family tailor in Inverness so had sent him the cloth and my measurements, as recorded by my mother. The result was a hideously badly cut suit with trousers whose behind sagged pendulously. I must have looked quite a sight next to the dapper courtiers.

At Balmoral, Sunday church was a special occasion. For reasons of security and convenience we were generally driven down to Crathie Kirk, which is just at the gates of the castle, and then the royal family were driven back while the household walked back with the younger guests. In that summer of 1947 our present Queen and Prince Philip were in the final stages of courting, and they had a small number of regular visitors of their own age. The two that I remember best were Johnny Althorp, later Earl Spencer and Princess Diana's father, who was such an expert fisherman that I often watched as he popped down to the Dee in the castle grounds for half an hour and invariably caught a fish. The other regular visitor, certainly at Sandringham if not at Balmoral, was Porchy, Lord Porchester, later the Earl of Carnarvon, who became the Queen's racing manager. His skills were more social and very amusing, but I never saw him walk an unnecessary step.

In the Easter of 1947, when I was at Coppins, the French government decided to elevate me to the *Légion d'honneur*, with the degree of *Chevalier*, with the presentation to be made at the French Embassy. Princess Marina, Duchess of Kent, very kindly lent me her ceremonial car and chauffeur for this occasion, and off I went, decked for the last time in full Cameron Highlander uniform, with Special Forces badges upon it, to receive the insignia. Curiously enough, many years later the French government, recognising my work for ex-Resistance fighters and several other high-profile duties, like opening monuments in France, elevated me to the grade of *Officier* in the *Légion d'honneur*, but Geoffrey Howe's Foreign Office refused permission on the grounds that they couldn't permit the accepting of foreign awards retrospectively, although my understanding was that this was for current activities. That particular excuse was later blown away by the award of the *Légion d'honneur*, accepted by the Foreign Office, to remaining veterans of the 1914–18 war in Britain.

The master of the Duchess's household was Lord Herbert, a kindly and experienced man with a lifetime of royal service. In the same way that Dr Elliott tempted me with the offer of a job at Eton, I certainly considered continuing in royal service at a higher level. Lord Herbert advised very strongly against it, taking the kindly view that I was capable of rising to a more eminent position in the wider world. He told me that I would become stifled by an atmosphere he described as inward-looking, parochial, locked in precedent and out of touch with the modern world. That turned out to be good advice, which is why strenuous efforts have recently been made by two prominent lords chamberlain – Lord Camoys and Lord Luce, both good friends of mine – to modernise the organisation.

26

Domestic Bliss

On leaving Oxford, I passed over the options of teaching, being a courtier and turning to the law to join William Mallinsons in October 1947. My social life was also very active, with 1953 turning out to be a genuinely landmark year. In fact, one night that year changed the course of my life.

It was a Saturday towards the end of March, and I was trying to cram two dinners into one evening. The first was the annual dinner of the London Scottish Rugby Club, which was always enormous fun in those days, with everyone turning out in Highland dress. From there I rushed up to Gunters, near the Dorchester, which was where the Achilles Ball was being held after the Oxford and Cambridge athletics match. By the time I arrived, the ball was in full swing and I was also in very relaxed form after my earlier dinner.

My good friend Roger Bannister was at a table entertaining a party of ladies, so I joined them and was immediately persuaded by one of my new friends to climb onto the table so that she could study the differences between my knees, one of which was hairless due to having had a plaster on it until recently, while the other was as nature intended. From that vantage point I noticed that two of the girls at Roger's table were twins, Jean and Anne Butler-Wilson. I'm told regularly that they are identical and that it is extraordinarily difficult to tell them apart, but, from that first meeting, I had no trouble at all, and my eyes lighted on Jean in a way that left no room for doubt in my mind.

We danced, we talked and I discovered that she was studying teaching at the University of Edinburgh and was at that time on a work placement at a school in Gloucestershire that had a famous arboretum. On the Monday morning my secretary soon identified the school as Westonbirt.

I got in touch with Jean and persuaded her to join me for the London Scottish dance a fortnight later at Ripley, out near Woking. When she got there, we talked and danced until our feet hurt, but I also discovered that she was unofficially engaged to a very nice but rather boring and rather deaf architect. Needless to say, I worked hard to dissuade her from what was quite clearly an unsuitable fate. She had one of those bubble-shaped Morris Minors on loan from her father, so we drove up to London, where I thought that she had relatives with whom she was staying. On the way it became clear that this wasn't the case and that she had no roof over her head, having thought that I was inviting her to stay with my family. I was in digs in Hampstead with a very nice family called the Braithwaites, so she crept in with me in the middle of the night, and I installed her in the bedroom of their son, who was away at school. The following morning there was some surprise on the part of my landlord and landlady, but they took it all in good part and assumed that an engagement would follow. Life was like that in those days, and an engagement, I'm happy to say, did follow quite quickly.

After that, whenever we could, we went up to her parents' home in Alderley Edge, near Macclesfield, for the weekend. Jean's father, David Butler-Wilson, was a proud Scot who had served in the Royal Scots during the First World War before transferring to the Royal Flying Corps and flying his plane so high on one sortie that he burst his eardrums and became permanently deaf. Jean's mother was small, neat and extremely intelligent and welcomed me into the family with surprise but no suspicion.

In her childhood Jean had been severely asthmatic and immediately before the war had been sent to convalesce in the clean air of the Swiss Alps. One of the doctors there was a Canadian, Dr Campbell, one of Jean's father's fellow Rotarians who was on an exchange from Canada. When the war broke out, Jean and her twin, Anne, were sent off as evacuees to stay with him. The girls grew up with the Campbell family and have maintained a loving association with them, although they were lucky to have got to Canada at all: the sister ship of the *Duchess of Atholl*, on which Jean and Anne sailed from Liverpool, was also transporting evacuees but was torpedoed and sank with very few survivors.

By the time the twins came home via the United States and Portugal, they were long, leggy girls, and, arriving at the railway station where they were to be met, they were totally unable to recognise their parents. However, the reunion was made and was successful. Jean's asthma had also improved greatly, although it occasionally returned in times of emotional stress, such as our wedding. There was one occasion, after her term had ended, when I visited Alderley Edge and could hear her pathetic voice from her bedroom saying, 'Don't let him see me, don't let him see me!' Of course, I went in, because, while her face was swollen and her voice and cough were harsh, to me she was still beautiful. So, on 26 September 1953 we were married in Edinburgh, and life was never the same again.

After the service, beautifully conducted by Dr White Anderson at St Cuthbert's Church on Princes Street, followed by the reception at the North British Hotel – now The Balmoral – we went to my sister's home at Cargilfield, near the airport, to rest briefly before the flight to London. I wasn't feeling terribly well and put it down to the fact that I'd come up on the Friday-night sleeper directly from work and was tired. In the aeroplane, however, I began to pour with sweat and to shake like a jelly, with my brand-new wife looking on in horror. I soon realised this was a recurrence of sandfly fever, which I'd had many years before and which does come back once or twice before you get rid of it completely. I staggered into our hotel on the Cromwell Road, spent a restless night soaking the sheets with perspiration and then staggered onto the plane to Majorca the next morning. Only by the time the car from Palma arrived in the beautiful new resort of Formentor at the north end of the island was I finally feeling human again.

After a glorious honeymoon we returned via Paris, because we had been invited to spend a weekend with Field Marshal Montgomery at the Château de Courances, on the south side of the city. I had first met him at my boss Stuart Mallinson's home, The White House, which was the scene of countless summer garden parties for one charity or another. At one of them Prince Philip came along and was delighted to find that there was a cricket net in the grounds, where, among other things, Stuart was trying out a plastic-skinned, cork-centred practice cricket ball invented by a neighbour called Colonel Coote. This plastic-coated ball swung violently in the air and, off an uneven surface like the hessian wicket at The White House, could kick unnervingly. I was instructed to keep wicket for Prince Philip's batting, which I did, and then to bat for him to have a bowl. I was also told that, for heaven's sake, hit him about as much as you like, but if there is a straight one let it hit the stumps – it so happened that his first ball was straight as a die and, to everybody's delight, duly hit the stumps.

It was around that time, in 1951, that I found digs in Argyle Square, near King's Cross, with a very nice Italian family. I was surprised to find that the elder daughter of the house – whom I only once clapped eyes on but who did some of the domestic cleaning, bed-making and so on – worked an evening shift in a factory that made what were known as French letters and would regularly leave me a little present on my pillow. I never discovered whether this was a gentle hint or whether she was simply encouraging a young man's libido out of the goodness of her heart.

From there I moved in with a business colleague, Braithwaite, who kindly offered to take me at the same modest figure of five pounds a week that I had been paying in Argyle Square. This also included supper and a lift to work, a huge improvement on the bus or walking home when it was foggy.

It was while living with the Braithwaites in 1952 that I met Jean. We were soon engaged, and shortly after it was official I took her for the weekend to see the Mallinsons at The White House, only to find that Field Marshal Montgomery was also staying. I never served under him, but he was a legend and was also deputy supreme commander of Supreme Headquarters Allied European Forces (SHAEF). He took to Jean right away, and when she teased him that it was pointless us getting married when people like him were about to make a war in which I would be sent away, perhaps never to be seen again, he said, 'Bring me a bit of paper!' On it he wrote, 'In order that the wedding and future years of Jean and of Tommy may be more fruitful, I will arrange that the outbreak of World War III is postponed for at least ten years. Montgomery of Alamein – 16 May 1953.' A few days later Winston Churchill was staying at The White House, and Montgomery persuaded him to endorse this. He wrote, 'Hear, hear on 31 May,' and initialled it 'WSC', upon which Montgomery said, 'No, no, this will go down in history. They don't know who "WSC" is; you must make it Churchill.' So he turned the 'C' into 'Churchill', and the signature 'W.S. Churchill' is a rare one, not normally used by him.

This led to our invitation to stay with Montgomery during our honeymoon. It also led, on future visits, to his reviewing what he had written, and under it he wrote, on 23 November 1957, 'This prophecy seems to be maturing in the right way. I hereby make it 15 years from this date. Montgomery of Alamein, Field Marshal.' That wasn't the end of it. Again, with Churchill's approval, some five years later, he wrote, 'This is to declare that life at Woodford Green in The White House will continue on an even keel and secure from all war for the next 15 years.'

When our son Angus was aged about eight or nine, we were invited to visit Montgomery in his Hampshire home, and I treasure a photograph of the boy with him. Montgomery was determined to instil in him the will to be a soldier, which may be one reason why he eventually joined the Scots Guards. But in that year of 1962 he seized another piece of paper and wrote, 'The words written by me in The White House in 1953 have all come true. It now remains for Angus to become a soldier and carry on the good work in preventing war when I have passed over Jordan. Montgomery of Alamein, Field Marshal.'

He had, of course, a fearsome reputation for correctness, for being very demanding of his staff and his subordinate commanders, but he was essentially an extremely kind man, undoubtedly lonely from the early death of his wife, wrapped up in the future of his son, David, and extremely good to us.

When we arrived at Orly, on our way back from Majorca on honeymoon, we were met by a senior aide-de-camp at the airport and whisked off to the Château de Courances just in time to wash and change for dinner. We had, on our brief excursion to our rooms, discovered that, although on honeymoon, we had been put in two enormous adjoining rooms with no connecting door. Jean was apparently the first female ever to visit the Château de Courances to stay as a guest of the Field Marshal, and, according to the aide-de-camp, he was adamant that the soldiers' morale must not be impaired when they brought up breakfast by seeing the two of us in bed together. Fortunately, there was a balcony between the two rooms, and, when we had duly said our goodnights, I made my way safely along the balcony. Jean opened the French windows, reversing the process in the morning just before the appointed hour for our breakfast to arrive. During dinner our unpacking had been meticulously done by the military batman. It was noticeable that Jean's frilly smalls were laid out about one to a drawer all round the room, while my normal soft garments were all stuffed into a single drawer.

Montgomery was an excellent host, and, again, it was a very interesting time with equally interesting guests. On the day of our departure, which was to take place after lunch, between courses the Field Marshal whispered an order to his aide-de-camp, who came back bearing a truly magnificent decanter-sized bottle of splendid perfume as a wedding present for Jean. This was most gratefully received, but the Field Marshal insisted personally on removing the glass stopper. I understand it can be quite an art to remove a tight-fitting glass stopper from a glass bottle when it is new, and the Field Marshal certainly did not have that art. With the dogged persistence that was a feature of his military strategies, he persisted and eventually demanded that the waiter bring a bucket of very hot water and a bucket of cold water. He alternated between these buckets with the splendid crystal, and eventually, with a shout of triumph, the stopper came off in his hand, unfortunately bringing with it quite a flood of highly perfumed liquid, most of which ended up down the front of his day uniform. This was to astonish the guests who were arriving for a garden party just as we were departing. We could see the members of the line coming to shake hands turn up their noses and look at each other in wild surmise.

Montgomery's later home at Isington Mill was extremely simple, and his library was full of memorabilia and records. He was very generous in giving and signing for us all that he had written up to that time, including the splendid manuscript diary that he had kept of major events during the war.

When we arrived back in London, it was to a small furnished apartment in Hampstead that I had hurriedly acquired before we left for Majorca. Yet we weren't to stay there long because, within the six months that the lease provided for, Jean had managed to find a wonderful flat in Hyde Park Square, the 200th she had looked at. This flat, on the first floor of an old mansion in the middle of the north side of the square, looking south into Hyde Park, must be the most comfortable and luxurious place we have ever lived in. Its huge drawing room and balconies were perfect for entertaining, and one of the parties we gave in the following year, 1954, was for the Achilles members who were to travel to Vancouver in July of that year for the British Empire Games. It was a beautiful summer's night, so we opened the huge French windows so that our guests could stand out in the balmy night air, looking at the gardens just below us. The following morning we received a letter from the landlord saying that, by the way, he had forgotten to tell us that the balconies were dangerous, were shortly to be repaired and that under no circumstances should more than two people ever be on them. It was a fortuitous miracle, therefore, that half the British Empire Games team, including famous names like Bannister, Chataway and Stacey, ever made it to Vancouver.

There was also an earlier incident in the Hyde Park Square flat. After we had signed the lease, we decided to do the place up completely, and my father-in-law recommended a family of decorators from Alderley Edge who would come down and do the job for us, sleeping in the flat on camp beds. We fixed all the details with them and arranged to be away for ten days, staying with our friends, Michel and Yolande de Bourbon at Montchevreuil, near Paris. I had been at their wedding not long before, and a very grand affair it was, conducted by a splendid fellow who was then the papal representative in Paris but who later became Pope John Paul II. The intricacies of the Mass were pure theatre: I was sitting next to the American ambassador, who, at the point at which the white gown was placed on the future pope, said in a loud voice, 'Gee, he's about to have a shave!' Incense boys moved to and fro, with the papal legate and the other priests changing robes from time to time. Dark and slim, Yolande looked quite beautiful at her wedding. She was from a very interesting Normandy family called the de Broglies: one uncle was a Nobel Prize winner, and she was also descended from the Napoleonic War hero Marshal Soult, which was why the chateau of Montchevreuil contained a vast, unused ballroom full of rolled-up oils and furniture that Soult had liberated from Spain during his campaigning there.

After a happy time with them in the chateau we caught our plane home, eventually turning the key in the door of our Hyde Park Square flat at half past eleven at night, expecting to find the place in pristine condition. It was not to be, though: the decorators had got the date wrong and were not going to complete until the following day, so we were greeted by snores from the various camp beds. We put down all but a small overnight case and headed off to the nearby Cumberland

Hotel, which had a certain reputation at that time. When we got there, there was a rather elderly gentleman with pince-nez behind the reception desk. When I enquired whether there was a double room available, he looked slowly up at me over the top of his glasses and said, 'Yes, sir, and what name shall we say tonight?'

Jean and I were very happy in our Hyde Park Square flat, but as the years passed we began to long for a family. We were, however, having some difficulty, until we enlisted the help of a wonderful doctor, Robert Kennedy, whom I had known through athletics for many years. Suddenly Jean was pregnant, and our firstborn son, Angus, arrived just before Christmas in 1958. We were extremely fortunate to locate a newly redundant nanny from a doctor's family in the West Country. Nanna, as she liked to be called, arrived looking dignified and fiercely defensive as we eyed each other with mutual suspicion, but she soon became one of the family and was to remain so for over a decade.

Angus's arrival produced a significant headache in that the lease for our flat stipulated, 'No cats, dogs, children or prostitutes.' With a break clause soon coming up, we had been frantically looking for a house. Our neighbour in Scotland, Captain Peter Lindsay, who was fast becoming a very close friend, had promised that we could buy his London house at No. 4 Gloucester Square for just over £10,000 as soon as he found a suitable flat to move into, but there were endless delays and we faced a very difficult situation. Thankfully, my boss, Stuart Mallinson, once again rode to the rescue, renting us an empty wooden cottage in the grounds of The White House in Woodford Green for a nominal sum until we found a house. While it was a beautiful spot, neither of us expected the arrangement to last 18 months, given that it was a favourite haunt of mosquitoes in the summer and was seriously cold in the winter.

Our time in the wooden cottage came to an end when I happened to be driving near our old flat in Hyde Park and saw that No. 10 Somers Crescent had a 'For Sale' sign outside it. The agent was just round the corner, so I arranged to see it at once. The house had been built in 1938 for two bachelors, but before they could move in the place was requisitioned, first for women's services and then for returning evacuees. A couple had bought it at the end of the war, when it was little better than a bomb site, but after the husband suffered a heart attack and could no longer manage the stairs they decided to sell up. The asking price was £15,000, but having been looking for so long I wasn't missing out again and went back to the agent's office to put down the deposit there and then, telling Jean what I had done when I arrived home.

Fortunately, getting a mortgage on satisfactory terms and finding a good builder was helped by my customer contacts through Mallinsons, although the rebuilding still cost nearly as much as the house. We had expected to move in by September but had to make do with the top floor while work carried on, although the builders were out in time for us to have a very jolly house-warming party just before Christmas. We were in that house for over 25 years, and it was a huge success. We built a proper staircase to the roof, put a small bedroom up there and surrounded the whole flat roof with high wiring so that it was safe for children. Another change was an involuntary one when the Greater London Council decided to alter our address from No. 10 to No. 4, a bizarre decision that, it turned out, was within their powers. Still, it was a beautiful house, five windows wide with the door in the middle.

Eighteen months after Angus's arrival, our daughter Ishbel was born in Westminster Hospital. Jean had had a miscarriage while we were in The Wooden Cottage, so we took great precautions over this pregnancy, admitting her to hospital ten days before the baby was due. I got the all-important call while I was at dinner with my old Cambridge contemporary and later High Court judge John Woods and his wife, Anne, with the coffee being interrupted by the hospital ringing to inform me that I was the father of a second fine son. I roared down to the hospital and arrived just in time to see a white-coated chap come out of the labour ward carrying by the ankle an extraordinarily unattractive and manifestly female baby with bright-red skin and almost covered with black hair. I turned to a father who was obviously waiting for his child to appear and said, 'Well, I don't know if that's yours, but thank goodness it's not mine.' Minutes later I was summoned to find this hairy female child being cradled in Jean's arms, with my wife looking extremely pleased with herself. Thankfully, the black hair eventually disappeared to be replaced by a handsome brown mane.

When Angus was coming up to three, the question of kindergarten raised its head. Somers Crescent was a big house with a flat roof and a small paved back garden, and, given that Nanna was a qualified kindergarten teacher and Jean was a qualified teacher, she decided that we would have our own kindergarten. As well as our own two, there were three of the famous Mitford family plus two children from a local family called the McEwens. Word soon spread, and within no time at all Jean was effectively running a fully fledged kindergarten from Somers Crescent. It soon became obvious, however, that it wasn't big enough for such an operation, and she began looking for somewhere larger.

The answer lay with St John's Church in Hyde Park Crescent, yards away from our house, and a deal was quickly reached whereby we could take their basement for storage and use their halls as a nursery during the morning and early afternoon. That was only possible because Jean and our American neighbour, Rita Beale, had saved the church from extinction when its congregation dwindled to single figures thanks to an extraordinarily bone idle old Welsh rector. Bishop Montague Stopford – who had a very narrow head so that his mitre looked as though it was entirely supported on his enormous butterfly ears – had been determined to close down the dilapidated old church before Jean and Rita enlisted the help of Ivor Bulmer-Thomas, an influential man who was chairman of an organisation called the Friends of Friendless Churches.

Faced with Ivor, the bishop relented and agreed to put the rent that the nursery school would pay towards renovating the church, which has since gone from strength to strength, as did the nursery. In 1970, as well as renting the church, Jean managed to secure a 500 ft-long, narrow strip of ground at the back of Connaught Street that had been part of the old Tyburn graveyard but which had been used as a dumping ground for builders' materials while the housing association built flats of remarkable unattractiveness after the war. It looked like a bomb site, and there were also gravestones lying in all directions, but once it had been deconsecrated a succession of dumper trucks carted away the bones, dropping the odd thigh bone here and there. It took an enormous amount of determination and persistence, but Jean certainly got it done. It is now one of the largest and most beautiful private gardens in London.

At its height the school had over one hundred children aged from two and a half to seven, but Jean's management and quality standards were impeccable. She kept the fees low and granted a lot of free places to those in need. This made it impossible to make money, especially as the set-up costs – such as taking over a shop that backed onto the garden for use as classrooms – were considerable.

Meanwhile, as the kindergarten grew, so did our family. We had longed for a third and fourth child, the idea being to have them in two pairs, and after considerable problems Duncan appeared, hale and hearty, just after Christmas in 1968. Alas, there was not to be a fourth. Jean had a severe miscarriage when we were staying near Stamford with a friend called Barbara Brassey for the weekend, which destroyed our hopes of extending our family further.

It was during this period that Peter Lindsay came to the fore and was extraordinarily helpful and kind to us. We both wanted to bring up the children as Scots with a love and knowledge of the Highlands, and so we holidayed in Scotland each summer, partly with our great friend Jean Fforde on Arran and partly with my mother in Newtonmore. As the rest of the family wanted to head to the Highlands in August, this proved to be a problem, because the presence of small children, even with the nanny looking after them, was a sore trial to the other members of my family, particularly Niall, who liked total peace and quiet in his life. After one especially tempestuous holiday, he wrote to my mother to say that it was impossible for her to expect the rest of the family to come to their home if it was going to be virtually taken over by Jean, our nanny, two small children and two small dogs.

So, the next year, when I was not there, Jean and the family were banished to the old, cold, damp coach house and steading at the bottom of the garden, where there was a groom's flat above where the horses had been kept. This flat, which was where I used to play with my Hornby trains as a boy, had such a low ceiling that Jean could hardly stand up, and to make matters worse it was reached by a glorified ladder, which she eventually fell down, breaking a bone in her foot in the process.

Peter turned up one day during this miserable period and found her clearly in the aftermath of weeping. He had always been very fond of Jean, and without hesitation he turned to my mother and said, 'I see, Lady Macpherson, that you are really overburdened with numbers at this time. May I take Jean and the children? I have room in the house. Jean, go and pack.' And, without further ado, he whisked her off. She had a succession of very happy summers in Cluny Castle, near Newtonmore. One of her pleasures was to occasionally drive Peter to Inverness in his magnificent 1927 Rolls-Royce, an extraordinarily long vehicle that was in splendid condition but which found the steep hills on the road up to Inverness a considerable trial, so that Jean had to stop periodically and pour water into the steaming radiator. Peter had promised to leave her the Rolls in his will, but at the last minute he changed his mind, saying that he didn't think we could possibly afford to run it – which was sad but true.

Peter was a remarkable man. He had come to Scotland from Austria as a schoolboy – his Jewish parents escaping what they saw, before the First World War, as an inevitable move to anti-Semitism – and by 1914 he was at Cambridge, where he quickly changed his name, choosing that of his landlady when he was stuck for an alternative identity. He then joined the British Army and fought with considerable distinction in the First World War before building up the engineering firm of Morgan Crucible so that, when the owner of the 12,000-acre Cluny Castle estate went into liquidation in 1943, he was able to buy the whole place, complete with house, stables, cottages and walled garden, for less than £1 per acre. Peter was also a keen skier, and when he could no longer go to Austria he founded the French resort of Méribel. He also had a splendid but formidable wife called Eugenie, who rode side-saddle to the Quorn hounds well into her '80s and in spite of dickey knees. She seemed to be keen that I should marry Patty, her second daughter, but neither of us was terribly keen on the idea, although I have remained extremely good friends with both Patty and her sister, Sonia.

If Jean spent her summers at Cluny, Christmas and New Year were spent with our friend Jean Fforde on the Isle of Arran. She lived in a nice house called Strabane, right on the sea, surrounded by a spacious and secluded garden, which was big enough for the three children and two dogs to make as much noise as they liked without annoying anyone. They were a rumbustious lot, and Jean soon christened the children and dogs the 'yellers and yappers'.

We only got two weeks of holiday in those days, so my visits were very brief. New Year's Day was not a bank holiday in England, so we would spend from 27 December to 2 January in the painful business of interviewing every salesman and sales department in the company and building up the subsequent year's budget. That meant that I had to travel down by train on Boxing Day evening at the latest, and on one occasion, as we climbed over Beattock on the way from Glasgow to Carlisle, there was a shuddering bang and everything came to a stop, with the train lights going out. We had run into the back of a stationary freight train, and while no serious damage had been done it meant that we eventually crept into Euston 23 hours after leaving Glasgow. Needless to say, no provision of food or water was made by British Rail on the way.

27

Balavil

While Jean and I were incredibly grateful for the hospitality of friends like Peter Lindsay and Jean Fforde, we decided that we needed our own base in Scotland, preferably in the Highlands and ideally in the Badenoch area, where my family came from. We studied every advertisement, but we had not accumulated capital, and, until I became assistant managing director and my holiday entitlement increased to four weeks, my salary was negligible and my holiday limited. We began to put a little money aside but also knew that school fees were looming. We examined a strange square tower called Garth Castle in Perthshire, an ancient Stuart stronghold just south of the Inverness-shire border, and contemplated buying it in conjunction with Rob Kennedy, our doctor. When that fell through, we looked as far afield as Ardnamurchan on the west coast, but a close study of Messrs Bartholomews' rainfall maps of Scotland dissuaded us from that.

Then, just down the road from Newtonmore, towards Fort William, a house called Craig Dhu came up for sale. We were hugely enthusiastic, made our financial arrangements and put in a bid on the advice of Ewan Ormiston, a villager who was reputed to know everything in those parts. He advised us that the owners were expecting £13,000 and that a sealed bid of £13,500 would surely do it, advice we followed only to find that we had lost out by £500. We were able to buy it 30 years later but at a huge multiple of the price at which it had originally been sold.

Shortly after the frustration of that missed opportunity, Jean was at a social event and met a remarkable lady called Mrs Brewster Macpherson. The widow of Balavil, who had been friends with my grandfather, was already touching 75 but was extremely vigorous and very much in command of her estate. They hit it off, and one day Mrs Macpherson took Jean up to

Balavil, a magnificently placed mansion whose drive was the old road. The front, on the north side, faced what had been the road, and the rear faced the valley, with a splendid view of the Glen Feshie hills and Cairngorms.

The house had been built in the late 18th century by Robert Adam for James Macpherson, who was known as 'Ossian' and was a big man in every sense. The son of the schoolmaster at Ruthven, across the Spey, he graduated from Aberdeen University and became tutor to various noble families in Edinburgh, where he met many of the intellectual giants of the Scottish Enlightenment, men such as Blair, Hume, Robertson and the Adam brothers. He had the idea that he could accumulate the bardic tales of the Highlands that were handed down orally in every remote village, a tradition that still existed particularly in the West Highlands and the Islands. These bardic lays were extensive − a single bard would be expected to know over 2,000 lines of Gaelic verse, which he would then embellish − but together they represented a direct link to the great deeds of violence, love and culture from the time of St Columba. Just as importantly, they were hugely popular and very profitable.

Ossian eventually moved to London and became William Pitt's pamphleteer, but only after a varied career that included serving as paymaster general in the British Army in North America at the beginning of the War of Independence and then working as the London agent for the fabulously wealthy Nabob of Arcot. His friend Sir John Macpherson of the Skye branch of the clan was governor general of India, and he and James Macpherson corresponded a great deal, often in Gaelic to fox the censors. Sir John made himself enormously popular around the Highlands by helping to place many Highlanders in the East India Company and in the military, and his writer friend James basked in the reflected glory.

At the height of his reputation, James commissioned his friend, Robert Adam, to build him the house of Balavil − or Belle Ville as he originally called it − and it had many typical Adam features. When Mrs Brewster Macpherson introduced it to us and invited us to take a 25-year lease, provided we put it in liveable condition, it was in an appalling state. One red-brick wing had been added in the 1920s and was already a ruin, with a tree growing inside it and out through the roof. The house had been empty for 29 years and had last been used as a convalescent home for the Army. Doors, where they existed, were usually off their hinges and had six-inch nails driven into them. The old lady, who had been the sole guardian of the estate and the house, had taken a saw and cut huge holes in the dining room and drawing room floors to prevent the dry rot that we found in the windows from spreading. The holes were so large that you could have lost half a normal house in them, and in her enthusiasm she had cut through the main wooden beams that supported the rest of the floor.

The lead roof, mercifully, was not as bad as we feared, but you could have driven a Land Rover through the gap that existed between the slates and the wooden eaves. There was no electricity, and the water supply, which once came off the hill a mile and a half behind the house, had long since been destroyed by the planting of forestry and the natural erosion of time. Although the formidable grey granite walls were intact, a fire had burnt out the whole core of the house, which was totally bare and ruined. The fire had immediately been reported to the local fire brigade, who had brought their horse-drawn fire engine up from Kingussie, three miles away, and installed it at the door, only to find that their hose was not long enough to go down to the water supply, which was by then in a glen at the entrance. They had little option but to watch the house burn and try to contain the spread of the flames and stop them from consuming everything.

I went up and viewed the house with Jean and the old lady when I came for my summer holiday. I was frankly appalled and simply wouldn't have touched it, except that we couldn't find anything else and I was all too aware that Jean was desperate to have her own place.

There followed a very difficult and expensive period of years of reconstruction. We pulled down the 1920s wing and used its red bricks to make a terrace where the wing had stood. The ground floor of the Victorian wing at the east end of the house was turned into a large garage, with the rooms above it used for storage. My friend and colleague George Hughes, at our Manchester branch, had a trade in western red cedar, a fantastic wood, which we used to make the roof watertight. To start with, we had no heating other than the big fires on the ground floor, and in spite of cleaning the chimneys we still encountered problems, on one occasion only preventing the whole house from going on fire by chucking vast quantities of water down the chimney from the roof. Putting in a new water supply was also hideously time-consuming and expensive and involved a row between the plumber and Jean that led to our plumber driving away in his Land Rover in a rage and running over our Shetland puppy. He was, to his credit, genuinely contrite.

So, by that first Christmas, with 15 subcontractors still on site and a generator installed, we had electricity, some water and lots of fires. I vividly remember sitting round the hall fire with six children – our own and three Mitford children – their mother and Jean, singing carols to the accompaniment of Angus on his recorder, which was very effective. I have a permanent vision of Jean kneeling by the children, upright in her back, clad in a slightly religious-looking grey dress with a white lace collar, lustily singing a Christmas carol with a face so full of innocence and beauty that it was a memory I will never lose.

When the electricity finally came, we were able to begin decorating the place. One of the company's salesmen down in London called on all sorts of obscure builders' suppliers and directed me to Jacksons on the south end of Putney Bridge. I took down some samples of the cornicing and walked in to find an elderly gentleman wearing pince-nez perched on a high stool. It was some time before he looked up and asked what I wanted. When I told him, he examined the moulds carefully and said, 'Robert Adam, sir, Belle Ville in Scotland, you said. If you'll forgive me for some minutes, I'll see what we can do.' He was gone for a good half-hour but finally came back with my samples in his hand and said, 'Yes, sir, we have the original moulds.' That was astonishing enough, but so was the price, which at half a crown per foot was more modest than I ever imagined. So the cornices from the original moulds, made in the original fashion with plaster of Paris strengthened by horsehair, still adorn Balavil today.

The original designs for Balavil, which I found in Sir John Soane's Museum in Lincoln's Inn Fields, did not show colours at all, so we visited a large number of Adam houses to find out what colours he might have chosen in the north of Scotland. Eventually, room by room, we were satisfied: for the small drawing room we were adventurous and took some bold multicoloured Adam designs from other houses; the drawing room was a conventional green, with gold accoutrements; we used a dark-blue-based fabric for the dining room; while the hall was basically red. All the decorating was done by a local man, Douglas Mackintosh, an ex-Cameron Highlander whom I had known since boyhood. I have a mental picture of him lying on his back at the top of very high scaffolding, looking like Michelangelo in the Vatican and trying out the colours for the mouldings until we got a handsome result.

We had been both far-sighted and fortunate in furniture. Friends of ours in the Kingdom of Fife – Sir John and Ursula Gilmore – were about to sell up their very large house, which was so long and narrow that Ursula used to say that she had to wheel the dinner 70 yards from the kitchen to the small drawing room and dining room at the other end, where they lived and where the heating was concentrated. So, in selling, they were going to have an auction of the furniture, and they very kindly invited us for a night to see what we would like to take. In that way we managed to acquire a lot of the furniture that was to serve us extremely well at Balavil.

If things were moving ahead on the housing front, there was also a real sense of the children getting older and life in general racing on. By the time we had renovated Balavil, Angus had gone off to board at my old prep school Cargilfield, near Edinburgh, while Ishbel had gone to the French Lycée with Emma Mitford. The headmistress told us that, if children went before five years, they would absorb French rather than have to learn it, and she was absolutely right. Ishbel and her friends went at four and a half and were soon talking perfect French, so that when Jean collected the girls from school they would chatter away to each other in French until the first child was dropped and then, immediately, as if by a signal, chatter in English.

There's a famous family story from that time. When Ishbel was six she came home with a handful of pennies – quite a haul. Jean asked how she got these, and she said, 'Oh, well, Mummy, I'm a very good climber, and there is a tree in the playground, and the boys said they would give me a penny every time I climbed to the top. So, this is my reward.'

Her mother said, 'Oh, Ishbel, you are silly. They only wanted to look at your knickers.'

Ishbel had an air of weary sophistication and replied, 'Mama, of course I know that, but I fooled them – I took them off.'

The incident reminded me of the last time I remembered her appearing unclothed in public, when she was two and a half or three. It was bath-time, and I was having a business conference in Somers Crescent with four very solemn gentlemen in dark suits when the door opened and in marched Ishbel, stark naked, waving a bottle of whisky and saying, 'Papa – milk, milk, milk.'

Of such memories are families made!

28

The SAS and Dark Arts

Although I left the Army after the war, I didn't sever my ties completely. In the autumn of 1947 the Territorial Army reopened for business and the SAS was reformed as 21 SAS (Artists), based in the drill hall of the Artists' Rifles near St Pancras Station. My Special Forces contacts asked me to get in touch with the 21 SAS so that they could make use of my experience, with me becoming an attached officer within their instruction programme. I was, however, soon adopted by the SAS, who made me a full member even though in reality I continued to function as an attached instructor.

We had great fun with this wholly volunteer body of experienced ex-SAS and Special Forces people, and the camp we went to in Devon, where we did a series of independent exercises, proved to be remarkably enjoyable. I started off being considered by the SAS rank and file – the hard men of the regiment – as a rather bogus interloper, but during and after that camp I am glad to say they accepted me thoroughly, and I still have some very good friends as a result of it.

As an ex-SOE member, I was technically always on call. I didn't, however, expect to hear from them unless it was for advice on issues such as the Italian–Yugoslav Border Commission, onto which I was briefly co-opted. So it came as a major surprise when, the year before our wedding, I got an urgent call from Alan Clark in Intelligence, a man whom I had met before and who, indeed, was responsible for one of the inadequate briefings I had received before being dropped into Europe during the war. Clark required me to go to Norway for a fortnight and had already cleared it with my employer.

Once in Norway I was to pose as a civilian, travelling under the name of Martinson. My job was to contact those members of the Norwegian armed forces who were responsible for setting up resistance points, called stay-behind parties, in case their country was invaded and overrun by the Russians. It was easy to see why I had been selected, because my main tasks – setting up cells of trained personnel and building dumps of armaments and communication equipment – were a throwback to my days in France and Italy.

At that time a Russian attack on the West seemed imminent, with an invasion of Scandinavia sure to be a key target. The Norwegian, Finnish, Danish and Swedish armies would inevitably have been overrun, so the stay-behind parties were viewed as an important element of the resistance. Their aim was to spread as much mayhem and disruption as possible, through a campaign of sabotage, intelligence and assassination, and generally make it difficult for the Soviets.

I was equipped with a camera, a pistol and maps on which I could record my movements. After the most cursory search of my luggage at Northolt Airport, with the customs man's broad wink telling me that all was well, I picked up my contact in Oslo. I would travel alone, and he would meet me on my return journey at Trondheim, taking me to one or two secret places on our way back to Oslo.

A good part of my journey was by air, travelling by the old three-propeller German Heinkel bombers that were then used for the internal air service. Journeys were freezing because the plane's fuselage was made of a sort of corrugated iron, which always leaked. The seats were extraordinarily uncomfortable metal deckchairs that had been welded upright, but at least we had an excellent view as we flew low over the countryside.

The other part of my journey was in what the Norwegians call a *hurtigruten*, which is an express steamer that acts as a bus up and down the coast. It was in this steamer that I found my way north from Trondheim to Tromsø, which is on an island deep inside the Arctic Circle. The boat was absolutely packed, and, running late, we descended on the one hotel in the little town of Tromsø like a pack of ravenous wolves. Fortunately my room had been kept for me, but there was a howling mob of disappointed people. Those who couldn't persuade guests in the hotel to double up – one almost hysterical young Norwegian lady whom I had chatted to on the boat billeted herself with me, making for a strange and platonic evening – ended up sleeping communally in the local school.

Tromsø, which is effectively the first major port of call for ships heading out of the Russian naval base at Murmansk, is so far north that I tried out my camera by taking a photograph of the town clock at midnight, to show the night sun. When the photograph was developed, it looked more like midday. From there I went 350 miles to the south to Bodø, a big American airbase on the mainland just north of the Arctic Circle. My main memory of the place is that the Gulf Stream hit the coast right there, making the water warm enough to go for a dip, which I did. How many people can say they have swum in the sea north of the Arctic Circle?

Travelling by plane and bus, I went via Alta Fjord, which had been such an important German base for the U-boats raiding the Arctic convoys, to the small port of Kirkenes, right on the Russian border. From there I was able to patrol the Norwegian border of the Pasvik River and study the military installations on the Russian side. After I left Kirkenes, I travelled by bus through what seemed like endless birch forests to Kautokeino, where I stayed at the only local hotel. On my way to my room I stepped past a young, blonde Norwegian lady who was washing the floor, and I smiled, I hope pleasantly, bidding her good morning. I thought nothing further of it until two months later when I received a love letter from this lady, whose name turned out to be Vesla, which I've always treasured as the only unsolicited affection ever to have come my way.

In the summer those birch forests were thick with mosquitoes and the stinging black birch flies. The local remedy was to cover your face in greasy, malodorous whale oil, which you would later scrape off, flies and all, with a sort of wooden paper knife. As if that wasn't bad enough, I also bounced the Land Rover I had been lent by the Norwegian Army off an oncoming military truck in the early hours of the morning while driving down a narrow country lane.

I met my Norwegian contact at The Victoria, the smartest hotel in Trondheim, the town whose fjord is famous for the crippling of the battleship *Tirpitz* by mini submarines, one of the most gallant actions of the war. I was pretty dishevelled by the time I arrived at the packed lobby to find the hotel claiming that I had no reservation. I resolved the stand-off by insisting they rang the British Embassy, but it was an uncharacteristic moment in a fascinating trip among a people who had proved themselves beyond doubt to be extremely gallant folk during the Second World War. They would have demonstrated that again had they been called upon to do so, which, thank goodness, they were not.

Apart from any other considerations, while I had been extremely enthusiastic about this challenge and had arrived in Norway with an open mind, I found the Norwegians wanting in important areas. They weren't happy with my report, which criticised their plans for the mobilisation of stay-behind parties, the concealment and location of arms dumps and their domestic communications and those to Britain or the United States, but the visit itself was fascinating.

So, too, were some of the private individuals who sought my help. One of those was the explorer Sir Ranulph Fiennes, a larger-than-life character whom I met through the SAS. He and his team came to stay with us at Balavil in early January to test their equipment and were extraordinary weekend guests. They would disappear outside late in the evening to sleep in the open in the deep snow that surrounded the house during that hard winter, which at least meant that the new gear they were to use on their polar journey had been well trialled.

The same exploration team later came up with the idea of an expedition to circle the globe on the zero meridian and invited me to join the board they put together to raise money and arrange all the necessary support and logistics. All went extremely well through the Antarctic up to the North Pole and for most of the Arctic leg, but, as they drew near to their destination of Spitsbergen, panic broke out when an early thaw meant they were drifting about on a large iceberg and unable to make further progress. Despite several members of the board pushing to send in a helicopter to rescue them, the view of myself and another couple of the board was that they should be given time to get to the pick-up point and meet the small Norwegian relief vessel. Fortunately this was what happened, and the remarkable Ran Fiennes managed to circumnavigate the meridian without ever leaving terra firma.

Even after heart surgery, he has since done further amazing feats of exploration and endurance, including running seven marathons in seven days. He is a remarkable man and, inevitably, is missing the odd finger and toe from frostbite – and, occasionally, his friends would say, the odd glimmer of self-preservation and common sense. His late wife, Ginny, was hugely supportive and went on many of the expeditions as advance radio contact and organising officer. She was one of the most mentally and physically resilient individuals I've ever met, but I still don't know quite how she did it.

29

Timber!

It was by sheer accident that I drifted into the firm of William Mallinson, which was to be my life for nearly 30 years. As the time came to leave university, vague career thoughts began to enter my mind. My brother Phil was always careful not to influence me, which meant that his advice was often so vague that it left me completely confused. On the one occasion he mentioned a specific job, it was with the merchant bank Lazard, who had told him they were interested in me. Unfortunately I was so ignorant that when he said they were a bank I pictured myself standing behind a counter counting pound notes and stupidly declined an offer that promised nothing but a life of extreme wealth.

The other job I turned down was as a management trainee with the John Lewis Partnership, which was offered to me by Lord Woolton, the ex-food minister. No matter which way I looked at it, shop life just didn't appeal. My other option was going to the Bar. Because I had done some desultory reading for the law exams in my prisoner-of-war camps, I was exempted from all of them except the finals. However, I soon found that in my first two years I could count on only one police court case per week at two guineas a time, giving me a hundred guineas a year, about a third of the amount I had been getting at university. That was a non-starter.

Stuart Mallinson was a man of great size and forceful character who collected people like other people collect books. Among his house guests while I was working with him were Winston Churchill, Field Marshal Montgomery, a whole host of politicians and astronaut Neil Armstrong, fresh from walking on the moon. I met Stuart through Phil, whose bank, Benson Lonsdale, had floated Mallinsons as a public company just before the war.

Phil and Stuart got on well, and Stuart had also taken an interest in my sister Rhona. As the country woke to the fact that a conflict might be pending, health and fitness had become all the rage in 1937 and 1938, and as head of a voluntary organisation promoting fitness in Essex he appointed her to manage the campaign. So he knew our family well.

His eldest son was, sadly, killed at the Rapido River in Italy while serving with the Essex Regiment during the war. His middle son wanted to be a farmer, and the youngest one was some ten years younger than me, so Stuart was looking for someone to fill that gap and his eyes lighted on me. I was only vaguely conscious of this until the night before my final examinations, when this formidable figure arrived in my room at ten o'clock in the evening at Vincent's Club, where I was living. I was doing the usual frantic last-minute revision, and he wouldn't go away until I agreed to join his company that October. He described the training I would undergo and forecast a rapid movement through the management ranks to take what he had thought would have been his son's place at the head of the firm. It later became obvious that Stuart was locked in the past and viewed William Mallinson as a family company rather than a growing public concern with outside shareholders. His number two in the company was the distinguished Scottish international full-back Dan Drysdale, who had played alongside Phil on numerous occasions.

I started my training by being sent to various stations around the country where I would learn about wood, how it was harvested and prepared. A key part of my education was arriving at a wood and learning to estimate how much timber we could get from it and what it was worth. My first posting was to Oundle in the Midlands, followed by a stint at the company's main timber mill at Bury St Edmunds and then back to head office, where I worked my way through all the departments: buying, finance, selling, manufacturing and so on.

On the buying side, purchases from abroad were extremely limited at first because of currency restrictions, but, finally, there was an opening to make purchases from France, and it was decided that I should go, as interpreter, with one of our stalwart timber foremen to buy French walnut. I was able to fit that in with one of the French rugby tours, and I joined him at Périgueux, the heart of walnut country, where we bought some walnut planks and gunstocks, which were an interesting sideline. I also managed to attend the marriage of my good friend Freddie Cardozo in Tours, on the Loire, wearing, as insisted by Freddie, my uniform of

Cameron tartan trews and Blues jacket. He had two best men: me and Denis Truscott, a stalwart of the All England Lawn Tennis Club at Wimbledon and later to become lord mayor of London.

While at head office I spent a considerable amount of time down at the London docks and, more specifically, the timber wharves. I was learning how to judge timber by its character, odour and feel, often manhandling it into place so that it dried properly. Because we often started very early or very late, I found digs in the heart of the East End in the rectory of a church that had been bombed, close to Bishopsgate Goods Station, deep into Bethnal Green. I played table tennis with the curate, a muscular Australian, on a huge marble slab that used to carry the coffins before they were interred, and tried to keep out of the way of the black marketeers who used the graveyard as a cache for the goods they stole in bulk out of the trucks in Bishopsgate Goods Station.

At night I used the Victoria Park running track for training a bit, and in my lunch hour I became a regular at a pub where you could get a pie and a half-pint for a very modest fee. Just around the corner from the pub was a pawnbroker, and one day I saw four dusty white-wine bottles in the window and, looking at them closely, saw they were Château d'Yquem 1945. The pawnbroker told me that they were 'not much good now; they're getting a bit old,' so I bargained him down to eight shillings for the lot. I'm not very fond of sweet Sauternes, but, over the years, Jean and her guests managed to get through three of the bottles, and when we eventually moved house in 1986 I auctioned the remaining bottle at Christie's and got £250 – not a bad return.

Mallinsons provided much of the timber for the rebuilding of important panelled or timbered buildings in the City, with ancient monuments a speciality. They kept enormous piles of huge oak logs, felled for 15 to 25 years, which could be cut into magnificent beams. Some went into Windsor Castle, York Minster and the roof of Westminster Hall at the Houses of Parliament. As well as working with architects, I would be sent out to see customers such as engineers, car manufacturers, shipbuilders and a variety of industrial users.

I was often sent to stand in for regional salesmen who were sick or on holiday, and I remember going down to South Wales and travelling by bus around Cardiff, Newport and Swansea before heading up into the valleys to visit Abergavenny and Merthyr Tydfil. One night I stayed in

Abergavenny and found that, by some extraordinary luck, an early Peter Ustinov film called *Hotel Sahara* was playing in the village hall. For those days, the film was quite risqué, and I laughed loudly throughout, only to find that the hall, which had been packed with townspeople wearing their Sunday best, had emptied at the first of the risqué moments.

Things were done differently then, but I still remember my surprise at visiting a family firm in Huddersfield to find a black-coated clerk in white shirt with hard collar and black tie sitting at a high desk. He took me to the boss, who bade me good morning and, as it was eleven o'clock, offered me a glass of Madeira and a slice of plum cake. In Sheffield I would visit the firm of Stevensons, whose eponymous boss, Henry Stevenson, was a contemporary of mine who kindly put me up, which made a marvellous change from the rather seedy hotels where I generally had to stay.

Further north were the shipyards. John Brown on the Clyde were building superb liners and buying everything from teak decks to mahogany panelling. The main feature of Clydeside was that the labour force was robbing the company blind: in the local town of Gourock a stream of gentlemen would knock at your door offering you tablecloths, cutlery, glasses, a carpet – all looted from the liners.

Tyneside was also extremely busy. The foreman ruled the roost there, doing the purchasing for the ship and strutting the quayside in his bowler hat, very much the martinet. Tyneside also made liners and a lot of naval vessels, and they were extremely important customers. Unfortunately, many of the foremen were all too ready to take a bribe, a practice that we were not prepared to enter into. They also had to be entertained and were extremely heavy drinkers, as I found on the only occasion I tried to keep up with them.

The shipyards on Wearside were fascinating, being smaller, less well equipped and used generally for cargo ships. The Wear was so narrow that the ships had to be launched sideways, which took an immense amount of control.

My next major overseas excursion was to West Africa in 1956, when Jean and I were still installed in our happy flat in Hyde Park Square. Jean had resumed part-time teaching at a ladies' finishing establishment in Knightsbridge called the Monkey Club, which was all the rage with smart young ladies, domestic and foreign, at that time, provided they had enough money to pay the huge fees. She went there nominally as a teacher but became a teacher of British customs and behaviour, which some of them, particularly the overseas ones, badly needed.

I set off to Africa in a four-engine propeller aircraft called a Constellation. We travelled in reasonable comfort because the fare differential between economy and first class was so modest that most businessmen automatically went first class. The highlight of the flight was dawn, when we peered out to see the infinite African jungle spreading as far as the horizon.

Our first port of call was Leopoldville, now Kinshasa, in the Belgian Congo, and we disembarked to find an airport that was a total shambles. Thankfully I had travelled lightly and had so little luggage that I was able to make a quick getaway. There was no sign of any taxi rank, but I knew my hotel was expecting me, and when a local taxi driver came up to me shouting 'Mackeson' I hopped into his vehicle and was whisked off to the correct hotel, where a very handsome first-floor suite awaited me. I later discovered that the taxi was intended for the brewing magnate Sir Ivan Mackeson, who was presumably unamused by my intervention.

As soon as I got to my suite in the boiling midday sun of Leopoldville, I threw open my French windows to look at the turbulent street below. I immediately heard a disturbance and saw a stark-naked lady – presumably, from her voice, an American – driving a large open vehicle up the street with her hair draped Lady Godiva-like in strategic places and screaming at the top of her voice. It was remarkable that the locals barely batted an eyelid, although she was apprehended by the police at the end of the street. I was later told that the poor lady was suffering from sunstroke.

The Congo has been both blessed and cursed with an enormous wealth of diamonds, which has led to endless wars, but the diamonds are up-country in Katanga while the timber I wanted was mostly in the lower Congo. After a day or two in the pleasant city of Leopoldville, at which point the river is so wide that it looks more like a lake, with the French Congo city of Brazzaville on the far side, I flew downstream to Matadi, the highest easily navigable point of the Congo River and the country's main port.

As we travelled downstream, I could see that the riverbanks were infested with crocodiles. At one stage, while we were waiting for a car ferry – which was no more than a platform on which two cars would be towed on a wire across the great river – a canoe-shaped boat came speeding downstream with the current. Suddenly it hit an awkward wave, capsizing and throwing the three natives in it into the water just below us. In a flash, one of the men was seized by a crocodile. It was an unnerving sight.

After we reached the other side, we headed northwards through many miles of jungle until we reached the Kabinda border, where the Belgian forestry company Agrifors was exploiting a magnificent stand of the timber agba, which we at Mallinsons believed could find an important future in Britain. I spent days walking around and marvelling at the tropical jungle, with its old trees standing like huge soldiers and forming a canopy of leaves well over a hundred feet in the air under which virtually nothing grew.

The Belgians lived in fairly basic huts with a mess room in the middle. Most of them were long-term foresters and had their wives with them. In the midday and early afternoon they had a siesta, but because my hut was unventilated and stiflingly hot I would go for a walk, only to find that during siesta time the Belgian ladies took all their clothes off except their pants and would wander openly about their rooms in full view of anyone passing.

From Leopoldville I travelled to the French Cameroon port of Douala, which must be one of the most unpleasant places in Africa: extremely hot, almost on the equator and with the highest humidity. After the briefest stay possible I flew up to the capital, Yaoundé – which was mercifully in open country on a hillside, well inland – and from there to one of the main mills in the country, called Eséka, which was halfway between Yaoundé and Douala and the source of an extremely hard, smooth, almost black timber called ekki. I flew up to Eséka in a single-engine plane chartered from the local aeroclub and piloted by a gentleman in a tropical city suit, a bow tie and pince-nez glasses who turned out to be the local dentist and who relied on me reading the map. His determination to follow the railway line, which took us miles out of our way but which meant that 'They'll find us if we crash' put me in such mortal terror that I caught the train back to Douala and was quite glad to fly safely out of the country to Nigeria.

My time in Lagos was very comfortable and enjoyable, thanks in large part to a namesake of ours, Sir John Macpherson, who was the second-last governor-general before Nigerian independence and who, having heard of my trip, invited me to stay at Government House. He even sent his chief of police to meet me, with the man coming onto the plane and leading me off – the rest of the passengers clearly thought I had been arrested. We drove directly to the diplomatic beach, where the Governor General had a large picnic each Sunday after church. As we arrived, there was a terrible commotion, which turned out to be because one of the wives had had a large chunk of her backside bitten off by a barracuda. 'Mind you,' said the Chief of Police, 'she can well afford it.' So that was my introduction to Nigeria, and after that very informal picnic I had a couple of days in the luxury and formality of Government House.

From there I was driven up-country and away from the extraordinary bustle and confusion of Lagos's markets to Ije-bode, where Mallinsons harvested mahogany. After a breakfast of fruit picked straight from the trees, I walked into our piece of jungle to watch our axemen and sawmen skilfully felling the gigantic mahogany trees. The fascinating thing is that the forest is full of insect and wildlife noise until a great mahogany tree falls with a tremendous crash, at which stage there are 90 seconds of absolute dead silence until, suddenly, it all begins again.

Nigeria is the most populous country in Africa, and there is a huge vitality about it but, equally, a degree of tension between the people: the majority Yoruba around the capital, the Ibo in the east and the stately Hausa in the north. The Muslim area in the north, and the area round its capital, Kano, is particularly charming and encompasses both jungle and desert. The Hausa travelled to join Saladin's fight against the Crusaders, and as a result the sheikhs in the small villages have jesters and jugglers in their processions – obviously borrowed from northern climes – and relics of captured Crusader armour that have been preserved by the sand and dry climate.

I visited the coastal town of Sapele, which was the headquarters of the United Africa Company, the dominant company of British West Africa, before heading further up-country. Ever since the early missionaries handed out beads and trinkets whenever they wanted something, the Nigerians had expected to be paid, which presented problems for us. We tried to counteract this by building good relations with the local chiefs, which brought me to one memorable ceremonial banquet in our honour in a small village up-country. All went well until it became clear that the huge cauldrons bubbling on top of a brazier in the middle of the village contained monkeys.

As the feast began, the chief sent one of his very young sons to fetch me a piece of the monkey because, as the honoured guest, I had to eat before it could be distributed to the host and the villagers. I watched him take a monkey out of the pot, and there it was, looking like a boiled baby. He wrestled with it, and eventually an arm came away, which he proudly handed to me. I gingerly held it round about the elbow and eventually dug my teeth into the biceps, to a roar of approval from the assembled villagers. But, to my horror, as I dug into the biceps the little hand at the other end flicked its fingers to and fro with the reaction of the sinews. Our long evening ended with the discovery, when we got back to our hut, that the chief had provided two of his daughters to be our 'handmaidens' for the night. Fortunately they were persuaded to lie on the floor, but they left us wreathed in smiles in the morning.

After Nigeria I visited the Ashanti gold mines and the large plywood mills of the Gold Coast – now Ghana – before climbing aboard one of the Union-Castle liners that regularly sailed between Cape Town and London. The result was a relaxing journey up the coast in beautiful, calm weather, with me arriving in London refreshed and revitalised.

My department did a huge number of interesting jobs – such as refurbishing burnt-out City livery halls and helping to construct great new buildings such as the Abbey Theatre in Dublin, the Festival Hall and the new BP and NatWest Headquarters – but there was always something special about overseas travel. It could also be very demanding, as I found when I was almost arrested in Saudi Arabia when I unwittingly went straight from the plane to my hotel's pool, only to find four armed guards sticking their guns into me as a way of letting me know that I had intruded on 'ladies' day'.

But it could also be very lucrative, and one of my favourite business memories is of an occasion when we received an enormous tender document for the resupply of the naval dockyard in Valletta, Malta. Two of our serious rivals had already bid for the work, but I really wanted the order – and, let's face it, I also wanted to visit Malta – so I got myself on an aeroplane, immediately went out there and scooped the order. The return journey was on the Comet, one of the most beautiful and comfortable aircraft of all time. It was an absolute tragedy when a subsequent one mysteriously crashed in the Mediterranean, virtually writing off the whole project in favour of Boeing.

30

The Boss

In 1965 Stuart Mallinson retired, and it was not before time. He had never been a real businessman nor a strategist. He was a great asset to the business because he loved it, was extremely good with people and had an enormous list of personal contacts. The business, however, was going downhill, and Dan Drysdale was unable to correct the slide.

Dan decided to retire two years later, so in 1967 I became managing director at what turned out to be the nadir of the company's performance, when profits had gone down to a mere £167,000 before tax. I am happy to say that, from the following year onwards until we were taken over in 1981, every single year showed a rise in profits, culminating in a pre-tax profit of over £10 million, which in those days was a huge sum.

I persuaded our competent but conservative finance director to take early retirement and appointed his deputy, John Dyke. In 1969 we got our first real break when our rivals Gliksten bid for Denny Mott & Dickson, a company with which we had a lot of overlap through its softwood activities. Thanks to an ingenious financial device devised by our merchant bank, Kleinwort, we managed to sneak in and win the day during a very exciting takeover battle. We had suddenly gone from being a small company to a substantial operation, and things would never be the same, because not only did the stock market view us very differently but, unlike a small family company that can't risk the family silver, we could now afford to fail. This meant I had the ability to follow my instincts, and from that time on we were acquisitive and built up a substantial network of companies, not only in Britain but in Europe, Australia and the United States.

Not that it was all plain sailing. As Denny Motts were bigger than us, we had to take aboard some of their senior staff and directors, and while we were delighted to have men like Peter Hine, the well-regarded head

255

of their softwood operation, this wasn't always easy. In particular I had remarkably little in common with their chief executive, Richard Jefferies, who had come in as joint managing director alongside me, although as the chief executive I had the final say. Most of the Denny Mott staff except Jefferies soon left the company, and I was also able to sell their smart, expensive head office on London Bridge.

I made several changes, making Peter Webster, who had been a contemporary of mine as a trainee at Mallinsons, the boss of the Australian operation, where he was at that time the number two. But it was Thailand, where Dennys owned the company of Louis T. Leonowens, that gave me most food for thought. This was a name to be conjured with in Thailand for reasons that anyone who has watched the film *The King and I* will understand.

Anna Leonowens, who moved to Thailand with her son, Louis, was nanny to the royal family of Thailand and tutor to their small son immortalised in that film. Although the film is a Hollywood travesty of fact, Anna Leonowens did establish herself at Court and her son Louis did become firm friends with the heir, Chulalongkorn. When Chulalongkorn succeeded to the throne, young Louis was in a restless phase and serving in Canada with the Mounties but was recalled to Thailand, where his new king asked him to raise and train the Thai Army's first cavalry force.

Louis became an influential figure but eventually tired of soldiering and decided that trading would be more profitable. The King gave him huge trading concessions that included logging in the teak forests, one of the great wealths of the country both then and now. Louis lived to a ripe old age, travelling the country – buying, selling, exporting – and the Thais developed quite a veneration for him because he had the three qualities they particularly admired: an enormous capacity for alcohol, an equally enormous capacity for women and the venerability of bearded old age. So Leonowens, as a company, was a household name in Thailand, and during my tenure there we obtained the right to use the Royal Arms, the only company with that privilege.

Back in London it quickly became quite clear to everyone that any sort of joint management by me and Jefferies was not going to be possible and, even if possible, would not be efficient. An ultimatum was put to him by the board, who offered him the chance to run the Australian and Far East operation from Australia, which he accepted. That enabled me to make the necessary changes in the UK and to get rid of inferior performers among the management, but complaints from Australia and Thailand meant that Jefferies was soon given early retirement. So, finally, I had the whole company in hand, for better or worse – fortunately it turned out over the years to be for better.

It was an interesting time, with lots of fascinating products. The big franchises that we held were Colgate Palmolive and Massey Ferguson tractors, which we actually assembled, while in Singapore and Thailand we had the Moët Hennessy franchise, in which I naturally took a close personal interest.

In London, at about this time, I made my first incursion into what might be called public life. Peter Runge – who married my cousin Fiona Macpherson and whose sister Peggy married my brother Niall – was the first president of the Confederation of British Industry, which had been formed from an amalgamation of the Federation of Manufacturers and the Commercial Federation. Peter invited me to join the London and south-east region. In due course I became chairman of the region and soon realised that it had a lack of influence because it and the organisations representing the City were often at variance. Dick Lloyd, a colleague on the London and south-east committee, and I suggested a joint committee of the main City bodies and the CBI, an idea that was eventually accepted by David Nickson, who was the chairman of the CBI.

Shortly after that I received a visit from Ian McDonald, who had been an employee of mine in Leonowens and was now senior administrator in the London Chamber of Commerce. He invited me, on behalf of the Chamber, to join them as deputy chairman for two years and then to take over as chairman. After considerable thought, I agreed, unknowingly setting my foot on a ladder that would lead to the presidency of the British Chamber of Commerce and eventually to the enormously prestigious post – at least, for continental countries – of president of the European Chambers of Commerce.

I was conscious at this time of the need to broaden my experience further, and the opportunity came when Peter Kininmonth, a long-standing friend of mine from my rugby days at Oxford who went on to captain Scotland, introduced me to Micky Resnick of Allstate Insurance Company of Chicago. Micky was in the UK to head up a small Manchester-based insurance company in Britain called Federated, which had been bought by Allstate and renamed Allstate Insurance UK, and he was looking for a British chairman to keep them in touch with the way business operated here and to form a link for them with the City of London.

I got the job, setting up a connection with the United States that I have certainly never regretted. Indeed, my role expanded, as I became the UK liaison man for Allstate's owners, Sears Roebuck of Chicago. On one occasion their chairman was coming over to London and I was asked to get the chief executives of the four main London banks to dinner with him – no mean task considering how full their diaries were. However, the chief executives of Lloyds, National Westminster, Barclays and Midland duly came to a dinner I had laid on at Le Gavroche, which was very highly regarded and recommended, although I had never been there. It turned out to be an absolute disaster: the service was appalling and the food of a not very high standard. Fortunately there was plenty of wine, and we managed to create a good atmosphere, but I very much regretted having gone there.

Although Micky had a profound culture shock on moving from Chicago to Manchester, I grew to love Chicago and still believe that the wide boulevard of Michigan Avenue, which is lined with high-rise skyscrapers in rococo, Gothic, Tudor, Arabic, pure-engineering and classical designs, is one of the greatest streets of the world, encapsulating the go-getting ethos of the interwar years. Allstate Insurance Brokers wasn't a success and was eventually sold to a consortium from Edinburgh led by the Noble brothers, Ian and Tim. Hence was born New Scotland Insurance, of which, after a proper interval, I became a director while also continuing as chairman of Allstate Insurance UK in the City.

That wasn't my only commercial tie with Scotland. I was approached to become a director of Scottish Mutual Life Assurance in Glasgow. I had wanted to get into the financial sector and into business in Scotland and was delighted to join, which meant 13 visits a year to Glasgow. I was surprised to find that the life of a director of a mutual life-assurance company seemed to consist of little more than keeping the show on the road, keeping everything legal and avoiding trouble.

At the same time I was also approached to join the board of TSB Scotland, based in George Street in Edinburgh. Again, this proved less demanding than I had expected, this time because the bank was run by able people and the last thing they wanted was too much interference by non-executives. We were given enough information, but only just enough, so that we could do our job but not create any waves.

All this happened against a background of change at Mallinsons. I was determined to take a back seat and had instructed professional recruitment agents to find my successor as managing director. It took a long time because, even for a leader in the sector, we were still only a medium-sized company and the sector itself was unfashionable. Much to the headhunter's surprise, I eventually chose a rough-diamond Scotsman from Edinburgh called Frank Andrew, who was an accountant and entrepreneur but also, more importantly, a real go-getting type.

The timber world was changing, and instead of bulk sales of timber to the building trade I saw we would be moving to selling machined timber to the general public. We built the finest sawmill in the country, at King's Lynn, in preparation and made repeated efforts to buy a firm called Travis & Arnold to provide us with retail outlets. They have since gone from strength to strength and would have been marvellously complementary, preferably with the young Travis in charge as managing director. However, his father Ray was locked into the philosophy of family companies and refused to sell.

As a medium-sized market leader with an outstandingly successful record we were very vulnerable to takeover, and when we received an approach from the Brooke Bond Group, the largest player in the tea and coffee sector, the writing was on the wall. I met their chairman, Sir Humphrey Prideaux, on several occasions, but all seemed to go quiet. Shortly afterwards we decided to fund a rapid expansion with a rights issue, only to find that Brooke Bond bought most of the new shares, a move that was inevitably followed by a bid. Given the attraction to shareholders, there really was no purpose in opposing it – and Mallinsons ceased to exist as an independent entity.

It is amazing the way perfectly rational boards of directors get carried away in boom times by the thought that they must grow by acquisition and that they can manage anything. Unfortunately, it soon became clear that the synergies between Brooke Bond and Mallinsons were non-existent and that the companies had such different philosophies and ways of working that any meaningful integration was impossible. To make matters worse, Humphrey Prideaux had retired and had been replaced by an overly aggressive executive called John Cuckney. I became a director of Brooke Bond but was only a non-executive director of Mallinsons and therefore unable to influence strategy or operations.

Economic circumstances were poor in that year, and that, coupled with severe managerial disruption, saw Mallinsons' profits take a sharp downward dive after having risen annually every year since 1967, when I took over. The Brooke Bond board reacted by refusing to rubber stamp the acquisition of a company called Addison, which was based in Atlanta, Georgia, a crazy decision, as proved when one of our competitors took over the company for a far greater figure and still considered it a steal. Still, at least I had some fun before the deal collapsed: first, when the head of the Addison family took me to a small French restaurant for dinner and I saw a bottle of Château Pétrus 1964 on the wine list for $15, and later, when we examined the company's outpost in Augusta, Georgia, and the manager, who was a member of the Augusta National, got me onto that famous golf course, where I was allowed to play the first and the eighteenth.

The decision to kill off that deal was petty and malicious, and it came as no surprise when, not long after my year was up, Cuckney made it clear that it would be considered a favour if I resigned. I was only too glad to do so as soon as a severance package was agreed, which happened remarkably quickly. Shortly after that, Brooke Bond were taken over by Unilever, whose boss, Sir Ken Durham, was an old acquaintance from the CBI. He came to see me and asked me a whole series of questions on the company, the last being whom he should keep. I told him that the only man he should keep would be the ex-Colonial policeman who ran the cattle-to-carnations East African venture, because nobody else knew anything about it, but that he should get rid of the rest. He laughed at me, thinking I was simply venting my spleen, but I was absolutely right because he kept none.

I arranged to stay on in a private office in Brooke Bond's rather lavish head office for six months as part of my severance plan so that I could look round to see where I would base myself for my various non-executive and consultancy activities. Jenny Coles, my faithful secretary, remained with me. She came to me as a newly married, very raw 20 year old and proved an absolute treasure with extremely fast shorthand, a very fast brain, excellent French and a mind that handled all sorts of details almost before I had thought of them myself. After she had been with me a month, she gave me a 'male chauvinist pig' tie as a present, but there must have been some compensations because she stayed with me until her fiftieth birthday, with a short break of seven years in the middle to raise her own family.

At the end of the six months, a good friend from my Oxford and Achilles days, Derek Steele, offered me a place in the offices of his insurance company for at least another six months. During that time, however, John Pelling, who ran the Sears Roebuck-owned banking firm Dean Witter, approached me. He was a little mystified by the way financial business was done in London and invited me to come and take an office next to his in Leadenhall Street. My base remained with Dean Witter, both there and later in Broadgate, until they merged with Morgan Stanley and moved off to Canary Wharf, when I decided to move in with Boustead, a company of which I was to become the chairman.

As well as charitable work, such as my long association with the Worshipful Company of Dyers and the Worshipful Company of Carpenters, plus other roles, such as being High Sheriff of Greater London, my list of non-executive directorships was also expanding. As well as joining TSB and Scottish Mutual Life Assurance, during the early stage of Mallinsons' takeover by Brooke Bond I was approached by the directors of Birmid Qualcast. Robin Leigh-Pemberton, who was later to become the governor of the Bank of England, had just been appointed chairman of the National Westminster Bank and felt compelled to resign from his role as chairman of Birmid Qualcast. He was asked to suggest a successor and recommended me to his board. Jimmy Insch, a Birmingham Scot with an engineering background who had taken over as interim chairman, and the entire Birmid Qualcast board came to lunch with me at Mallinsons headquarters and seemed to view me with considerable suspicion. They nevertheless invited me to join the board as a non-executive director, with a view to taking over almost immediately as chairman.

I was keen. The company was headquartered in Birmingham, and I knew that the imminent takeover of Mallinsons by Brooke Bond meant that I would have time on my hands. Birmid Qualcast was a very interesting company that had originally been based in heavy engineering but had successfully branched out into Potterton boilers, Atco and Qualcast lawnmowers and later into bathroom equipment. As a family company that had gone public, it felt very much like Mallinsons. Part of that was a conservatism that could be problematic: it took two years of drifting before I was confirmed as chairman and then another long hiatus before I was able to remove the managing director who had been responsible for a decline in the share price since Leigh-Pemberton's departure. However, once Peter Prateley, an executive with a background in marketing, took over as managing director, the company prospered in all our markets, bought New World Kitchens and became healthy and profitable.

As with Mallinsons, a medium-sized company performing so well inevitably had the bigger companies circling. First Hepworth Engineering, led by the future Manchester United chairman Professor Roland Smith, and then Blue Circle Cement made offers for the company. However, where Hepworth had taken no for an answer, Blue Circle refused to give in and launched a hostile takeover bid. It was such a close-run thing that the outcome seemed to depend on one company with 2.5 per cent of the shares, a company that turned out to have as its chairman Sir Martin Jacomb, a very old friend whom I first met when he was working for the merchant bank Kleinwort, who agreed to vote for us. The count was nerve-rackingly close, with the vote at first going against us and then for us on a recount. That, however, turned out to be a pyrrhic victory, because Blue Circle had in the meantime bought 43 per cent of the company's shares, which made a buy-out inevitable. All that was at stake was the price, but when they tried to bully us into accepting 390p a share it really put our backs up and we made them pay top dollar. A year later it was sold at 460p per share.

Without a major role once more, I began to get a whole raft of invitations to join boards as a non-executive director or chairman, and, while I was glad to remain active, I became very selective. I turned down more offers than I accepted, and the ones I took on were often because of conscience or duty. Some weren't a success, such as Société Nantaise, a French laminate manufacturer run by an old Mallinson colleague, Peter Pedley, which ran into cash-flow difficulties and went bust. Similarly, I and distinguished stockbroker Jock Douglas were non-executive directors for CH Industrials, a middle-ranking engineering plc that had been too acquisitive and which owed money to a consortium of 50 banks led by Barclays. Despite our best efforts to sell some bits of the company and accelerate key contracts, Barclays pulled the plug and sold the parts for a fraction of their worth just to ensure they got their own money back. My other problem job, taken on for a friend, was the headhunting business of Michael Webb-Bowen, a brother of one of Jean's best friends. An extremely likeable person and a very capable headhunter, he seemed to have absolutely no business sense, and after ten years struggling along his health broke down almost completely and we wound up the company, although with no loss to any creditors this time.

But the vast bulk of my directorships were happy and successful ventures, such as asset managers Candover, who eventually asked me to become chairman of Keller, an up-and-coming organisation in the field of foundations for large buildings and stabilisation of soil. The idea was for me to prepare the company to be a plc and then to float on the Stock Exchange. This was partly achieved through the acquisition of Case and Company in Chicago, a sizeable Irish-managed company in an Irish-dominated city, which seemed, miraculously, to get an awful lot of public contracts in the US, no doubt on merit.

Chicago was also the base of Allstate and of its parent, Sears Roebuck, who wanted to develop a credit-card business in England. The Sears House credit card was the largest in the US, but with 10 to 15 per cent of their holders travelling abroad they needed an international dimension. They had, however, had their fingers burnt in their only two previous ventures into Europe so asked me to be their consultant, dealing with London bankers and with the Bank of England as regulator. They couldn't decide whether to launch independently or go for a joint venture, even looking at the possibility of buying one of the small private banks. In the end they opted for partnership with one of the major credit-card issuers.

Between Allstate, Sears and Case, I got to know Chicago reasonably well, even attending a baseball game with the then Sears chairman, Ed Brennan. Chicago has an awful climate, with ice piled high along the lakeshore in the winter while August is almost unbearably hot and humid. Yet I grew to love the place and was very sorry when Allstate was sold to an Australian company and my involvement ended.

An equally successful episode occurred when Sir Peter Rawlinson, who had been attorney general in Ted Heath's Conservative government, approached me to succeed him as chairman of Owl Creek Investments, an on-shore oil exploration and production company in the United States but based in London and British-owned. A small company, Owl Creek relied on its percentage of oil strikes, and although it was high in the first couple of years, it fell away after that and we were forced to sell the company on – at a profit, but not as high as we had hoped. On the plus side, I had acquired some experience of the oil industry.

At about the same time, I was also approached by the founder of management consultants Bain & Company, first as a member of their international consultancy board and later as a member of their British advisory board. I spent a decade with Bain, working alongside high-powered minds such as the then chairman of ICI, Sir Denys Henderson, and Govi Mallinckrodt of Schroders. I am generally extremely sceptical about consultants who, all too often, are called in by chairmen or chief executives simply to disguise their own failings, but Bain's strict emphasis on results, the measurement of results and payment by results was impressive.

My roles were wide-ranging and usually very interesting. As well as TSB, Scottish Mutual Life Assurance, Birmid Qualcast, Société Nantaise, Michael Webb-Bowen, Candover, Keller, Case and Company, Sears Roebuck, Owl Creek Investments, EMAC and Bain, I also chaired Employment Conditions Abroad, a company that advised major companies on the treatment of their ex-pats. Then, at the age of 70, when I retired from TSB, I was immediately approached by the head of the London operation of the French merchant bank Société Générale. However, despite the occasional excellent dinner in London or Paris, I never did work out what they wanted the UK merchant bank to do.

Boustead, a Far Eastern company of very ancient lineage, was the longest running and among the most interesting of my non-executive chairs. Edward Boustead arrived in Singapore on the heels of Stamford Raffles, and it was Boustead's number two, William Farquhar, who really created Singapore out of nothing. The UK company was a plc in London, but changes in the Malaysian governance rules after independence made it essential for the Malaysian sister company to be a Malaysian-registered and -listed company in its own right.

Boustead presented enormous challenges and considerable worries and exertion, and Jean often quizzed me about why I stayed there. I suppose it was an obstinate determination to get the company running smoothly once again after finding it in a parlous state. Its problems included the fact that the previous chairman and chief executive had gambled heavily with the company's money on the Singapore Stock Exchange and had lost and that, in restoring the finances, they had issued new equity to a Singapore Chinese businessman called Ching Poh, a man of somewhat equivocal reputation. Ching Poh had joined the board and was endeavouring, quite clearly, to make himself the dominant factor, holding some 22 per cent of the equity.

I believed that the previous chairman, Charlton, had dissipated the company's money and taken a course of action that had not been authorised by the board. Despite the difficulties of prosecuting a previous chairman and chief executive in Singapore, and Helena Kennedy QC's gloomy prognosis, we opted to pursue him and secured a very substantial settlement from Charlton moments before the case was due to be held.

The next step was to recruit a managing director, and in Michael Noakes we seemed to have found the right man. The company accelerated its growth, and its shares shot up from single figures to 70 pence. And then disaster struck, with personal problems forcing Ching Poh to sell his shareholding to an extremely aggressive Singapore businessman by the name of Jack Chia. A cultured and civilised man who had a remarkable collection of oriental porcelain, he was ruthless in the pursuit of his own interests and began to buy up shares in the company. When serious problems were unearthed in the trading of the Singapore operation, Chia was able to buy enough shares to gain control of it.

Arguably the most interesting of my non-executive appointments arose from a casual meeting in Moorgate with Sir Ian Fraser, the deputy chairman of Lazard, shortly after the Brooke Bond takeover of Mallinsons when I mentioned to him that I would have free time and would like an interesting and challenging non-executive directorship. I heard nothing for quite a while and then received a call from him asking whether I would like to meet Sir Ian MacGregor, then chairman of British Steel, who was about to take over as chairman of the National Coal Board. I had heard such amazing things about MacGregor that I jumped at the chance, and he and I got on well. He appointed me to his new board, which turned out to be the beginning of a very interesting but difficult period from which the board and the industry emerged strengthened and with a future. Obviously, the strike under Arthur Scargill dominated the period, but I had already had the opportunity to make considerable contacts with the Scottish and Welsh coalfields and to descend into the depths of the mines.

The first descent was in Wales, and I found it immensely interesting because the conditions down the mine were not nearly as bad as I expected. Indeed, there were long, tiled, well-lit corridors leading to the faces where the coal could be worked mechanically, with lots of dust and noise but no gross discomfort. If, however, you were unlucky enough to be away from one of the main, easily accessible seams, there was also a great deal of hand work, propping up, awkward angles, lowered roofs and so on, and everywhere one had to be extremely conscious of the imminence of possible disaster and the necessity for safety. Coming out of the mines on the little trains loaded with coal, you had to lie very flat with your face pressed into the coal in order to get through the small openings without being scraped off the top of the truck.

My regard for the miners themselves was immense. In Wales we all had the common interest of rugby, but whether it was Wales or Scotland – the two areas that I got to know best – the miners were the salt of the earth, and, in spite of the fact that they would vote for anything wearing a Labour rosette, they were extremely conservative, conventional, upright, honourable people. The tragedy was that their loyalty led them to follow irresponsible and self-seeking leaders with ulterior motives. When the strike eventually came to an end, it was impossible not to feel a deep sympathy for the miners who marched back to work in orderly and 'heads-high' fashion.

The seeds of the strike lay in the miners' success in bringing down the Heath government and in the management of the previous board of the National Coal Board, which subsequently avoided confrontation of any sort. Made up of brilliant mining engineers rather than businessmen, their idea of a triumph was to extract coal from virtually impossible faces rather than extracting coal that gave the greatest profit and the highest possibility of the industry being in the black instead of in the red.

In spite of the efforts of propagandists to build him up as a fearsome, ruthless capitalist, Ian MacGregor was an enormously kind man. A difficult time for him, however, was not made easier by the fact that the minister Peter Walker seemed to be playing both ends of the pitch, passing information that we'd given him to the strikers and giving them unrealistic hope of a settlement on terms that would never be acceptable.

Our cause had been helped by the fact that the strike had been so long coming that we'd been able to build up considerable reserves, and also by the fact that the anti-Scargill Midlands miners decided to go on producing. This infuriated Scargill, who not only persuaded the miners to picket the Midlands pits but also unleashed what I would describe as mercenary violence as he transported thugs from one area of the country to another to try to harry the police and make deliveries difficult. Fortunately the police remained steadfast throughout.

I like to think that I contributed two important ideas that helped resolve the dispute. The first was to persuade the National Coal Board to replicate a scheme run by British Steel, which had created a foundation with the specific purpose of helping the creation and growth of businesses in areas that were severely affected by closures. I also managed to persuade Ian MacGregor – who had been fronting the Coal Board's television presentation but whose American accent and eccentric mode of presentation didn't play well with viewers – to stand down in favour of a home-grown presenter. The man chosen was a colliery manager called Eaton, who turned out to be a natural, although he was rather corrupted by the fame, changing his modest lifestyle into something of flamboyance that wrecked his future career.

If Eaton has cause to regret his part in the dispute, I don't. Unlike Scargill and his cronies, I didn't have any doctrinaire reasons for wanting to win the conflict, just a belief that to have a future any industry needs to make a profit. Indeed, that principle was my guiding light throughout a business career that lasted from my mid 20s right up to my 90s.

31

The European Dimension

Business occupied my time very fully, with a lot of travel for over two and a half decades, and so it was a long period before I was once again mixing with politicians of stature, partly when I was president of the London Chamber of Commerce and then the British Chamber of Commerce but mainly when I was president of the European Chamber of Commerce. It's often difficult for British businessmen to grasp just how big a deal this organisation is in Europe, in part because membership of the various chambers of commerce was compulsory in many countries. This meant that most of the European chambers of commerce had huge numbers of members and considerable standing.

As a result, with the rotating presidency of the Council of Europe, the European Chamber of Commerce was generally among the very first to be received by each new president who was, of course, also the prime minister of his national state. We therefore saw characters like Andreas Papandreou of Greece, Anders Rasmussen of Denmark, Carvalho da Silva of Portugal, Giuliano Amato of Italy, John Major, and Helmut Kohl of Germany. All of them were extremely welcoming and interested: sometimes the reception was for me and our secretary general in a private meeting; sometimes we were asked to bring a delegation.

Chancellor Kohl presented me with a case of his favourite Moselle wine, which we later drank with extreme pleasure. There was also Jacques Santer, with whom I was later to work closely when we both became founder members of ERA Trier, the Academy of European Law. He received us as prime minister of Luxembourg just before he became secretary general of the European Community. Of them all, I was most impressed intellectually with the Portuguese premier Carvalho da Silva, who had been at the University of York. He spoke perfect English, grasped concepts quickly, had an impressive clarity of thought and was unusually positive for a politician.

During that period, I happened to sit on the left of Mrs Thatcher at a dinner during the run-up to the 1987 election. After talking to her right for a bit, she regally and graciously turned to me and said, 'Well, if you were me, how would you think I should set about winning this election?'

Partly stimulated by a couple of preprandial glasses of champagne, but also speaking from real conviction, I said to her, 'Prime Minister, if you really want to carry the voters with you in great numbers, you should say to them, "If elected, for four years I promise to do absolutely nothing at all."' She gave me a piercing look, said not a word, turned the other way and never spoke to me again.

After my stint representing London and the south-east on the British Chamber of Commerce, I was then invited to become chairman of the British Chambers, which was a great responsibility, especially as it often meant advising ministers of the Thatcher government. Because I was colonel of the London Scottish TA and then the London and south-east division of the TA (and later chairman of the Territorial Army Volunteer Reserve Association), I was also asked to advise the Ministry of Defence and successive Tory defence ministers, including Michael Heseltine, George Younger, Tom King and Malcolm Rifkind, on how to reward employers when their employees were released for TA service. It was for this that I was knighted, the Lord Lyon inviting me to take up the title of Sir Tommy Macpherson of Biallid in recognition of my ownership of Biallid, the second-oldest continually inhabited house in the upper Spey Valley and a Macpherson stronghold.

As chairman of the British Chambers, I was their representative on the European Chambers of Commerce in Brussels, a body comprising all the 15 Common Market countries as full members and the 18 or so countries associated by trade treaties with the European Union. Because Great Britain was one of the few countries where membership of the local chambers of commerce was voluntary, we were relatively weak numerically and financially compared with the major chambers of the Continent, so it was with some surprise that I found myself elected as president of the European Chamber of Commerce.

Getting elected was one thing, but I expected that the feat of navigating the fiercely competitive national chambers would be well-nigh impossible. Surprisingly, I was wrong, and despite the misgivings of the secretary general, a German called Von Bülow who was a scion of the famous military family – bizarrely, the German delegation also contained a Hindenberg and a Von Moltke – we managed to persuade all 15 countries to back a reform to the constitution to give the president more power to get things done and to raise money.

During my time as president, we made huge progress in expanding our influence, which was largely due to the work of a German called Frank Friedrich, whom I recruited as secretary general. With his organisational skills, the influence of the Eurochambres – the French name of the European Chambers of Commerce – expanded rapidly, and we became the first organisation to meet each new six-monthly president of the European Union. This included John Major, who met us in the Cabinet Room at No. 10 Downing Street at the start of his presidency. He was extremely interested to hear just how influential the European Chambers were in general and with their own governments in particular, asking me to support discreetly various ideas that the British government had for the presidency.

Every six months I attended Eurochambres' general meeting in Brussels, and at the end of each year a member country hosted us for the annual general meeting. While at those yearly meetings, in charming places like Venice, Vienna and Nicosia, I found that the continent was united in wanting a European free-trade area but that there was almost unanimous aversion to the centralising bureaucrats of the Commission, who believed they could solve all ills from their ivory towers in Brussels.

One of the biggest trends in the EU during my time as president of Eurochambres was the French resistance to the gradual but unremitting erosion of their power. France had been the driving force behind the creation of what was once called the Common Market and had gone into the enterprise with the express intention of dominating this new organisation. French remains the official language, but even in the 1980s and 1990s, when I was involved with Brussels, the French were still striving to preserve their predominance, so it was always the French National Chamber of Commerce who bucked the consensus view. Yet nothing they did could stop English becoming the accepted language of general exchange.

Another subtle way in which the French tried to maintain their powerbase was a new constitution proposed by my close friend President Giscard d'Estaing and his committee. This new constitution contained many good things but skirted around the problem that the enlargement of the EU meant that unanimity in voting would have to give way to qualified majority voting (QMV) if Europe was not to become institutionally paralysed. The French wanted the number of votes each country had under QMV to be based on gross national product and population, which would have favoured them, while I always believed that it should be based on each country's net contribution, on the basis that he who pays the piper ought to call the tune. This would have left recipient countries like France at a disadvantage and given more power to nations like Germany, Britain, Sweden and the Netherlands, which I thought was absolutely fair. Instead, we're stuck with a ruinously expensive Common Agricultural Policy benefiting the Mediterranean nations yet being paid for by a coterie of contributing nations.

National rivalries were never far from the surface during my time as president of Eurochambres, and, as my tenure approached its end, the Dutch and Spanish were both keen to have their man succeed me. The Dutchman was the right man for the job, but the Spaniards assembled a Mediterranean alliance to push their man, so we did what European institutions invariably do and compromised: the Dutchman and then the Spaniard each did two years instead of four, at which stage the extremely able German Dr Jörg Mittelsten Scheid took over, with an Italian as secretary general to maintain the balance between northern and Mediterranean countries.

Those last few days at Eurochambres were extremely emotional for me. After all, they neatly encapsulated and intertwined the various strands of my life, from going out into wartime Europe in an effort to bring peace and harmony in the long term to working assiduously to oil the wheels of industry in peacetime. That, I believe, is a legacy of which I can be proud.